THE
POLITICIAN

THE
POLITICIAN

An Insider's Account of
John Edwards's Pursuit of
the Presidency and the Scandal
That Brought Him Down

ANDREW YOUNG

Thomas Dunne Books
St. Martin's Press ⚏ New York

THE POLITICIAN. Copyright © 2010 by Andrew Young. All rights reserved.
Printed in the United States of America. For information, address St. Martin's Press,
175 Fifth Avenue, New York, N.Y. 10010.

www.stmartins.com

Library of Congress Cataloging-in-Publication Data Available upon Request

ISBN 978-0-312-64065-1

First Edition: February 2010

10   9   8

For Cheri, always

Note to the Reader

Quotes from e-mails, text mails, and voice mails mentioned in this book are offered verbatim, from the author's records, which have been made available to federal authorities investigating events, individuals, and transactions related to John Edwards's personal, political, and financial activities. Public statements quoted here have been confirmed with media reports and other contemporary sources. Where conversations are reported, quotations are based on contemporary notes made by the author and on his personal recollections of direct encounters with the parties involved.

Contents

Acknowledgments

Having never written a book before or, more specifically, a page of acknowledgments, I looked at a number of other books to help me decide what to write here. It seems a normal note of acknowledgment represents a nod of thanks to those who endured the author's long hours of research and an expression of gratitude for those who have been supportive during the writing process. That is not what I intend here.

Every single person mentioned on this page deserves more thanks than I can ever give because they were loyal to me and my family at a time when the national media descended upon us and many negative things were being said about me. Many "friends" turned their backs on us, but the people listed here gave us unconditional love through two years of hell, and unending inquiries from press, friends, and neighbors.

To Cheri, Brody, Gracie, and Coop, you are everything. I have always said I would kick the devil in the teeth for each of you, and I hope this book accomplishes a bit of that.

To my dad, who passed away while I was writing this book, may God bless you and keep you. Thank you for everything, and I will talk to you always.

To my mom, I love you so much and I am so sorry that the storm that overwhelmed my life came while Warren was dying. Thank you for always being there for us.

To my mother-in-law, Susie, and my father-in-law, Roger, I am so sorry I put you and your daughter through this hell. I can't make it right but I will try to give her the best life I can.

To my stepmother, Virginia, and her family, thank you for everything, and I love you.

To my sister Sherri, her husband, Dean, their son, Dustin, my sister Terri, my brother, Rob, and his wife, Julie, thank you, thank you, thank you. I love you so much. Let's all work to keep our family together.

To Cheri's sister, Deana, her husband, Dale, and their children, Arielle, Cali, Mackenzie, and Camden, your love and support carried Cheri and me through so much. We deeply love you.

To Cheri's brother, Roger, you are a brother to me. Thank you for everything.

To Glenn Sturm, thank you for jumping into the foxhole with me when no one in your world would. You are one of the best people I know, and I love you. I would not have survived this without you.

To Leo Hindery and Jim Heavner, thank you for your advice and friendship.

To my brother-in-law Joe Von Kallist, you saved me and my family. I will never forget it.

To Tim Toben, I love you, brother. And I love Megan and your family like my own.

To David Geneson, much thanks. You enable the little people to have a say against the big people.

To Bryan Huffman and Bunny Mellon, you are incredible.

To Heather and Jed McGraw, only the two of you understand the depth of this book—thank you. Congratulations on Nannytucket, and best of luck in everything you do.

To the folks at St. Martin's, Tom Dunne, Karyn Marcus, and my new dear friend John Murphy, thank you for helping create this work. I wanted to write something that would help my kids to someday understand why I did what I did, right or wrong, and I think we accomplished that.

I would like to thank the FBI agents, IRS agents, and the officers of the U.S. Attorney for the Eastern District of North Carolina for treating us fairly and professionally.

To the Edwards and Anania families, with the exception of John and Elizabeth, thank you for many years of friendship.

Thank you to Mark and Amy Friedman, Dave Badger, Kerri Drury (an angel to our kids), Claudia Kelsey, Greg Pruitt and his family, Uncle Perry, Sarah B., Melissa Geertsma, Bill and Susan Walser, the Sartor family, and the folks we didn't even know in California who took us in.

There are two other people whom I cannot thank by name, but thank you and I love you.

This journey has taught me to appreciate what I already had, the few people who love me unconditionally. I love each of you more than you will ever know. I was hurt by the many people who turned away, but I was blessed by you who stood by me.

The person who can give us a sense of hope is the one who knows the human condition and can encourage us to face the realities of life.

—From a sermon by my father,
Reverend Robert T. Young

THE
POLITICIAN

Prologue

Late on a spring afternoon, the soft Carolina sunlight filtering through the pines around our house reminds me of why I have always loved my corner of the world. The great universities in Raleigh-Durham and Chapel Hill draw extraordinary people from around the world, but like us natives, most of them stay, at least in part, because of the quiet, natural beauty. There is no better place to make a home, raise a family, and enjoy the simple pleasures of life. I thought about this as my wife, Cheri, packed some snacks—juice, apples, Goldfish crackers—into a cooler and I helped our eight-year-old son, Brody, pull on his Yankees uniform and find his mitt. It was time for the last game of the 2009 season, and he was excited.

Along with Cheri, Brody, and me, the crew in our minivan included our six-year-old daughter, Gracie, our four-year-old son, Cooper, and Tugger, the new chocolate Lab puppy. As we drove down the winding dirt lane that cuts through thick woods to the main road, Brody talked about whether his team would beat the Mariners and remain undefeated. Gracie and Cooper anticipated finding other children to play with on the sidelines. Cheri and I wondered whether we would meet, face-to-face, the former friend and boss who had betrayed my devotion and trust—given freely for more than a decade—and then made our existence a living nightmare.

Halfway to the ball field we passed the Bethel Hickory Grove Baptist Church, where the man in question had married his wife, Elizabeth. I knew the story as well as anyone. She showed up carrying a soda pop. He gave her a ring that cost eleven dollars. They had a one-night honeymoon in Williamsburg, Virginia, and then quickly settled into a life built around their law practices and then their children. In those early years, Elizabeth, who had grown up in Japan as a navy brat, was the sophisticated one and he was the diamond in the rough. She bought his clothes, coached him on his courtroom presence, and advised him on how to navigate the social scene.

We reached the end of the road and turned left onto Highway 54 and then left again at the park entrance. On one side of the lane, a few people walked dogs in a specially fenced area. On the other side, a couple of kids hacked away on a tennis court. My throat tightened a bit as we approached the baseball field and I saw kids and parents clustered on the bleachers and near the backstop.

It was an all-American scene—kids in baseball uniforms, families gathered on the grass, fireflies flashing in the air. But as any team parent knows, social intrigue often lurks beneath the Norman Rockwell surface. Real life comes with pettiness and gossip that can make people feel uncomfortable. In our case, the idle and mean-spirited talk wasn't about some neighborhood dispute or a run-of-the-mill extramarital affair. Oh no. We had been caught up in one of the seamiest national political scandals in recent history. And just about everyone in the country, if not the world, believed they knew enough to judge us in the harshest terms.

I had hoped that the man at the center of the story would have had the sense to stay home. But as we parked I saw his familiar silver Chrysler Pacifica, which I had helped him purchase. (I was startled to see that the rear bumper of the car, usually plastered with half a dozen campaign stickers, was bare.) Cheri and I braced ourselves emotionally as we got the kids out of the car seats. When we closed the van doors and walked toward the diamond, it felt as if every head turned toward us. Every head, that is, except one.

Out on the field was the man who had once promised me the brightest future I could imagine and then abandoned me to national disgrace, hiding behind his sunglasses, talking on his cell phone and chatting with the boys on the Mariners team, including his own son Jack. The players, with big ball gloves on their hands, seemed as cute as floppy-eared puppy dogs as they chased pop flies and grounders. My former friend, who beamed at them with his world-famous smile, looked like America's Father of the Year, an award he actually won in 2007.

We joined the Yankees sideline, where everyone except the kids felt the tension. Cheri and I sat alone, ignored as the other parents chatted. As the innings passed, we marveled at the way our old friend and his wife—two people who had been as close as family—refused to even look in our direction. Once we would have hugged as we said hello and then spent the entire game side by side, laughing and talking. Half the people at the park would have wandered by just to say hello. A few would have asked for favors, which were granted with a simple "Call Andrew and he'll take care of it." And I would.

This time there were no hugs and no jokes, and no one came to ask either of us for anything. Jack and his sister Emma Claire, who used to play with our kids, looked at Cheri with confusion in their eyes. We had no idea what their parents had told them about us. We overheard one of the mothers in the crowd whisper something about "the Youngs."

When the game ended with our guys a few runs behind (so much for an undefeated season), my old friend, boss, and mentor walked the long way to his car so he could avoid us and everyone else. While other parents were still collecting empty juice boxes and tired little ballplayers, he and his family were halfway to their home. It was the last time I would ever see my former boss, John Edwards—once one of the most powerful politicians in the world. But it was hardly the last time I would be forced to deal with the shame, distress, and anguish that came out of my own dedicated effort to help him become president of the United States.

As I write this, on a sunny midsummer morning in 2009, I am waiting for the Federal Bureau of Investigation to come sweep our home for listening devices. I called them after a couple of mysterious break-ins. (They will find nothing, but they wanted to make sure we weren't being bugged.) I'm in regular contact with the United States Department of Justice because I have just completed testimony before a federal grand jury investigating allegations of corruption in John Edwards's recent campaign for president. After I swore an oath to tell the truth, federal prosecutors questioned me for hours about huge sums of money that had quietly changed hands, and just who knew what, when. The process of giving testimony is what you might expect. I sat in the witness chair, and as the men and women of the grand jury scrutinized me, the prosecutors pressed me for exact information about checks that were written, the way the money was used, and the timing of events. They wanted names, dates, and amounts in very specific terms. The ordeal was grueling but also reassuring, because it forced me to recall and try to understand the people, events, and decisions that had almost ruined my life and the lives of people I love.

I found some real peace in finally telling the whole truth in the grand jury room, and I am continuing to follow this process as I write this book, which will set the record straight, and try to salvage some positive lessons from the scandal that brought down one of the most promising leaders of a generation. My critics will say I am writing this book for money. They are partly correct. The Edwards scandal has left me practically unemployable, and as a husband and father, I have serious responsibilities I can meet by publishing my story. But I also have every right after three years of silence to tell my story and clear up the many lies that have been told about me and John Edwards. I believe that anyone who cares about history and the way things work in politics has a right to the truth.

Of course, the lawyers in the office of the U.S. Attorney for North Carolina weren't interested in my family responsibilities or my desire to make something worthwhile out of the ordeal of the last few years. They wanted to hear my story in order to resolve potentially criminal issues around the Edwards affair and its cover-up. And no one in the world knows more about these events, and more about the real John and Elizabeth Edwards, than I do. I was the man who "took the bullet" for then-candidate Edwards by falsely claiming that I had fathered the child he had with a mysterious woman named Rielle Hunter. It is an indisputable fact that I willingly participated in this ruse. I joined in the deception, and at the time, amazingly, I believed it was the right thing to do. Once the decision was made, Cheri, our children, and I went on the run with Rielle to escape the press. Flying in private jets and changing locations several times, we managed to disappear, under the direction of Senator Edwards and his biggest political backers. During this time, I arranged for Edwards and Rielle to stay in constant contact. I also played a key role in keeping the truth—about the depth of their affair, the paternity of her child, and his ongoing commitment to Rielle—from the candidate's cancer-stricken wife.

Without knowing more of the details, anyone looking in from the outside would consider what I did and conclude that I must have been a cold-blooded schemer who was motivated by ego or greed or the desire for power. It's true that I had hoped my sacrifice would be appreciated. Everyone who works in politics wants prestige, status, and a good salary. But when this misadventure began, I didn't request a single specific thing. On his own, when he asked me for this favor, John Edwards did promise to tell the truth within a reasonable amount of time.

I was paid well while I was on the run, but I also took a huge risk with my reputation and my family's future. In fact, I might have abandoned John and Elizabeth Edwards many years before, when I had proven myself as a fund-raiser, campaign aide, and overall political operative, and could have sold my services to the highest bidder. Instead I stayed with them for ten years, watching others come and go on to bigger and better things. I did this for one primary reason—I believed in John Edwards and all the things he said he stood for, especially his commitment to equal rights and opportunity for all, including the people who have been traditionally pushed to the side in Southern politics. Although it might be hard to recall in the Obama era, at one time John Edwards was heralded as a potential savior for a Democratic Party that had been hammered by Karl Rove, Dick Cheney, and the conservative noise machine. Like many others, I believed he was destined to lead the party and the country.

In the beginning, and through most of our time together, John Edwards had given me an outlet for the powerful idealism that I had first felt as a small boy who sat awestruck every Sunday as my father, a big, charismatic Southern preacher, filled the prestigious Duke University Chapel with words of hope, wisdom, and inspiration. As university chaplain in the turbulent seventies, the Reverend Bob Young challenged prejudice and small-mindedness in a booming voice that was one part professor and one part Bible-thumping preacher. He confronted a comfortable white congregation with the legitimate grievances of the poor, blacks, and women. But he also offered hope and understanding. "Accept your mistakes, errors, failures, sin," he said one Sunday. "Acknowledge them, know them, and live."

When my father was pastor, the formerly staid chapel welcomed to the pulpit greats of the civil rights movement like Martin Luther King Jr. and heroic leaders like Terry Sanford. A former governor, president of Duke, and U.S. senator, Sanford was once John Kennedy's choice to replace Lyndon Johnson as vice president in 1964. I often sat on his lap at the chapel while a thousand people listened in rapt silence to my father's message. No experience could have been more inspiring. As light streamed in through stained glass and the great pipe organ literally shook the pews with sound, I learned to imagine myself as a part of something bigger. My father, Terry Sanford, and their friends had been involved in the civil rights movement and had witnessed and participated in historic events. Their stories gave me chills.

At home, I spied on my dad as he wrote his sermons late on Saturday nights and then practiced the lines. I came to walk and talk just like him, and his example became my guiding star. Of course, I knew I could never match my dad's achievements. A tall, powerfully built man, he was the twelfth of thirteen children born to a farmer in the tiny town of Woodfin. With his intelligence, talents, and determination, he rose to the top of North Carolina society. My mother, a smart and beautiful woman, was equally accomplished and driven. At the University of North Carolina, when Dad requested a visit with her at her sorority house (back then the "house mother" played gatekeeper), she came downstairs to meet him only because she thought he was a basketball player named Bob Young. Confident and charming, my dad nevertheless swept Jacquelyn Aldridge off her feet. Soon they married. He was elected president of the UNC student body, and she was elected secretary.

In contrast to my outgoing parents, I was a naive, bookish kid, the youngest of four, who found adventures and heroes in books and got so nervous when called on in class that I could barely speak. I started to come out of my shell at fourteen, when I served as a page at the state legislature. I saw enough whiskey bottles and sexual intrigue in the statehouse to realize you take the good with the bad in politics. (From Raleigh to Washington, the bad always seemed to involve infidelity.) But I remained idealistic. I also developed into a young man who threw himself heart and soul into every challenge. When my brother insisted I try out for football, like every good Southern boy, I hated it at first but stuck it out and eventually started. I made friends easily, and the experience reinforced my belief that everything good was possible.

Then, when I was seventeen years old, came a series of events that shook me to the core. My dad, always strong as a horse, had several heart attacks that led to his first double bypass. It changed Dad and my family forever. The following year, my senior year in high school, my parents attended counseling and traveled extensively in a futile attempt to save their struggling marriage. The week after I graduated high school, my father left his Duke job for a much lower-profile pulpit in the little city of Statesville. Soon after, he was caught in an affair with a church deacon's wife. The deacon videotaped my dad and his wife at a Red Roof Inn. I'll never forget my father calling to tell me, "They caught me, Andrew. They caught me." The scandal became widely known. My hero was exposed as an adulterer, and our family broke apart. While my father's brilliant career was destroyed, my neat little world spun out of control.

Disillusioned and heartbroken, I stumbled through my early twenties, dropping out of Furman University and then opening a sports pub (ironically named Winners) in Asheville, which thrived until I lost control of the finances and it went belly-up. Bankruptcies were rare and shameful in those days, and when I locked the door and ran away from my debts, I left behind a great many angry and disappointed people who thought Andrew Young was the lowest son of a bitch in the world. I would have agreed with them. The lowest point may have been the night I used an expired key card to sneak into a hotel room and slept hidden on the floor between the bed and a wall because I was broke and desperate to get in out of the cold. During this time, I drank way too much and got into plenty of minor-league trouble, the worst of which involved a stupid attempt to steal a fifty-dollar sign from a bar. It seemed like a good idea at the time.

When I finally grew up and got serious about life, I went back to school for a bachelor's degree at the University of North Carolina and a law degree at Wake Forest. The most difficult thing for me at law school was responding to the professors when it was time for me to stand in front of the class to review a case. Whenever this happened my heart would pound, I'd grow flushed and sweaty, my voice would tighten, and I found it almost impossible to express myself coherently. Despite this problem, I managed to get through the program, and along the way, I realized I didn't want to practice law. I was far more interested in politics, especially the politics of my home state.

North Carolina has a unique, almost bipolar political history. In 1898, the coastal city of Wilmington saw the only violent coup in American history when a mob of white vigilantes called "Red Shirts" wielded a Gatling gun bought by the famous Daniels publishing family to take over the city and drive away thousands of black residents. (From that day to the Jesse Helms era, fear-based racism played a big role in the state's political affairs.) But North Carolina is also home to great progressives like Terry Sanford, who broke down racial barriers and built some of the best public and private universities in the country. We gave the country Sam Ervin, chairman of the Senate Watergate Committee, and we went for Barack Obama in 2008. Regressive, progressive, and everything in between: That's North Carolina.

My first full-time involvement in politics came in 1994 when I became part of Democratic governor Jim Hunt's campaign. As a volunteer, low-level fund-raiser, I saw old-fashioned politics firsthand. The four-term governor was a progressive, and his policy priority was a terrific education program called Smart Start. He was also a hard-driving politician who knew how to run his machine. At his quarterly fund-raising conferences—staff called them "Come to Jesus" meetings—Hunt would work himself into a lather urging his people to raise campaign funds "for those kids." He would then display a color-coded map of the counties, which showed who was winning in the money game and who was losing. People would be publicly praised for meeting their quotas—like star salesmen at a convention—or criticized for falling short.

Everyone knew that campaign donations were rewarded with jobs or public works projects. More than a few men got rich because they knew to buy land where a new road was going to be built or received contracts to provide goods and services to the state. These connections also explained why one county might get a big new bridge or an eight-lane highway and another did not. Although this kind of horse-trading was common, it was obviously unfair to outsiders, and the participants liked to keep it quiet.

After Governor Hunt's reelection, I worked briefly for the state Commerce Department, then with the North Carolina Academy of Trial Lawyers in the state capital. My boss was the group's main lobbyist, and my work revolved around fund-raising, staging events, and helping to keep the office going. It wasn't the kind of work I had dreamed of doing while I listened to the sermons at Duke Chapel, but it was a responsible job in politics—by now I was a full-fledged political junkie—and I was on my way toward building a career. I knew I would never be a candidate or a very public figure, because my anxiety about speaking in front of people wasn't getting any better. (If anything, it was worse.) But I could dream that I might one day become an insider who could have an exciting career and perhaps make the world a better place.

The pieces were coming together in my personal life, too. After I spent more than a decade as a committed bachelor, a kind and beautiful woman had finally broken my complacency. The chance meeting happened in the spring of 1997 in Cancún, in one of the most famous bamboo tourist bars in the world, Señor Frog's. We had both gone to the bar to fetch drinks for friends. Cheri wore a sexy black dress. I wore a red polo shirt and a baseball cap. We fell to talking, and I was completely taken by her beauty, warmth, and openness. We forgot our friends and danced the night away. When I got back to my hotel, I was so partied out that I couldn't remember her name or the name of her hotel. All I could recall was her room number—312—and I couldn't find anything to write with. Finally, in desperation, I laid out three bottle caps (for the number 3) next to a single credit card and two room keys so I could remind myself in the morning and then fell asleep.

The next day, I telephoned hotel after hotel, asking for room 312 and then hoping that whoever answered would help me. Finally, on about the fifth call, I reached a room where a young woman answered and said, "Oh, is this Andrew? You must want Cheri." Bingo!

Cheri spent almost all the rest of her vacation with me. She was the sweetest and most beautiful woman I had ever met, and I could tell we were falling in love. When the time came for her to depart, I met her in the lobby of her hotel and we waited for the airport shuttle to arrive. As the driver called for passengers, she started crying. I kissed her, told her I already loved her, and impetuously told her I believed we would get married someday. Cheri's eyes grew wide, and she gripped me tightly. We both had been hurt in bad relationships, and as much as she wanted to believe me, it was crazy. I can't explain it, but I already knew. She was unlike anyone I had ever met. "Just believe," I whispered. For some reason, I knew it would happen.

Our long-distance romance took place in Denver, Raleigh, and Los Angeles, with side trips for a cruise and vacations along the California coast. Seven years younger than me, Cheri was twenty-three and had just begun a career as a traveling nurse. An agency booked her on three-month assignments that moved her from city to city so that she could see the world while making a living. After growing up in a small town in southern Illinois, she was pursuing the life of adventure she wanted. It was full of new friends, new sights, and new experiences. She was not ready to fall in love or settle into a serious relationship, but we had fallen head over heels.

We were so crazy in love that I skipped my family's Christmas celebration and went to meet her family in the tiny town of Highland, Illinois. My first impression of the town was that it was small, cold, and windy—and had a lot of cornfields. When we got to her house, a gust of wind caught the door of my SUV as I opened it, and it banged me hard in the head. The blow opened an old wound, which started bleeding profusely just as her mother, father, and thirty close family members came to greet us. A bandage and some compression stopped the flow, but I wasn't finished making an impression on my in-laws-to-be. I tossed and turned all night and finally got up early, took a walk, and bought a newspaper. As I was reading it at the kitchen table, her mother came in to cook breakfast. She lit a candle that was on the table. The paper went up in flames, singeing all the hair off my arm. Adding insult to injury, that night her mom walked in on Cheri and me as we were "making up" after having had a little spat.

Despite all the mishaps, Cheri's family decided they liked me, which, given how close they all were, was extremely important. She and I settled into a life together in Raleigh, where we shared a little apartment in an old downtown building with huge windows, hardwood floors, and posters of Jack and Bobby Kennedy on the walls. Cheri's favorite bit of decoration was a slogan I had found on a paper bag, cut out, and taped to the refrigerator. It said, "Never Confuse Having a Career with Having a Life." To me, it meant that happiness could be found in a balance of work and love, and it seemed like a great piece of advice.

It was pretty easy to stick to the refrigerator motto in those days. Cheri worked long shifts as a nurse at the hospital—I usually drove her there and picked her up—but she had lots of days off. I put in my eight-hour days for the trial lawyers association, jogged at lunch, and at night I would cook dinner and we'd sit on the little balcony at our apartment, where we could watch the sun set over downtown. We'd spend weekends at a lake or the beach or traveling. We felt like the luckiest people in the world.

I offer all this background not to explain or excuse any choices that I made later, but to reveal, as best I can, the man I was before I tied my fate to John Edwards. I had been blessed in many ways. I had grown up in a comfortable home as the son of a prominent family who had introduced me to people and ideas that were exciting and inspiring. My mother and father both loved me and taught me that I should try to make the world a better place. I had the support of friends and extended family. I had a good big brother, two loving older sisters, a dog, and a horse. And in the community of Raleigh-Durham/Chapel Hill—known as the Research Triangle—we were respected even when my father's more liberal ideas rubbed people the wrong way.

Life inevitably brings change, loss, and trauma to everyone. Growing up requires us to accept that people are deeply flawed and that sometimes, at least in the short run, evil seems to triumph over good. In my case, these realizations came in a shocking way as my father's affair took away my hero, my family, and my community. I didn't respond well at first. But in time, I recovered my equilibrium. By age thirty-two I had finished my education, started a career, and found someone to love (who also loved me), and I had begun to see a brighter future. It was the summer of 1998.

One

THE SPELLBINDER

That summer, the members of the North Carolina Academy of Trial Lawyers went to Myrtle Beach for a meeting where they would network, do business, and attend professional seminars at a beach-front hotel called the Ocean Creek Resort. A palm tree paradise with secluded cottages, hotel towers, pools, and a white-sand beach, the setting was ideal for a working vacation. My job would require putting on a party where the group could meet political candidates and organizing a five-kilometer road race. Otherwise, Cheri and I were free to make the long weekend into a minivacation.

We were dressed in bathing suits and flip-flops when we walked through the hotel lobby and I insisted on stopping in one of the meeting rooms to hear at least the start of a presentation by a Raleigh-based lawyer named John Edwards, who had surprised the state a month before by winning the Democratic Party's nomination for the United States Senate. (Edwards had spent millions of his own dollars to defeat a big field that included favorite D. G. Martin, who had run for Congress twice before.) It was one o'clock in the afternoon; even if we wasted an hour on this talk, there would be plenty of time for the beach.

In this crowd, Edwards was a superstar. He had amassed a personal fortune in the tens of millions of dollars by suing on behalf of those who had been terribly injured by corporations, hospitals, or individual defendants. By the mid-1990s, he was so highly regarded that other lawyers jammed into courtrooms whenever he made a closing argument. His most famous case involved a little girl who barely survived after being disemboweled by the suction of a pool pump. At the end of the trial, Edwards gave a ninety-minute closing in which he evoked the recent death of his teenage son, Wade, who had been killed in a freak car accident in 1996. His performance won a $25 million verdict for his clients and solidified his legendary stature. But it was just one of more than sixty victories—totaling over $150 million—that he won in roughly a decade. This record helped him become the youngest person ever admitted to the prestigious Inner Circle of Advocates, a group comprising the top trial lawyers in the nation.

All of Edwards's success had given him the means to do anything he wanted with his life, but he would say that it was his son's death that pushed him toward politics. By all accounts, sixteen-year-old Wade was a smart, talented, and high-spirited young man who loved the outdoors and music, collected sports cards, and owned a future that was as bright as a star. Three weeks before he died, he had attended a White House ceremony for finalists in an essay contest. The theme for entries had been "What it means to be an American." Wade wrote about accompanying his father to a firehouse to vote.

Wade's death devastated John and Elizabeth Edwards, who grieve to this day. But as John explained when he ran for office, Wade had often told his father he should consider public service. After a period of mourning, Edwards began to think about his son's advice. He made his decision to jump into politics after watching the movie *The American President*, in which a widowed president falls in love with a lobbyist. The movie helped him imagine a life of purpose following a great personal loss.

Wealthy, powerful men don't think small, so when John made the decision to follow his son's advice, he focused not on the city council or state legislature, but on the United States Senate. He then hired a staff of more than two dozen workers, bought help from some of the top consultants in the country, and easily captured the 1998 Democratic primary.

Edwards's talk at the Ocean Creek Resort was a chance for people to hear a potentially powerful new political figure, but less than half the seats were filled when Cheri and I entered the conference room where he was going to speak. We took seats in the back, on the aisle, so we could escape quickly, if necessary. (Cheri, who is apolitical, did not want to be stuck in the middle of the crowd.)

Edwards came into the room from behind us, and as he passed me, on the way to the podium, he put his hand on my left shoulder. For a moment, I thought it was my boss trying to get my attention, but when I turned I saw a young-looking guy in a blue suit, white shirt, and striped tie, grinning as though he were my best friend. He had a head of thick, perfectly combed brown hair, steel blue eyes, and a cleft chin. On his lapel was pinned not the usual enamel American flag most politicians wear, but a pin showing the compass-style symbol of the wilderness program for kids called Outward Bound. It had belonged to Wade.

At age forty-five, John Edwards looked like he was in his mid-thirties and moved with the energy of a college quarterback. He brimmed with confidence, but there was nothing overbearing in the way he presented himself. The way he looked at the people in the room, as if he knew each and every one of them, made it easy to understand why he was successful in the courtroom. Juries gotta love this guy, I thought.

Having been a candidate and politician for less than six months, Edwards didn't have many policy specifics to offer. But the trial lawyers knew he would be on their side in upcoming battles over so-called tort reform efforts by insurance companies, doctors, and Republicans who wanted to restrict our rights to sue when we are harmed. He was one of them and could be counted on to fight for the preservation of the tort system. With this in mind, they were satisfied with his generalizations about other issues like health care and education and helping out the poor and the middle class.

Having grown up the son of a millworker in the textile company town of Robbins, North Carolina, Edwards spoke about these issues with some personal authority. ("I'm the son of a millworker" was a staple phrase in his speeches.) Robbins neighbored the exclusive Pinehurst Resort area, and the contrast between the two communities—one working-class, the other extremely wealthy—was a stark illustration of what Edwards later called "the two Americas." During high school, he worked cleaning the soot off of ceilings in the mill. In college, he was a package deliveryman. Burdened with the insecurity of coming from a rural town, he found it difficult to believe in himself; thus, whenever he started at a new job or a new school, he thought he was going to fail. He studied textiles as an undergraduate with the thought of returning to Robbins. He was surprised when he got into law school and surprised again when the most worldly, sophisticated, and beautiful woman in his class, Elizabeth Anania, agreed to marry him.

As someone who had heard preaching and speechifying my whole life, I noticed right away that Edwards had a gift. He didn't just talk about kids who needed help. He painted a picture of a poor kid without health insurance who goes to a rundown school without books and lives in a violent inner-city neighborhood needing somebody's help to beat the odds and succeed.

Edwards took control of the room, and people started to come in and fill the empty chairs. Trial lawyers are a tough audience, but he captured them so completely that when he came to the end of his talk and asked everyone to "humor me a minute and close your eyes," they actually went along with him. (I know, because I sneaked a peek.) As the spellbound crowd grew quiet, Edwards asked us to picture in our minds all the people—children, poor families, millworkers, middle-class parents, older folks, and so forth—who had been left behind in the era of Reaganomics and Wall Street booms, and who deserved better. He then borrowed a quote from Gandhi and told us we could "be the change" that we all hoped would make things better.

"We are a country that speaks out for those without a voice," he said, "a country that fights for what we believe in. When we stand up for people without health care, for people who live in poverty, when we stand up for veterans, America rises."

At about this moment, with everyone practically hypnotized by his words, Edwards stopped and asked us to open our eyes and stand. "Come on now," he said, "just join me." As the audience complied, Edwards's voice got a little stronger and he scanned the crowd, trying to catch every eye he could and connect, if just for a second.

"I promise you, if you join me, we will change this country!" he said. "And the folks in Washington and on Wall Street will hear you loud and clear. They will know that their grip on power and money is coming loose. They will know that America is rising. Thank you for standing up."

The applause that answered Edwards's speech was loud and sustained. In a room filled with litigators who considered themselves to be highly skilled advocates and public speakers, he had proven himself to be in a league of his own. I was as impressed and inspired as anyone, and I turned to Cheri and said, "This guy is going to be president one day. . . . I'm going to find a way to work for him." She looked at me, unimpressed, rolled her eyes, and said, "Let's go to the beach."

After the noise died down, a crowd of people gathered around Edwards. Although I would have liked to talk with him, I knew I wouldn't be able to get close. Cheri and I stuck to our plan, heading for the sand and the ocean. But later in the afternoon, I spotted Edwards as he left the hotel and headed for his car alone. I couldn't help but notice that it was a beat-up Buick Park Avenue—dark blue, dirty, and dented—and that when he opened the door, an empty Diet Coke can and assorted papers fell out onto the pavement. Edwards chased down the trash and picked it up. The dirty car and the fact that he was so dedicated that he was driving it himself to campaign stops helped convince me that he was entirely sincere. He really did want to make the world a better place, and believed he could. (Much later I would learn that the car was a bit of a ruse. A multimillionaire, Edwards started driving the Buick and put away his BMW and Lexus coupe to effect an "everyman" image.)

Money—for advertising, travel, events, workers, and the like—is the lifeblood of politics at every level, and while John Edwards would pour millions of his own dollars into his first campaign, he also needed donations, which would fill his war chest and show he had serious support. Trial lawyers were a natural target for his fund-raising effort, and soon after Edwards spoke to the trial lawyers academy, I was asked to put together a phone bank operation that would contact our members and raise money to help his campaign.

Although almost everyone hates working the phones to raise campaign money, I don't. My usual fear of public speaking doesn't affect me on the phone, and I actually enjoyed the challenge. I would gather a group of six or eight telemarketers and back them up with the candidate and a few of our prominent academy members like Edwards's law partner, David Kirby, and Wade Byrd, who was a big Edwards supporter from Fayetteville. (A character and a half, Byrd was a profane, boisterous guy who looked a lot like the actor Nick Nolte, roared around in a convertible Jaguar, and enjoyed expensive cigars and The Macallan single-malt Scotch.) The telemarketers would do the work of trying to get folks on the phone, which was roughly a one-in-five proposition. Whenever they got through, they'd pass the call to me, Edwards, or one of the prominent attorneys. It was a bit like fishing. Sometimes the clock would tick for half an hour and you'd get nothing. At other times we'd hit a lucky streak and everyone would get a bite at the same time. I added to the buzz by posting tallies on big sheets of paper stuck up on the wall. This made the whole thing like a game.

The keys to success with a telephone bank include conviction—you absolutely must believe in your candidate—keen listening, and a sense of timing. You aren't going to raise much money if you spend twenty minutes on the phone with each person, and if you listen carefully, you can tell fairly quickly whether someone is likely to respond. I got pretty good at figuring out when I was wasting my time, and then saying, "Lordy, I've got another call coming in. I've gotta go." I also knew how to land a fish when I got him hooked. Once, as I talked to a guy who was offering to give us the maximum donation allowed, I realized he thought he was actually talking to John Edwards, who was sitting next to me. I passed him a note that read, "He thinks he's talking to you." When I tried to hand him the phone, Edwards laughed and mouthed, "Keep going." I did, and the fellow wound up "maxing out," which meant he sent checks for the maximum amount under his name and his wife's.

Edwards took a lot of calls during our first phone bank session, which he attended with his chief fund-raiser, Julianna Smoot. A native North Carolinian, thirty-one-year-old Julianna was just beginning to establish herself as a political consultant and finance expert for Democrats. With blue eyes and brown hair streaked with blond, she looked a little like Hillary Clinton and could match her when it came to smarts and intensity. In a business dominated by type A personalities, she was type A+ and an extremely effective and loyal right-hand woman. She helped Edwards home in on the health-care issues—a lot of people were angry with their insurance companies—and pick apart the weaknesses in the positions and campaign of the incumbent, Lauch Faircloth. Edwards was also guided by a first-time campaign manager named Josh Stein. A sincere, talented guy who grew up in Chapel Hill and graduated Harvard Law School, he was the kind of guy you want working for you in politics. Edwards also hired a top consultant/pollster named Harrison Hickman.

The incumbent, Republican Faircloth, was rich like John Edwards, but the similarities ended there. A seventy-year-old who had made his fortune in hog farming, Faircloth was an uninspiring speaker, and he looked terrible on television. After thirty or more years as a Democrat, he had switched to Republican in order to win the support of Jesse Helms. In 1992, he ran a nasty campaign where he used coded racist messages to unseat Terry Sanford. In Washington, Faircloth gained notoriety as a rabid critic of President Bill Clinton. He was obsessed with the Whitewater real-estate deal and Monica Lewinsky. In North Carolina, he failed to respond to constituents with the efficiency that made Helms so popular, and his plodding style was a handicap on the stump.

From the start of the campaign for Senate, Edwards stressed education, health care, and Social Security and was so good at rallies and on television that he excited even lifelong Republicans. (Typical was a "man on the street" named James Walker, who told the Winston-Salem paper he felt as though Edwards was "talking to me" when he appeared on TV.) Edwards spoke about restoring "integrity" in Washington, and his support for the death penalty helped him deal with charges that he was "ultraliberal." He used his inexperience to claim to be a true outsider who would shake up national politics.

In his campaign, Faircloth had to do without his former guru/consultant Arthur Finkelstein—a slash-and-burn strategist—because Finkelstein had recently been outed as gay, and a superconservative senator couldn't allow himself to be associated with a homosexual. Nevertheless, he followed the Finkelstein recipe, painting Edwards as an irresponsible ambulance chaser and running incendiary anti-Clinton TV ads attempting to make Edwards guilty by association. Both national parties threw big resources into the race. Clinton campaigned for Edwards. Former president George Herbert Walker Bush and his son, the future president, stumped for Faircloth. The last independent polls of the campaign gave Faircloth a slight lead, within the margin of error.

Like everyone else volunteering on the campaign, I threw myself into the effort, especially in the final weeks. I made hundreds of phone calls and used every connection I could to drum up donations and votes. Julianna had me put out hundreds of yard signs, including daily replacements of the signs in the Edwardses' yard, which were shredded nightly by his Republican neighbors.

On election night, Cheri and I went to the ballroom of the North Raleigh Hilton, which was the Democratic Party's headquarters for the evening. We were settling in for a long night when suddenly the results were announced by CNN at 8:45 P.M., with a graphic that showed Edwards the winner, 51 percent to 47 percent. (A third-party candidate got 2 percent of the vote.) Analysis would later show that Edwards won with a big majority among blacks and women and that he benefited from a national backlash against the Republican moralizers who had hounded President Clinton. (I also believed I saw in this the beginning of the end for the old Republican strategy of exploiting racism for votes.) But at the moment, all anyone knew was that Edwards had been elected. We shouted and hugged and cried as if we were members of a team that had just won the Super Bowl.

During the party that ensued, Wade Byrd brought me up to the Edwards suite in the hotel, where the senator-elect was getting used to the idea that he had won. Earlier in the day, he had refused to believe Harrison Hickman when he predicted a victory. In fact, he was so certain he was going to lose that he prepared only a concession statement and no victory speech. Now he seemed overjoyed as he celebrated with his wife, Elizabeth, teenage daughter, Cate, and infant daughter, Emma Claire, as well as his friends and campaign folks. But while he was the center of attention, Edwards impressed me when he noticed Emma Claire starting to cry and quickly picked her up and found a pacifier to help soothe her.

After a brief chat on the phone with President Clinton, Edwards went downstairs to the ballroom. Backstage, Elizabeth grabbed him and said, "You are a senator now. Act like one. The whole country is about to get their first impression of you." The place exploded when he appeared, and he had trouble controlling the celebration as he praised his opponent, paid homage to Terry Sanford, who had recently died, and thanked everyone who had helped him. But the lines that struck me in the heart were near the end of the speech. "A very important thing happened today," he told the happy crowd. "The people of North Carolina voted their hopes, instead of their fears." To native Tar Heel Democrats like me, long distressed to be represented by a divisive figure like Jesse Helms, this was an amazing outcome.

The rest of the night was a blur of celebration and optimism. More than a few people considered Edwards's smashing success, good looks, and obvious talents, and compared him with the Kennedys. Others wondered aloud if he might wind up in the White House. I certainly thought it was a possibility, and I was hoping to help him get there. Although Cheri was a decidedly nonpolitical person, she stayed by my side into the early-morning hours, listening to endless talk about the election and Edwards's future. I drank enough so that she handled the drive home, but I didn't worry about a hangover. On this night, Edwards had fulfilled my expectations and the state had, as he said, turned toward hope. I felt proud and happy, as if a great new dawn were breaking.

Okay. Is everybody ready to smile?"

"No. Not yet. Hold on just a minute."

This was take number twelve—or maybe one hundred and twelve—and once again the members of the Edwards clan were out of position and both Elizabeth and I were getting a little frustrated by the effort it was taking to get a nice photo of the family in front of a Christmas tree. The struggle, which also had something to do with Mrs. Edwards's perfectionism, included a little bit of sniping and complaining, and endless shifting and rearranging. In between shots, I found myself wondering, Just how did I get into this?

In fact, Julianna Smoot had called me at the last minute, asking if I could drive to the Edwards house in posh Country Club Hills (a rich Republican neighborhood he had failed to carry in the election) and take the Christmas photo because she had something else demanding her attention. Julianna had remembered sending me over on election day to put campaign signs in their yard. The picture had to be taken immediately, because the family had waited until the last minute and needed to place their order for cards. I happily agreed to do it because I had already applied for a job on Edwards's staff, and it couldn't hurt to spend some time with the senator-elect and to meet his wife, who everyone knew was his best friend and most important adviser.

Though small in stature—she's about five feet two—Mrs. Edwards was known as a powerful person in her own right. She graduated near the top of her class at the University of North Carolina Law School (just behind the senator) and had had a successful legal career under her maiden name, Elizabeth Anania. After their son Wade was killed, she retired and underwent fertility treatments and gave birth to Emma Claire when she was forty-eight years old. She changed her name to Elizabeth Edwards when her husband entered politics. When I saw her on photo day, she had been through an incredible couple of years that included losing a child, guiding her husband's election, and having a baby. (Another child, a boy named Jack, would come in the year 2000.) She wanted a perfect picture, and it didn't seem to be working out.

Part of the problem was the camera, or rather the guy working it. Mrs. Edwards had a fancy digital setup with a telephoto lens, and it took me some effort to learn how to work it. But the whole operation was also affected by the time pressure—we needed a great photo *now*—and Mrs. Edwards's desire for every detail to be perfect. I also thought that Mrs. Edwards, who looked like a normal woman of forty-nine—pretty but a bit overweight—was self-conscious about getting her picture taken with her husband, who was very youthful and photogenic. Finally, there was the pressure that surrounds every big politician's Christmas card. These cards are more than mere messages of good tidings. They promote the family's image, communicate Christian values, and signal who is favored by the powerful and who is not. People left off the list never forget it. People on the list feel honored, show off their cards to friends as status symbols, and keep them as historical mementos.

With so much riding on the photo, I had to struggle to stay cool as I snapped away and Elizabeth came over to check the images in the viewer on the back of the camera. She hated the way she looked in almost every frame, but in the end she had to accept one for the card. I had no idea whether anyone actually liked the picture. All I knew for sure was that it had not been the best time to get to know the Edwards family, and I hoped I'd get a second chance.

While I waited to see how my professional future might work out, I had no doubts about my personal life. Cheri and I had bought a house, and we moved in with my dog, a boxer named Meebo (a mash-up of My Boy), and a pair of cats named Pepper and Granny. We all got along so well that in January 1999 I ordered an engagement ring, which the jeweler told me would take several weeks to make. On the morning of Friday, February 12, a clerk at the store called to say the ring had been finished early and was ready to be picked up. I hadn't planned to pop the question so soon, but I was suddenly filled with inspiration and set about creating a night Cheri would never forget.

Fortunately for me, everyone, including the caterers I called—a company called the Food Fairy—loves a romantic. They agreed to go to our house at a little after five o'clock, find a key I would hide for them, and prepare both the meal and a beautiful table—china, crystal, flowers—and put Stan Getz on the stereo. (I wanted a violinist but couldn't find one who was available.) At about three o'clock, I called Cheri and said my boss had suddenly assigned me—which meant us—to attend a black-tie event that evening. She didn't like the idea of racing around to find something to wear and getting ready on such short notice, but when I told her that the governor would be there and it was important for me to attend, she agreed to do it.

By six o'clock, Cheri, who had worked until three-thirty, had somehow found something to wear, and she looked beautiful, although she was tired and a bit frustrated with me. I managed to get her in the car and down the road just as the Food Fairy truck whizzed past us. "I wonder where they're going," said Cheri. As she mused about the truck, I suddenly realized I needed to kill an hour so they could get things ready. I decided I'd drive to one of the city's few venues for black-tie galas—the Sheraton Raleigh Capital Center—and use up half an hour or so figuring out that it was "the wrong place."

The ruse would have worked better if the lot and entrance at the Sheraton hadn't been deserted, but as we drove up it was obvious that no one was having any kind of event there. Nevertheless, I had Cheri wait in the car while I ran inside to "check." When I came back out to report it was the wrong place, Cheri pushed for me to call my boss for the proper address. I resisted her. Finally, I said I didn't feel well and maybe we should go home. I don't recall her exact words, but they were something like "You don't ask me to get all dressed up like this on short notice and then just go home. Suck it up, buddy."

Since I needed to waste more time, I suggested we go to a McDonald's, where I could get a Sprite to settle my stomach (which to a nurse was ridiculous). When the soft drink didn't work—"I really feel bad; I think we should go home"—Cheri gave up on me and agreed to call it a night. She fumed on the ride home, though, and when we got to the house she got out of the car without saying a word. She was stomping mad, and I had to hustle to catch up with her at the front door. When I opened it she could smell our dinner cooking, hear the music, and see rose petals on the floor and a table set.

That night we had a candlelight feast that included the juiciest steak I ever had, topped with a concoction of crab and lobster. Cheri's dessert—a chocolate torte—came with whipped cream, raspberry drizzle, and her engagement ring. When I got down on my knees, my stomach didn't hurt, but it was filled with butterflies as I said, "You are the woman of my dreams, and I want to spend the rest of my life with you. Will you marry me?" She said yes. After dinner, we called our family and friends and gave them the news. (Her father wasn't surprised. I had asked for his permission.) We soon set September 11 as the date for our wedding.

On the day Cheri and I were engaged, the United States Senate acquitted President Clinton in his impeachment trial, ending thirteen months of crisis over his sexual affair with Monica Lewinsky and his stupid, lying attempt to escape the truth. Senator Edwards played a role in the investigation, helping to preside over depositions of Lewinsky and Clinton's friend Vernon Jordan. He also made his first speech to the full Senate during the closed-door impeachment trial, which was one of those rare moments when all one hundred members actually occupied the chamber. A lot of staff time and effort was put into preparing Edwards's remarks, but when the time came he put away the text and spoke, as he said, "from the heart." (He later authorized the release of a transcript of his remarks.)

In considering the charge, Edwards said, "I think this president has shown a remarkable disrespect for his office, for the moral dimensions of leadership, for his friends, for his wife, for his precious daughter. It is breathtaking to me the level to which that disrespect has risen." But he did not agree with those who thought Clinton acted with a criminal's intent to avoid prosecution. Instead, he saw a politician's instincts at work: "I suspect the first thing he thought about is, 'I'm going to protect myself politically.' He was worried about his family finding out. He was worried about the rest of the staff finding out. He was worried about the press finding out."

Urging the Senate to focus on the question of whether the evidence against Clinton exceeded the standard of "reasonable doubt," Edwards said he had poured long hours into studying the case, often staying up till three in the morning. In the end, although he suspected Clinton might be guilty of "a lot that has not been proven," he couldn't join those who thought the president had committed perjury or obstructed justice.

Considering John Edwards's gift for courtroom drama, I'm certain he held the Senate's attention with his explanation for his votes against the charges. But once I read the speech and thought about the clubby culture of the Senate, I realized that he probably won them over at the end, when he talked about how he had come to admire, respect, and even love his colleagues.

"An extraordinary thing has happened to me in the last thirty days," he told the one hundred senators. "I have watched you struggle, every one of you. I have watched you come to this podium. I have listened to what you have had to say. I talked to you informally; I watched you suffer. I believe in my heart that every single one of you wants to do the right thing. The result of that for me is a gift. And that gift is that I now have a boundless faith in you."

Edwards told me that after his address, he was practically bowled over by colleagues who wanted to congratulate him. Senator Edward "Ted" Kennedy, one of the great old lions, even wandered to the back of the chamber, where the newest members of the Senate were given their desks, to shake his hand. Kennedy saw almost unlimited potential in this young, energetic, well-spoken, and good-looking Southerner who shared his position on most issues. All the other freshmen in Edwards's class were veteran politicians who could be seen as part of the "system" that needed fixing. At a time when the public was sick of partisan politics and business as usual, this "outsider" status made him even more attractive.

Of course, you didn't need to be a Kennedy to see something in John Edwards. All you needed was a subscription to *Capital Style* magazine, which put him alone on the cover of its February issue with the cover line BUILDING THE PERFECT SENATOR. The article, titled "Senator Perfect," presented Edwards as an almost accidental politician. The author noted that Edwards had failed to vote in six different elections and couldn't recall if he registered first as a Republican or a Democrat, but also argued that this inexperience was balanced by Edwards's many obvious gifts. Quoting the political analyst Stuart Rothenberg, the magazine said of Edwards, "He may well be Clinton without the baggage. That's what we're watching and waiting to find out." At a time when the Republicans and Karl Rove looked unstoppable, the Democrats needed someone like John Edwards. This is why *Time* called him "The Democrats' New Golden Boy." Senator Edwards loved all the attention but was also wary of it. "Andrew," he told me, "they just build you up so they can tear you down."

Washington seemed to love Edwards, and from the beginning he attracted attention from the kingmakers in his party. But he was still burdened with the ordinary chores that come with joining the world's most exclusive club. He had to get up to speed for his committees—Small Business; Health, Education, Labor, and Pensions; Intelligence; and Judiciary—and hire staff for his Washington office on the second floor of the Dirksen Senate Office Building and for outposts around the state. To keep in touch with his constituents, he began holding weekly events called Tar Heel Tuesdays, which were open to the public. In D.C., he gave key jobs to his top campaign aides, Josh and Julianna, and then hired dozens more. In North Carolina, he tapped a mix of political pros and old friends and neighbors.

I first asked for a job with Edwards on the day after the election, but as time passed I started to worry that his staff was overwhelmed with applicants and might overlook me. I didn't have a strong personal connection to the senator, but Wade Byrd, Edwards's friend and top donor, had told me to call him if I ever needed help. I drove down Interstate 40 to I-95 South and found the stately Victorian house where he kept his offices. He brought me into his private study, sat behind his desk, and talked about his friend "Johnny" Edwards and how he'd helped plot his candidacy. At the end of our talk, he promised to call Johnny on my behalf. He followed through, and in July I joined the Edwards team in Raleigh.

We worked out of space on the third floor of the historic Century Post Office, which was the first federal building constructed in North Carolina after the Civil War. Mr. and Mrs. Edwards picked the building for its architectural character and because it was some distance from where North Carolina's other senator, archconservative Jesse Helms, kept his office. Equipped with used federal chairs and desks (I found old Helms papers in mine), the place was furnished in a drab government style except for the personal items people added to the décor. I put up a framed tourism poster from the 1930s that showed the U.S. Capitol and declared, "Your National Capital Beckons You." Some of the people in the office worked every day on constituent issues like passports and Social Security concerns. My job involved working with state and local governments and helping citizens with complicated issues.

Everything you can imagine flows through a senator's local office, from immigration appeals to reports about unidentified flying objects. One lady left rambling messages about her sexual fantasies—all of them involved Senator Edwards—on the office answering machine every night. Agents of the Office of the U.S. Marshal eventually paid a visit to her trailer and asked her to stop making these calls. She didn't. We heard almost as often from a federal inmate who wrote the senator on ten-foot stretches of toilet paper. Every sheet was filled with his carefully penciled grievances about the government. Each time one of these communiqués arrived, I got a kick out of watching an intern try to use an official stamp to record receipt of the letter without tearing it.

Most of the real business I did required me to steer questions to the right federal agency or untangle red tape. People who had seen campaign ads saying that Senator Edwards was going to Washington to use his trial lawyer experience to be an advocate for the little people called to seek clemency for relatives on death row. I did a lot of listening and a lot of sympathizing but could offer them very little concrete assistance.

I was so gung ho that I worked overtime almost every day and often left the old building so late that when I tried to take the elevator to the street level, it would get locked and I would be trapped inside. I'd use the emergency phone and call for help. The officers who responded probably thought I was crazy to work all alone so late into the night. In fact I was just a young, ambitious guy who saw a real opportunity in Edwards. At every chance I volunteered to do more, so when everyone else turned down the job of driving the senator when he came to town—picking him up at the airport, ferrying him around the state, bringing him back to the airport—I grabbed it.

Having been around politicians my whole life, I understood that when they travel, major political figures need an assistant—usually called the "body man"—who will be available during every waking hour. (You'll know him when you see him because he's the one who has to collect every gift or piece of paper handed to his boss and has a Sharpie marker at the ready for the hordes of autograph seekers.)

The person chosen for this job is granted a high level of trust and responsibility, and a good performance can lead to big opportunities. President Clinton's body man Kris Engskov became head of public policy for Starbucks. Reggie Love, body man for Barack Obama, has become a genuine celebrity in his own right. Since trust brings with it a sense of duty and responsibility, the job also encourages a fierce kind of loyalty that is rarely seen outside of families. The body man can develop a sense of mission and commitment that is practically fanatical, and his sense of duty, to a boss who may influence the fate of the world, could lead him to overlook, indulge, and even enable things he might not countenance in another person. For example, David Powers, who served President Kennedy, never uttered a word about JFK's many relationships with women other than his wife. Likewise, many of the people who served Governor and then-President Clinton knew about his affairs and said nothing.

I wanted to set a new standard for body men. Whenever the senator was flying in, I would call the airline and arrange for an agent to meet him at the gate. (Since airlines have a lot of dealings with the federal government, they were eager to help.) The agent would escort the senator through the crowds to baggage claim and out the door, where I would be standing at the curb beside my white Chevy Suburban, which was running with either the heat or air-conditioning on. Inside, I'd have a cooler with cold Diet Cokes (he preferred cans) and snacks. National and local newspapers would be displayed for him to read, along with briefing pages. If it was dinnertime and he wasn't going to be able to eat, I'd have a take-out meal and a chilled glass of Chardonnay. The menu would depend on whether he had made a request or was on the Atkins diet at the time. Diet meals generally involved salmon and a salad with ranch dressing and no croutons from the Glenwood Grille or 518 West. At other times it was ribs, or country fare from Cracker Barrel. He loved Cracker Barrel—once, he was so excited to see a new Cracker Barrel near his house that he almost made me crash.

Like many people who travel for work, the senator would complain about how much his life "sucked" because he was often away from home. Everyone on the staff did everything possible to make travel easier on him. We did it because our fate was tied to his. Every once in a while, he would notice one thing that I had forgotten and mention it. I would apologize, but he would quickly laugh it off, saying I so rarely forgot things that he was just giving me a hard time. It became like a game to me. My goal was to make things run as smoothly as possible for a man I believed was a future president of the United States. For this reason, I didn't talk unless he wanted to talk, and I learned how to say "Yes, sir" to every request he ever made. "No" wasn't in my vocabulary.

I quickly became the senator's "go-to guy," whether the task was to obtain last-second tickets to Leno for a niece, retrieve his daughter Cate's lost purse at Christmas (she'd left it on a flight), or borrow a private jet for some urgent flight in a few hours. John and Elizabeth Edwards both acted as if nothing were beyond my reach and tested me on it. I was proud when I passed their tests and proud to tell my parents and friends about my adventures.

The senator and I quickly developed a routine where he would get in the Suburban, take a deep breath, and then reach over with his left hand, pat me on the shoulder, and say, "Andrew, it's good to see you." Often he needed to vent about the frustrations of working in the Senate, which is ruled by seniority, moves slowly, and is set up to promote compromise. He also complained about the volume of work dumped on him every day, especially the so-called briefing books prepared by his staff. These binders contained background materials on major issues ranging from domestic economic problems to foreign affairs. Smart people put many hours of effort into these books, and they were designed for quick study. To their frustration, the senator never seemed to get around to reading them. Even when he had time in the car, he preferred to talk with me about local politics or Carolina basketball or family. The conversation was easy because we had so much in common. We were both small-town Southern boys who enjoyed the same food, loved the same sports, and cared deeply about our families. Unlike almost everyone else in his life, I *never* asked him for anything.

When we got to the house and parked, I jumped out and grabbed the bags. I had a key (he always misplaced his) and would open the door and follow him inside. Mrs. Edwards would light up when he came home and give him a big hug. I had rarely seen two people who loved each other more. She was his most trusted adviser—on everything from politics to wardrobe—and he would ask for her input on every important decision.

As she got to know me as a reliable aide, Mrs. Edwards couldn't have been friendlier. She was so at ease, in fact, that if it was late and she was already in bed, she told me to just come on into the bedroom and put the suitcases in the closet while her husband went to look in on the kids. "It's all right, Andrew," she would say. "You're family."

It was a warm but also surprising statement. I had worked for the senator for only a few months, and my direct contact with Mrs. Edwards couldn't have added up to more than a few hours total time. But they were exceptional people, and being with them made you feel you were putting your time and energy into a noble cause. We *were* trying to make things better for people, to make the country and the world a better place. And because this kind of mission couldn't be squeezed into a nine-to-five box, I saw the Edwards family in their home and at odd hours. If that didn't make me family, it made me something more than an employee, and it felt pretty good.

Even so, I resisted when the Edwardses told me to address them by their first names. For some reason—maybe it was to remind myself that we would never be on equal footing or that he might be the next JFK—I would always call him "Senator" and her "Mrs. Edwards." I did this even on the night I dropped the senator at his home and got an emergency phone call before I had reached my own house, asking me to come back right away.

When I got there, I found the senator and Mrs. Edwards dressed for bed and laughing. It turned out the kids had jumped into bed with them and the whole thing had crashed to the floor. They said they needed my help putting it back together. I tried to respect Mrs. Edwards's privacy—her nightgown was a bit revealing—while helping her husband get the slats and rails in place, lift up the box spring, and seat the mattress. In my mind, it was an oddly intimate and personal chore, but there seemed to be almost no limit to what the Edwardses might ask of me or the degree to which they would let me into their lives.

Two

INSTANT SUCCESS

Born off of East Africa in the middle of August 1999, Dennis wandered north and west to the Caribbean, where he flexed his muscles and became a full-blown hurricane. He reached the North Carolina coast on September 1, lashing the state with dangerous winds and heavy rains. The sense of relief that came with the return of the sun didn't last very long, as the storm actually came back a week later to dump as much as eighteen inches on towns at the shore. Much of what wasn't flooded the first time got washed away with the second pass, including our wedding cake.

The cake was at the Holiday Inn Resort at Wrightsville Beach, where Cheri and I held our wedding reception in a moment of quiet weather on September 11. Months of planning produced a nearly perfect ceremony and celebration. We were married in a historic church, surrounded by family and friends, and walked outside to fountains, a horse-drawn carriage, rice, and the sounds of the church bells. It was a beautiful day, but the true meaning of it all didn't hit me until we were on our honeymoon in St. Lucia. Marrying Cheri made me happier than I had ever been. I had gotten the girl of my dreams, and my tumultuous past seemed far away.

While we were in the Caribbean, North Carolina went through a nightmare as another hurricane, Floyd, slammed into the coast near Cape Fear on September 16 at three in the morning. Floyd packed winds over a hundred miles an hour and brought a ten-foot ocean surge that flooded towns up and down the coast. He dumped so much rain that rivers across the state overflowed their banks and flooded thousands of homes. Fifty-three people would die from storm-related causes, and the state would suffer more than $3.7 billion in property damage. More flooding came as a series of lesser storms swept through, and by the end of the month there was hardly a dry spot in the eastern part of the state. Cheri and I watched in horror from our honeymoon paradise as CNN showed footage of the steeple of the church where we were married being blown off.

As the news reports showed, Princeville, famous as the first community established by freed slaves after the Civil War, was hit the hardest. Every building in the town was flooded, and every citizen had to be evacuated. But it wasn't Princeville's displaced people and damaged structures that stuck in your mind after you visited, it was the coffins. The powerful floodwaters had undermined graves and lifted caskets out of the ground. The water was so deep that as it receded, some of the coffins actually got lodged in trees. Others were scattered in muddy yards and on streets that were strewn with debris. It was a ghastly sight, and something that no witness ever forgot.

I saw the destruction in Princeville and other communities as I drove the senator around the state in the aftermath of the storm, meeting with disaster officials and offering whatever solace we could. Floyd was such an intense storm, and the destruction was so widespread, that President Clinton visited two days after the rain stopped to assure people that federal help was on the way and to soak up some national media attention as he played comforter in chief. "We're going to stand with you," he told people in Tarboro, "until you get back on your feet again, as long as it takes."

Clinton would be followed by a host of other officials, none of whom could change much of anything on the ground. Disaster agencies, charities, and communities were already digging out and cleaning up, and unless he was willing to grab a shovel or a hammer, all a politician could do was offer symbolic support. Edwards, who was always aware of press opportunities, spent lots of time in the disaster area and got his share of attention from TV and print reporters, but he wasn't the only elected official looking for the limelight. A few days after the storm, while I was helping to shovel out a church filled with mud and debris, Congresswoman Eva Clayton scurried inside, noticed the Edwards staff T-shirt I wore, looked at the mask I was wearing to protect myself from fungus, and said, "Young man, gimme that thing, here come the TV cameras." She took it so she could look as though she had been working. As soon as the news crews left, I got it back.

Fortunately, my boss wasn't quite so brazen when it came to playing to the cameras. He knew they were there, but he also went out of his way to connect with the people who had lost homes and even loved ones in the storm. Almost every time we arrived at a site—church, school, or fire-house—he acknowledged the various dignitaries and VIPs but also made a point of heading for the back rooms and kitchens where the work was being done by folks most politicians overlook.

Given his interest in working people, I was a little surprised by Senator Edwards's reluctance to roll up his sleeves and get a little dirty himself. Instead of picking up a hammer and driving some nails with Habitat for Humanity or throwing around some cut branches with a road-clearing crew, he would say something about his tight schedule and depart without risking a blister. I thought this was a politically tone-deaf choice that opened the door to people who might say he was too much style and too little substance. Eventually, I learned that while he wasn't afraid of breaking a sweat, he was afraid of looking silly and wanted to avoid doing things that reminded him too much of the people he called "rednecks" that he grew up around in Robbins.

As I got to know the senator, I came to understand his ambivalence about his background. As a smart and sensitive young man, he had worked very hard to get an education, build a career, and separate himself from the rougher elements of the small-town South. He was proud of being one of Robbins's favorite sons, along with the astronaut Charles E. Brady, who was pictured on a mural in town. (Brady would commit suicide in 2006.) And when he ran for office, the senator harkened back to his humble beginnings with real affection. But while he may have still loved Robbins, or the *idea* of a place like Robbins, he didn't want to go back to being the boy who once lived there, even for a moment.

As flaws go, Edwards's fear of looking stupid and his ambivalence about his past were small. He presented himself as someone who understood the strain people felt as they lived paycheck to paycheck and said he found it easy to imagine what the flood victims experienced. He often said to me, "There but for the grace of God." I admired him for putting his arms around people and reassuring them. The Edwards staff worked overtime to help the victims of the disaster, and he returned to the area several times to check on the progress of the cleanup.

These inspections became part of an ambitious project—you might call it "The Hundred-County Campaign"—that I proposed to him a few months after joining the staff in Raleigh. The project, which called for the senator to visit every county in the state no matter how small and isolated, grew out of the basic notion that if he was going to accomplish anything in Washington, he would need the voters' support, especially in the next election. And while incumbency is usually an advantage, in the past thirty-five years no one in his seat had ever served more than one term. One of these senators, John East, had committed suicide. Another, Terry Sanford, was ousted when a close friend turned on him and ran for the same office. The job seemed jinxed.

I presented the idea of the hundred-county campaign with a written proposal that included a color-coded map showing where the senator had already spent time and where he had never shaken a single hand. I argued that with a deliberate effort he could get to all these places, where many people didn't even know who he was, and raise his political profile while doing some official business. Mrs. Edwards absolutely loved the proposal, and since she was the senator's closest adviser, it got the green light. The project would consume much of my time and put the senator and me in a car together for lots of long road trips. My job involved finding people and places to visit—we stressed education, medical care, the military, and law enforcement to beef up his standing on these issues—and all the logistics of getting him around. I poured days into the task of making sure everything went smoothly. In those days before people had global position systems in their cars, this preparation included actually driving the entire route, timing out the distances, and noting the directions down to a tenth of a mile on the backs of business cards. Sometimes I ran so short on time that I would have to make these test runs in the middle of the night on dark, windy, unlit country roads. I would often get lost, be forced to backtrack, and then find myself driving like one of the Dukes of Hazzard so I might get home in time to get a few hours of sleep.

The next day, I would have my Suburban all prepped with maps, cell phones, newspapers, briefing folders, Diet Cokes, water, and food, and we would attack the schedule like an army on the move. At each stop I'd reach into the backseat and grab a plastic plaque with the United States Senate seal and a roll of Velcro tape and make sure the plaque was fixed to the podium where he would speak. I tried to stage the events to capitalize on his trial lawyer's skills. This meant keeping his formal remarks short, leaving plenty of time for questions and answers, and surrounding him with people. But while I followed a set routine, the senator would often deviate in a way that would charm the crowd and let him connect with people in a more direct and emotional way. A classic case in point occurred at a school in rural Greene County, where the staff had begun to turn around a long record of poor performance. They had done this with a new program that involved building discipline and pride and used many unconventional techniques, especially songs, to help students learn.

As he often did, Edwards began his improvising by suggesting that the event be expanded. Feigning irritation with me, he said, "Andrew, we shouldn't be seeing just a few folks and leave everyone else out. Can't we bring everyone into someplace like the auditorium and get 'em all involved?" The principal of the school, eager to please the senator, loved his suggestion and announced that everyone should come to the cafeteria for a special assembly. You could feel the excitement ripple through the building as kids filed into the hallways. But I also noticed that these were the quietest, best-behaved children I had ever seen. No one ran. No one shouted. And they took their seats in the cafeteria without any ruckus at all. Walking with one of the teachers, I noticed there were no locks on the lockers and no graffiti on the walls. "We don't need locks—these kids learn trust," he told me. "And they learn pride. There is no graffiti."

When everyone was gathered together, the principal gave the kids a chance to show the senator what they knew. One small girl got up from her seat, and a hush fell over the room. Then she started to sing:

Two, three, five, seven, and eleven,
Thirteen, seventeen, nineteen, too,
Twenty-three and twenty-nine.
It's so fine,
Only two factors make a number prime.

When the little girl finished this first verse, every kid in the room joined her for the rest of the song, singing out prime numbers past one thousand. The performance took eight or nine minutes, but it was a breathtaking and inspiring thing to hear. These kids had a fraction of the resources of similarly sized schools and a hundred times the spirit. At the end, Edwards moved into the crowd and knelt to give the girl who had started the song a big hug. Whatever he might have said during a speech or question-and-answer session could never have the power of that gesture. Most important, it was moments like this (and there were many of them) that made me feel that my assessment of him as a leader was correct.

As we left the school, our hosts followed us to the car and waved goodbye. If anyone on the school staff had started the day with doubts about the senator, my bet is that they were resolved by the time he left. The same could be said for students who would go home and tell their parents about the assembly or cast their own votes in future elections. We were also happy to note that we had visited yet another county on the list. As we drove away in the Suburban, I said something like "Well, that's another county," and the senator responded by high-fiving me and saying, "Check!" with a wave of his arm, mimicking the gesture one would make to draw a huge check-mark on a blackboard.

On the day we visited Green County, we were close enough to home to sleep at our own houses. However, many of these expeditions were two- or three-day affairs, and we'd find ourselves spending nights at hotels and having three meals a day together. The first hotel I ever booked for us turned out to be a disaster. Located near Camp LeJeune, the Onslow Inn was very affordable and in the right spot. Unfortunately, every room reeked of mold and mildew. We stayed but the senator was miserable and he complained loudly.

In the days we spent touring the state, we talked about family, politics, our personal histories, marriage—like me, he said he loved his wife and was completely faithful—and everything else you can imagine. The subject of the senator's son Wade came up often, and he frequently asked me to drive by the cemetery so he could visit his grave, which was marked by a ten-foot-tall marble statue of an angel emerging from the stone, with what appears to be Wade's face cradled in her arms.

If we had company in the car, like a national reporter, the senator often discussed cases he had worked on as a lawyer, and whenever we passed a courthouse, he became nostalgic about performing in front of juries and judges and the thrill of winning a big victory for a deserving client. (He always gave some credit to Elizabeth for these victories, because she always studied his cases, offered advice, and even helped him with his closing arguments.) He would start to tell a story to a reporter, then stop and say, "Oh, have I told you this one, Andrew?" I would shake my head no. Then I would smile to myself and settle in to hear about another of his great legal conquests, for the twentieth time.

One of his favorite stories from his practice was about a case he tried in a small town close to Robbins. It was the first time his mother came to watch him work, and she was bursting with pride. Near the end of the trial, she ran into the jury foreman at the grocery store. She had known the man for years, and he told her, "We just think the world of your son." Even I knew this was probably grounds for a mistrial, but the story ends with a victory for Edwards.

At other times, we talked about University of North Carolina basketball (college ball is a religion in the state), and we planned routes for our daily jogs. Edwards was thoroughly addicted to running and would get cranky on the days he couldn't have an hour or more to change clothes, cover a few miles, shower, and cool down. I would join him, and as we pounded down city streets or dug our way across the sand at a beach, we would talk. Invariably, he'd say something about how much he preferred to be home in North Carolina and how disappointed he was by Washington and the life of a United States senator.

You're forgiven if you can't muster empathy for someone who complains about holding a prestigious elected office that brings him into the circles of power and requires him to be praised and honored wherever he goes. (Cue the world's tiniest violin.) The life of a senator is not digging ditches. But if you do it well, it can consume your every waking hour, and the travel back and forth to your home state can become exhausting. Senators spend an inordinate amount of time fending off lobbyists and begging for political contributions, which most find to be degrading. Finally, as a freshman, a senator has hardly any power. In his first years, Edwards was permitted to take up one real issue, a proposed "patients' bill of rights," and he got lucky when his colleagues allowed him to put his name on the bill beside that of John McCain, who really did believe in working across party lines to get things done.

The legislation Edwards and McCain proposed would have given Americans more say in their own medical care, making it easier for them to access services and giving them more power in dealing with health insurance companies. In the long run, the idea would be adopted by both the House and the Senate, but it was eventually vetoed by President Bush. In the short term, it gave Senator Edwards a very popular issue to talk about, and it brought him more attention from the national media than anyone else in his Senate class. Edwards couldn't have risen so fast without some help, and as time passed I would learn what a powerful friend and mentor he had in Senator Ted Kennedy, who was coming to believe himself that Edwards might be a future president. In a party that was short on charisma, the old warhorse saw promise in John Edwards and was going to do whatever he could to promote him.

More help would come from Senator Bob Kerrey of Nebraska, who saw great potential in Edwards and came to Raleigh in the fall of 1999 to attend a fund-raiser. Because I had to pick him up at the airport, I asked Cheri to take care of things at the Angus Barn steakhouse, where the event would be held, and she did. Kerrey, who insisted on carrying his own bag when I met him, couldn't have been nicer. He had just gotten a BlackBerry phone and was beguiled by its capabilities. "Look at this," he said, showing me the screen. "I just texted my whole staff."

Although he was a war hero who had run for president himself, Kerrey was unpretentious and undemanding. He drew a good crowd to the donors' cocktail party, where he made my boss sound as though he were already a key player in the United States Senate. Afterward, when Edwards asked him to share a dinner in the restaurant, he turned to me and said, "Andrew, why don't you and Cheri join us?"

For a local staffer with just a few months on the job, the invitation was like being asked to move up to the grown-ups' table at Thanksgiving. And unfortunately, I discovered what a lot of young people learn when they join the adults: It's not as great as you expect it will be. On this night, the Edwardses tried a little too hard to impress their guest, which was embarrassing, and then the senator put his foot in his mouth when he asked Cheri about her job as a nurse. Somehow he managed to get onto the subject of her salary and then insulted her by blurting out, "Jesus, how the heck do you survive on horrible pay like that?"

The comment bothered me on several levels, including the way it contradicted everything I had heard the senator say about how he respected working people. Cheri left the restaurant more than a little steamed. She actually made a very good living, just not relative to someone who made $10 million a year. Cheri never forgot it. I decided it reflected a flaw in a man who otherwise possessed a great many positive qualities, which balanced it out.

On the way home, as I agreed with Cheri about the senator's insensitivity, I also thought about how, in the course of the evening, Senator Kerrey had referred many times to Edwards's bright future as a national leader. It was hard for me to believe that a guy who had served less than a year in the one and only political job he had ever held was being described as a future star of the Democratic Party. It was so fast. But I also recalled what I had seen the first time I saw Edwards speak. Maybe, I thought, my intuition had been right.

Serious talk about John Edwards running for national office began long before the press and the public became aware of the possibility. It started in June 2000, when Vice President Al Gore came to North Carolina. As they planned the trip, Gore's people knew only that they wanted to get him into the graduation ceremony at Tarboro High School, which served one of the areas most affected by Hurricane Floyd. Besides that one stop, they wanted a second setting for what they called "an education event" and a third for "a tech event." The selection was complicated by the Secret Service, which required we consider sniper locations as we reviewed sites. I helped them settle on Broughton High School in Raleigh for a question-and-answer session with students and the North Carolina State University technology center, where Gore talked about the Internet. (I also pushed for these locations because the senator's children had gone to Broughton and he graduated from State.)

Senator Edwards and I accompanied Gore for the full day. It was my first experience with a motorcade operated by the Secret Service, and I got a sense of their readiness when the driver of a stopped car pulled onto the highway. Suddenly the rear windows of a black Suburban popped open and two agents, their firearms visible, leaned out. The stray car was surrounded by motorcycle cops, and the motorcade proceeded at full speed. (For fun I called my parents and told them what was going on.)

At each stop that day, the vice president excelled at meeting people one on one but put them to sleep with his public performance. The senator, in contrast, knew how to work a crowd. He knew when he had them, knew when they were getting bored, and knew when to wrap things up. At the last stop, when the crowd applauded the end of Gore's talk, I happened to be standing near two Secret Service agents. As Edwards and Gore waved to the crowd, one turned to the other and said, "If you ask me, the wrong one's running for president."

A few weeks later, the senator told me that he had gotten a few feelers from Gore's people, who said he was being considered for the job of running mate. Some of the hints came from Harrison Hickman, the political pollster and consultant who had helped Edwards beat Lauch Faircloth and just happened to be one of Gore's closest advisers. Edwards also shared a friend with Gore in Walter Dellinger, a prominent law professor at Duke. Both men knew how well the charismatic Edwards performed, how he could take apart a tough issue and explain it in terms anyone could grasp and win them over to his point of view.

In mid-July, on a day when I picked him up at the airport—Diet Coke chilling, AC blasting—and we stopped for some groceries, my cell phone buzzed while I was away from it. When I checked the message, I heard Warren Christopher's soft voice saying he was trying to reach John Edwards. (Former secretary of state Christopher was helping to guide Gore's vice presidential pick.) We took the groceries home and called him back. It was at just this moment that Emma Claire, the senator's two-year-old daughter, decided to raise the volume on the television so she could hear every word of the song "I love you. You love me!" being sung by Barney, the purple dinosaur. I raced to turn down the volume but couldn't find the remote control.

Between Barney's blaring voice and Christopher's exceedingly soft one, Edwards couldn't hear much of the call. Mrs. Edwards, who had been hanging on every confused word her husband said, pounced as soon as he hung up the phone.

"Well, what did he say?"

"I'm not sure."

"What do you mean, you're not sure?"

"Well, I think he was telling me I was one of two being considered."

"But you're not sure?"

"Well, the TV was so loud and I could barely hear him, but I think that was what he said."

"Why didn't you ask him to repeat himself?"

"I didn't want to embarrass myself. Besides, I was pretty sure I got what he was saying."

He was right. Christopher had called to say that while other names might be suggested, there were only two people under consideration, and Edwards was one of them. He and Elizabeth were thrilled by the news, and they asked me to arrange a little celebration with their "dinner club" friends at a local chain restaurant called Tripp's. I got on the phone and set it up, and by the time I was finished, I could hear him trying to temper his wife's expectations. He reminded her that he was still an inexperienced politician with no serious national profile. Like Gore, he was from the South, and most presidential nominees try to balance the ticket with a partner from a different region. Also, Edwards had absolutely no standing with party insiders across the country.

The man we believed was the other finalist, Dick Gephardt, had a political résumé as long as your arm. A member of Congress since 1977, he lost a bid for the presidential nomination in 1988 but became House majority leader the following year. He was from Missouri, which would give the ticket a Midwestern flavor, and he was both a policy wonk and a true insider with national party people. Everyone from New Hampshire to Iowa and beyond knew Gephardt, and half of them probably owed him a favor.

The main thing going against him was his style—he was almost as low-key as Gore.

When I got home with my news about the vice presidency, Cheri was shocked and a bit impressed. She had been skeptical about the senator. The idea that he might be moving up didn't change her opinion completely, but it gave her a bit of confirmation about my judgment, proof that I had placed my bet on a pretty good horse.

Days after Christopher's call, Edwards went to meet with Gore at the vice president's mansion on the grounds of the U.S. Naval Observatory. He did not think he had a good shot at the job, but he enjoyed the publicity he was getting. When I saw the senator next, he talked a little about Gore, saying he had been strangely shy and that there was no spark between them. He made fun of the vice president's pointy-toed cowboy boots, which he wore with a suit, and he said he thought Gore was much too cautious. Eager to be his own man and distance himself from the Lewinsky scandal, Gore had all but banished President Clinton from his campaign. Edwards, who had used the president to great advantage while courting the black vote in North Carolina, thought this was a big mistake.

But although he was lukewarm about the man he met, the senator was extremely impressed by the vice president's official residence. Built in 1893, Number One Observatory Circle is a three-story building with a round tower and a high-pitched main roof with dormers. It looks a lot like the faux Victorian mini-mansions you see in pricey developments all across the South, except it's the real thing. The senator thought it was a nicer home than the White House and would be the ideal place to prepare for a run for the presidency in, say, 2008. He didn't say what he intended to do if he became president, but as I came to learn, most big-time politicians don't think much about what they will do when they get to the top of the mountain until they arrive. Until then, it's all about the climb.

Of course, a place on the short list for vice president isn't a guarantee of anything, especially if you are the guy's in-state advance man. With this in mind, Cheri and I planned our future as if we were going to stay in North Carolina. She went off the birth control pill, and we hoped she would soon be pregnant. We had enough confidence in the future to buy a four-bedroom place on Lake Wheeler, on the south side of Raleigh, and start a major remodeling project.

We moved in at the end of July and were still unpacking on Saturday, August 5. I put a television on top of a cardboard box and turned on CNN. At some point while I was passing by, I heard a newscaster mention Edwards as they showed a video of the senator, Mrs. Edwards, and Julianna Smoot getting into his beat-up Buick in Georgetown surrounded by photographers. Minutes later, Julianna called to say that the Gore people had sent some sort of signal indicating Edwards was in. Then, almost in the same breath, she backed off a bit, insisting that while all the signs were positive, nothing was set in stone.

For the rest of the weekend, the cable news shows speculated about Gore's choice, which meant he enjoyed a bonanza of free publicity and everyone connected with the senator suffered with nail-biting anxiety. Most of the reports followed the themes that appeared in a *Wall Street Journal* article—"North Carolina's Edwards Gets a Shot at the Gore Ticket"—that ran through the pros and cons. The one line in the piece that stood out to me was, "When Republican nominee George W. Bush chose balding, 59-year-old Dick Cheney for his ticket, Mr. Edwards's youth became an even bigger asset."

The buzz had become a racket, and it was impossible to ignore the idea that John Edwards just might become vice president. (On Sunday, the *Daily News* in New York even published a story saying Gore favored Edwards and would take Massachusetts senator John Kerry if Edwards turned him down.) I had my own ambitions, and I thought about how well I had served the senator and the possibility that he might want me to work in the vice president's office. For me, an offer to work in a Gore/Edwards administration would mean an instant jump from the minor leagues to the majors. And as much as my apolitical wife loved the life we were building in North

Carolina, she said she would make the move and support me one hundred percent.

I tried to temper my own expectations, the way the senator had tempered his wife's on the day Warren Christopher called. Gore had other people under consideration, and presidential candidates always float a bunch of names to see how people react and to grab as much free press as possible. I also kept in mind that a jump to Washington would be disruptive. Cheri and I had just moved into a new house, and we were serious about starting a family. There was no sense in getting all worked up about something that might never happen.

Gore would make his announcement on the coming Tuesday at his campaign headquarters in Nashville. The senator and I began another road trip on Monday morning, heading north to Asheville, where we would stay overnight before heading into the Great Smoky Mountains and three remote counties that we could check off our list. When we got in the car, he announced that he was going to share something special, something he hadn't told anyone else. (I knew this wasn't true, but I played along.) He then told me that on Saturday he had heard from one of Gore's closest advisers, who said he was going to be picked for vice president. But then on Sunday, after the idea of Edwards for vice president was floated on the political talk shows, he got another call indicating the deal was not yet set.

"Today I don't know any more than you," he said. But this didn't make much sense to me. If he was going to be the pick, he would have been informed. So any hope we had was slender at best.

All day long we kept waiting for the phone to ring with Gore on the other end, asking Edwards to come to Nashville. In the mountains the cell phone signals are so unreliable that we often lost service, so I would check every few minutes for messages. We heard from staffers and political advisers and Mrs. Edwards, but not Gore. At the events we held, where the crowds were suddenly massive and we saw more reporters than usual, the senator made sure I arranged to have him jokingly introduced as "the next vice president of the United States."

That night in Asheville, we stayed at the historic Grove Park Resort, a massive hotel built in 1912 out of local granite by a patent medicine huckster who filled it with Arts and Crafts furniture and decorated it with quotations from Thoreau and Emerson and others. A few special rooms feature theme decorations. The "Great Gatsby" is Art Deco. The "Swinging Sixties" has a flower power motif.

As usual, I checked him into a suite and put myself in a regular room. Even though it was in the basement, it still cost hundreds of dollars for the night. Before dinner, we took a long run in the streets of Asheville and even cut through the parking lot attached to the building where my sports pub (now a Chinese restaurant) had, in the good times before bankruptcy, buzzed with life. At some point during the workout, I turned to the senator and said, "Doesn't it suck?" He wasn't sure what I meant, so I explained that I was talking about Gore and the all-but-obvious fact that he wasn't going to be selected.

In response, Edwards told me that his life experience, especially his son's death, had taught him to control his expectations and never take anything for granted. He had thought about what Gore had to consider as he made his choice and concluded that John Edwards was not the ideal pick. Since he never had the job and never expected to get it, losing out wasn't going to hurt. He also said something about how he had been a senator for only a short time and that the future would bring so many opportunities, it didn't make much sense to get upset about this one.

The next morning, as we drove west toward a meeting on the banks of an isolated reservoir called Fontana Lake, radio news reports from Nashville noted that Gore was going to make his announcement at noon. I began to feel like the one kid in class who wasn't invited to a birthday party. When we got to the lake, we were met by half a dozen officials from local communities and the Tennessee Valley Authority. The locals complained about the TVA's policy of drawing water out of the river to generate hydroelectricity. They thought it discouraged tourism and fishing and the economic benefits that come with visitors. I watched closely to see if the senator was bored or distracted, but if he was, he didn't show it. He left the lakeside assuring his hosts that he would look into the problem, and they were pleased.

Lunch was scheduled at a local school where the kids were on vacation, but we would meet with teachers and administrators. On the way there, we were shocked to hear that Gore had picked not Dick Gephardt, but Joe Lieberman, a senator from Connecticut with little national reputation and even less charisma than Gore. (We had heard rumors about Lieberman but had dismissed them as ridiculous.) In that moment, considering Lieberman's and Edwards's strengths, I believed that Gore had been afraid that if he picked Edwards, his running mate might outshine him. The senator insisted he never really expected to be picked and that he wasn't very disappointed. He repeated what he had said the night before about all he had seen in life and how he had learned to roll with the punches. I kept thinking about how the whole country was focused on Gore and Lieberman.

It was a punch to the gut. At that point, we all felt that Gore would win and any future hopes of a presidential run for Senator Edwards were a long way off. It was confusing working in politics at times like this; you want what's best for your team, but you want what's best for yourself, too.

At the school, we were met by the principal and given the usual tour. Somewhere along the way, Gore and Lieberman called and I took the senator into an empty room to congratulate them and agree that he would contribute to the campaign in any way he could. When he came back, it seemed as if nothing had happened. He sat down with a small group of educators and listened carefully to their concerns about the funding and technology needs of rural schools. No trace of disappointment showed on his face, and he was completely attentive. Looking back on that day ten years later, I can say he was never more presidential.

(Eventually, the senator told me what had happened with the Gore pick. According to Edwards, he *had* been anointed on the Saturday prior to the announcement, but the choice did not go over well among Democratic

Party insiders and with various pundits. The next day, the Gore family met behind closed doors, and when the session ended Lieberman was in.)

Realistically, the nomination for vice president was too much to expect for a guy who had run for office only once and had served a grand total of nineteen months in the Senate. Knowing this, I found it easier to focus on the chores Cheri and I had to finish at our new house and enjoy what the summer had to offer. We went to a Jimmy Buffett concert at an outdoor venue called Walnut Creek and attended a good friend's wedding at a country club down in Charlotte. Cheri wasn't feeling quite like herself, but I figured she was just a little run-down. Besides, we managed to have a great time at both events.

I was free to relax because the boss was in great demand out of state. In the middle of the month, he attended the Democratic National Convention at the massive Staples Center arena in Los Angeles. He had a minor speaking role: five minutes and not in prime time. But he also got to visit state delegations, where he met dozens of people who could help him in the future, and he socialized with the glittery Hollywood wing of the party, which was out in force. No matter what you might think of the Democrats at any given moment, you cannot deny that it is by far the entertainment industry's favorite party. Cher, John Travolta, Martin Sheen, Christie Brinkley, and many others turned out for the Democrats. Before he even left Los Angeles, the national media were describing John Edwards as a rising star and "the future" of the Democratic Party.

I heard all about the Hollywood scene when the senator finally returned and we resumed our routine, crisscrossing the state to meet constituents and officials. The senator was practically giddy with excitement about the convention and wide-eyed over the people he had met and the things he had learned. Always eager to tweak his technique, he was especially proud of learning how to address a vast but distracted audience like the crowd at the Staples Center. The party's media consultants had coached him on how to stop for applause lines and pretend that he had looked into the crowd and caught someone's eye. This bit of acting is essential for anyone who wants to look good while addressing weary delegates in midafternoon, and John Edwards was delighted to report that he had mastered it.

Others agreed with the senator's self-assessment. A little more than a week after the convention, Senator Edwards was the subject of a column in *The Wall Street Journal* by the paper's Capitol Hill veteran Al Hunt. The piece cited glowing assessments by big-name Democrats, but the comment that stuck out came from Alex Castellanos, a Republican consultant who had tried to help Lauch Faircloth fend off the Edwards challenge in 1998: "Edwards is the Robert Redford of politics, a 'natural.' " Of course, Castellanos was actually referring to the character Roy Hobbs, whom Redford played in a movie called *The Natural,* but his point was clear. John Edwards looked, walked, talked, and acted like a great leader, and he made it look effortless. And in a thirty-second sound bite age, these traits could be more valuable to a politician than decades of experience in public service.

I agreed with Castellanos, but I also knew the senator was sensitive about his natural gifts. He wanted people to remember that he came from a very small town and was raised in a lower-middle-class household where he got lots of love—his mom thought he could do no wrong—but no luxuries. "I've worked hard all my life," he would say. "This isn't easy."

As the senator and I went back on the road, he continued to hone his political skills. He was at his best when he encountered resistance in a crowd, like the time we went to an American Legion hall in a small town and someone asked why he opposed a constitutional amendment that would ban flag burning. The room was full of war veterans who had risked their lives and seen their friends die in defense of the flag, and they felt deeply insulted by the thought of anyone desecrating it. The senator opposed the amendment because he considered it a free-speech issue and he believed the Constitution was so sacred that amendments should be rarely enacted. Somehow in that hall he managed to listen respectfully, offer a differing point of view, and reach an understanding with a group that met him with real hostility.

The legion appearance left the senator feeling energized and engaged. He had a much more easygoing experience at a gathering called the Fatherhood Summit. At this meeting, he spoke a bit about the importance of fathers, and because I had spent so much time in his home, I knew he spoke sincerely. I had seen how he related to his children, making them feel nurtured, protected, and secure. Whenever he was home, he watched movies with the kids and took charge of bedtime, making sure stories were read, pillows were fluffed, and blankets were tucked in. And on many occasions when Mrs. Edwards had reached her limit with the kids, he would take over and restore harmony almost instantly.

The routine at the Edwards home was familiar to me because with every passing day I was getting more deeply involved in the family's life, even as I fulfilled my official duties. When they were in Washington, I took care of their houses in Raleigh and at Figure Eight Island near Wilmington. Home to about four hundred houses and no businesses, Figure Eight is a private gated community where seabirds outnumber people and security is so tight that it's a favorite for celebrities such as Tom Cruise, Andy Griffith, and Tom Hanks. A typical maintenance-related e-mail from Mrs. Edwards to me about this house included dozens of items, for example:

- Shower door in MBR replaced with something stronger.
- Painting the white exterior trim around windows, over the walkway.
- Have the kitchen stools sanded and primed. Base color can be white.
- Hot tub removed. Deck replaced. Poles for hammock added.
- Replace microwave (shelf where cabinet is presently is okay, so you can just enlarge existing space, and we don't have to buy built-in kit).
- Check all lightbulbs, replace those that need replacement (have 6-year bulbs for light fixtures in difficult locations), maybe label the switches as this is done.

- Have the crawl spaces on the top floor cleaned (presently too dusty etc. to use).

The Edwardses had similar expectations for their aides in Washington, who would often call me as they waited on the cable man, the repairman, or a delivery from eBay. (Strange as this may seem, many senators treat aides this way, as if they are personal assistants and not federally paid workers.) In North Carolina the list of chores was practically endless. I made sure the Edwardses were registered to vote and that their cars were properly inspected and maintained. More than once, I lent them Cheri's car to use while theirs was in the shop. At other times, I gave the senator my Suburban to use for errands.

These little favors generally went off without a hitch, but one incident stood out as an indicator of things to come. I loaned the senator my new Suburban, which I had just bought to replace the one worn out during the hundred-county odyssey. He drove it to the Village Draft House in Raleigh, where a blogger, who later reported what she saw, observed him shaking a few hands, signing some autographs, and waiting at the bar for a take-out order of salmon and vegetables. She watched as he departed, got behind the wheel, and backed my new Suburban into a parked car. He got out, looked around to see if anyone had seen him, and drove away quickly. The right rear bumper on my brand-new car suffered a dent the size of a dinner plate. The senator never said a word to me about it. I couldn't bring myself to confront him about the damage and ask him to pay for a repair. Cheri wasn't about to pay for it to be fixed or file a claim and watch our insurance rates go up. In this stalemate, the dent remained, and every time we went out to the driveway, we got a reminder of John Edwards's sense of entitlement.

In general, Cheri had trouble understanding why I worked long hours performing my regular duties for the senator and then serving as butler, personal shopper, and all-around handyman for the entire family. She thought the extra roles were demeaning for a man of thirty-four with a law degree. I saw her point, but I had reasons for my devotion. First, I was doing the job the only way I knew, saying yes to every request and doing my best all the time. Second, I truly believed that John Edwards was going to be president of the United States one day, and I thought that this would be good for the country and for our family.

Finally, I knew that I had become indispensable. I felt this because from time to time the senator would call from New York or California and ask me to perform some special duty, saying, "Anyone else would fuck it up, Andrew, but if I ask you to do something, I never have to worry about it again." (He had complete confidence in me.) I believed that by staying close to John Edwards, I might rise along with him and earn a secure, comfortable future for myself and my family. I say "family" because in the late summer of 2000, Cheri discovered that the physical discomfort she had felt at the Jimmy Buffett concert and at my friend's wedding was an early sign of pregnancy. We were going to have a baby come February, and I hoped it would be the first of many. Now that I had a family to support, I was especially concerned about being a good provider.

In the early months of the pregnancy, I was able to give Cheri a little extra attention because the senator was involved in the presidential campaign, speaking for the Gore-Lieberman ticket at different events around the country. Whenever I saw him during this time, Edwards complained about how lackluster the ticket seemed and said that by sidelining Bill Clinton, Gore was taking a star player out of the lineup. More critically, he was not using Clinton to attract every black vote he could get. It would cost him, he said. The way he saw it, people who liked Clinton might respond to him and go to the polls for Gore. Those who hated Clinton would never pull the lever for Gore anyway.

On election night, the senator asked me to watch the returns at his house in Raleigh with him, Mrs. Edwards, and their Country Club Hills friends. We all celebrated a little when some of the networks called Florida for the Democrats, because it was a key battleground state. Then, as more returns came in, the Florida count tightened, and by ten P.M. it seemed to belong to

George W. Bush. The senator and I were intrigued by the reports coming from the networks, but as time passed I noticed that we were the only ones talking about it. The party at the Edwards house started to thin out before midnight. The senator's former law partner and closest friend, David Kirby, departed before one o'clock, and then Mrs. Edwards went to bed. The senator and I were the last holdouts, and Cheri called a few times to ask when I was coming home. Every time I got up, he asked me to stay longer.

All night long, the senator had only hinted at the idea that he wouldn't mind too much if Gore actually lost. Now that we were alone, two teammates dissecting the game, he spoke openly about how the Democrats were so short on future presidential contenders that he ranked near the top, despite his lack of experience. A Gore victory would mean he would have to wait eight years before taking his shot. If Bush won, Edwards could make a run at the 2004 nomination.

I had assumed that Edwards would spend at least six or more years in the Senate and I would glide along with him. This greater ambition, stated so boldly, surprised me a little. I asked, "Do you think you are really ready?" I had in mind his lack of experience and what I thought was his reluctance to grapple with difficult new issues. (He still didn't like to read the staff-prepared briefing books.)

He answered by confessing that he knew he was pushing things a little too quickly, but he added that "there are only so many times when that door cracks open. When it does, you've got to take the opportunity and push your way through, whether you think you're completely ready or not. If you don't, the chance may not come again." He also spoke in a team mode, about "us" being in the White House. About "us" creating change. It was intoxicating.

At some point in our conversation, the senator noted, with the hint of a smile, that he was going to get serious about reading his briefing books and other materials on national and foreign affairs. In this moment, he reminded me of a bright but smart-alecky schoolboy who, upon hearing he's about to fail, promises his teacher that he's finally going to buckle down and do his homework.

That night, the topsy-turvy returns made it difficult to tell just who was going to wind up president, but the way Gore handled himself—conceding to Bush and then calling back to unconcede—did not bode well. As I left, in the predawn darkness, we both had a hunch that the Democrats would somehow be outfoxed and lose.

I considered what Edwards had said. There was merit to it. I had my own interests in mind as I turned the key to fire up the Suburban and realized that I was the one who had stayed up all night with the senator, watching and planning and scheming. If I stayed close to him, it was possible that I'd accompany him through national campaigns and, ultimately, find a job in the White House.

Sitting behind the wheel of the Chevy, I flicked on the wipers and let them clear the dew off the windshield. With sunrise still more than an hour away, I needed the headlights to get home, but as I drove my future seemed so bright that I could have used some sunglasses.

Two weeks after the election, more than twenty million Americans opened *People* magazine to find a glamour shot of John Edwards lounging on a sofa in a rust-colored Ralph Lauren sweater with a gilt-edged book in his hands. The magazine's cover announced its annual Sexiest Man of the Year award—winner Brad Pitt—and the senator appeared as Sexiest Politician. (I thought back to the day of the *People* photo shoot, when the photographer had asked him to roll up his pants legs and stick his legs in the Edwardses' backyard pool. Elizabeth had refused, saying it wasn't "presidential." The staff had just been glad they'd remembered to have the pool cleaned.) The brief article accompanying the photo quoted North Carolina secretary of state Elaine Marshall on his "clean-cut boyish charm" and noted that Mrs. Edwards said, "I feel very safe in his arms. He's someone who's there to protect you. That's more enduring than someone who just looks good in a suit."

For weeks, months, and even years to come, John Edwards would face some fairly merciless teasing about the *People* photo, and he would make a concerted effort to look less youthful and more senatorial. (The right hair-cut would help enormously.) But in a business where name recognition is essential to survival, his cameo appearance in the "sexy man" issue was priceless. This is because *People* reaches a huge number of people who never read a serious newsmagazine or tune in to *Meet the Press*. Short of appearing on a reality TV show, there was no better way to reach these voters than *People*.

Beyond the direct contact with the public, an appearance in a mass-market weekly can also influence the men and women who control other, more serious media outlets. Suddenly, they decided that Edwards was a high-profile politician with a big grassroots following. As a consequence, he got calls for interviews and pundits recognized his potential. (A month after the *People* magazine appearance, William Safire of *The New York Times* wrote that Edwards was the front-runner in the undeclared race to run for president as a Democrat in 2004.) All this happened because he had a great smile and was willing to pose for the political equivalent of a cheesecake photograph.

Three

I'M "FAMILY"

Brody Young took his time.

Cheri's due date came and went, and when her obstetrician finally decided to induce labor, the little guy still waited a full day to make an appearance. When he finally arrived at 2:40 A.M. on May 26, 2001, he had to torture us a bit—turning blue and refusing to breathe—until the medical team finally got him to take a big gulp of air and say hello to the world. At eight pounds nine ounces, he was a sturdy little guy, and Cheri, with her background in neonatal and pediatric nursing, seemed to me to be the most attentive mother in the world. She would need all of her strength and expertise, because in her first few months as a mother, life was going to challenge her in some extraordinary ways.

At the time Brody was born, our house was undergoing a major renovation. When we brought the baby home, we had access to the basement and the second floor, but the first floor, including the kitchen, was blocked off with plastic sheeting and the walls had been taken down to the studs. In the same period, my job was becoming even more demanding, and the senator and his family had come to rely on me—and reward me—in new ways. I was not just the senator's aide. In his eyes, I was a friend, and we spent increasing amounts of time hanging out like a couple of buddies. I knew that unlike Mrs. Edwards, the senator was not insatiably curious about policy and public affairs. She might read briefing books to relax. He liked to lie on the couch and watch stupid movies like *Tommy Boy* with Chris Farley or sports.

We went regularly to UNC basketball games together, usually taking our kids and giving Cheri and Elizabeth the night off. If we were traveling, I would call ahead and have the hotel staff tape the game and cue it up on a tape player in his room. If we happened to be at the senator's beach house on the coast, we'd take a run, buy some ribs, and follow a bunch of super-stitious rituals—changing seats or even moving to a different room—that we hoped would bring good luck to the team. In March, we went to Atlanta to watch the 2001 Atlantic Coast Conference tournament. When we checked into the Ritz, the staff thought I must have been with former United Nations ambassador and Atlanta mayor Andrew Young and put me in the presiden-tial suite. The senator quickly suggested I take his regular room and give him the suite, which I did. Duke beat UNC in the finals (by sixteen points—ugh), and after the game, as we eased out of the VIP parking lot in my Suburban, I revved my engine as if I were going to run over Mike Krzyzewski, the Duke coach, as he walked in front of us toward the team bus. "Don't do it, Andrew!" shouted the senator, and we got a big grin out of Krzyzewski.

For a couple of North Carolina boys, first-class treatment at the ACC tournament represented the ultimate male bonding experience, and I could feel, as we spent time together, that Edwards considered me a true friend. Occasionally, when he asked me to do something above and beyond the normal call of duty, he'd smile and say something like "You know how much I appreciate everything, Andrew. You aren't staff, you are family. You know that, right?" He said it like a big brother and with so much casual sincerity that I believed him and would, naturally, do whatever task he might request.

I had worked hard to win the senator's trust, to become invaluable. And the more I heard about his ambition and dealt with the staff in Washington, the more I began to believe that if I wanted to capitalize on my connection,

I would have to leave Raleigh. An opportunity arose days after Brody was born when Will Austin, the scheduler in the senator's Capitol Hill office, gave notice of his resignation due to a family emergency.

A senator's scheduler is far more than the keeper of the appointment book. He or she occupies the desk closest to the senator's private office and is the one who controls who will see him and who will be left waiting. In a business where "face time" is the most valuable currency, the scheduler gets a daily, if not hourly, supply. The scheduler is trusted to know a senator's whereabouts at all times and becomes the one person relied upon to settle conflicts or enforce a time-out when the demands get too great. Because of this power, the scheduler can be more important even than the chief of staff, legislative director, or press secretary. Will Austin was a great scheduler because he put the senator's needs first, juggling appointments and events to accommodate his need for rest and exercise and his low tolerance for boredom. There were times when Edwards would come into the office, tell Will to hold all his calls and meetings, and just close the door. Will kept the hordes at bay.

On the evening after Will had announced he was leaving, I met the senator at the airport in Raleigh. He got into the car, skipped the pat on the shoulder and "Good to see you, Andrew," and reached for the Chardonnay. "I don't know what the fuck I'm going to do about Will leaving," he said. "I don't have anyone I want to put in there."

"How about me?" I said without thinking.

"Would you want to do it?"

In fact, I had been thinking about a change for several months. My work in Raleigh had become routine, and I felt I needed a new challenge. I had even started to talk to Cheri about working on Capitol Hill, if only to see if I could keep up with the high-powered people on the senator's staff there and make myself available for further advancement. Will's spot seemed like the perfect option.

The senator responded with an eager smile, saying I could have the job if I wanted it. But he urged me to make sure that Cheri and I both knew what we were getting into. When I got home that night, she didn't hesitate. She said I had to try out Washington and that she would support me. I then took a quick trip to consult with the staff there, learn what the job entailed, and make my decision.

My visit took place on a typical June day for Washington, which meant ninety-degree temperatures and high humidity. The Edwards office was in the Dirksen Building, a big slab that occupies half a block along Constitution Avenue between First and Second streets NE. Built in the 1950s, the place is covered in marble that is so white, at certain times of day you risk temporary blindness from the reflected sunlight when you step outside.

Will Austin, the man I would replace, and my old friend Julianna Smoot met me at the Edwards suite, which was on the second floor. They showed me around, introduced me to the people who would be my coworkers, and talked about the job. Based on what they said, my assignment would be demanding, but I thought I could handle it. However, Julianna and Will didn't explain the real challenge involved until we had left the building for lunch and settled into an outdoor table at a little restaurant.

For several minutes, the two of them talked about the pressure they felt working on the Hill and the cutthroat nature of the competition both inside the Edwards office and with the staff who worked for other members of the Senate. A case in point was Josh Stein, who had done more to get John Edwards elected senator than anyone because he had run the Senate campaign. Josh had served as "acting" chief of staff or deputy chief of staff. But he never got the chief of staff job on a permanent basis because of Mrs. Edwards. She told me that she believed that Josh kept things from her, and that made her suspicious. (In fact, Senator Edwards often told key staffers to withhold things from his wife.) Eventually, her disapproval would drive him back to North Carolina, where he won election to the state senate.

Will and Julianna did their best to make me understand the environment inside the Edwards operation—they used the term *snakepit* and warned, "They'll suck you dry"—but I didn't really want to hear it. I was too busy thinking about how inspiring it would be to walk to work on Capitol Hill every morning and take my daily run on the National Mall in the shadow of the Smithsonian Institution. I insisted that Cheri and I were ready for the move, that everything would be okay.

"But Andrew, you have everything you could want right now," said Julianna. "You have a beautiful wife, a baby, a house, and the chance at a normal life. That's what we *all* want and don't have. Why would you want to come up here and give that all away? D.C. is miserable. The people here suck."

It was almost impossible for me to understand what they were saying. Washington seemed beautiful, exciting, and full of opportunities. The job was a perfect fit for someone with my skills, and it would put me at the center of the action. Cheri and Brody were going to come north with me. The senator was even giving me a big raise to go with the new title, and he insisted we use their condominium in Alexandria—just across the Potomac from Washington—rent-free while we got settled. What could possibly go wrong?

You know how most babies are lulled to sleep when you put them in a car seat and start driving? Not Brody. He hated the car and cried for much of the four-hour trip up Interstates 85 and 95 and into the District of Columbia. Cheri did her best to quiet him, and from where I sit now, years later, I have to say she also did her best to bury her own anxieties about moving to Washington and leaving behind a house still undergoing renovation and a good, stable life. I had asked her to "just believe" in the move in the same way that I had asked her to "just believe" when we met and got married. Things had worked out so far, so she set aside concerns about money and the fact that she didn't know a soul in Washington and came along.

When we got to the city, we went straight to the Embassy Row district and the Edwards mansion on Thirtieth Street NW, where the neighbors included the ambassadors from Italy, the United Kingdom, Brazil, and South Africa. A massive seven-bedroom house with marble walls and a sweeping central staircase, the place reeked of power and money, but when the Edwardses met us at the door, they seemed like the same people we knew in North Carolina. If anything, they were even more down-home friendly, and they welcomed us as if we were good friends. They insisted we have dinner with them, and the senator grabbed his car keys and said, "C'mon, Andrew, let's get some ribs."

When we got in the car, I realized that this was the first time I had ever ridden while he drove. And when we took off in the direction of Connecticut Avenue and his favorite hole-in-the-wall barbecue joint, it struck me that I had no idea where we were going. It was a little unnerving to give up control, and the experience made it clear to me that I had left a certain comfort zone. The senator and Mrs. Edwards seemed to sense what Cheri and I were feeling, and they talked about how much time we would spend with them and how they would help us ease into our new life. When they gave us the key to their condo and directions to Alexandria, they told us not to worry about using it and to stay as long as we wanted. No rent. No worries.

It was late evening when we finally got to our temporary home, and no doubt our first impression was affected by our fatigue. However, even after a good night's sleep, the free condo was still a dark and depressing space with furnishings from the 1970s, as well as an orange shag carpet, a bare-bones kitchen, a living room with a sofa and TV, and a tiny bedroom. It was on the second floor of an odd-looking building that had dozens of units, but we never saw a single other soul coming or going. The neighborhood struck us as cold, not family friendly, and we quickly decided it was not the kind of place where Cheri would be comfortable hanging out alone with Brody while I was at work.

Two days of house hunting with Elizabeth convinced us that we could not possibly afford to buy or even rent a house in Washington like the one we had in Raleigh. We eventually found something we could afford—a gutted condominium in the Watergate complex—and signed a contract to buy it. While we waited for the closing, we took out a month-to-month lease on a nicer apartment in a big complex in the Virginia suburb of McLean. It was the kind of place where almost everyone (me included) left so early in the morning and returned so late at night that it might as well have been a ghost town. Alone and isolated, Cheri spent her days with a brand-new baby who fussed and cried all day long and never slept through the night. As the weeks passed she grew more miserable, feeling she had lost her comfortable home, the support of friends, and even her husband.

I became one of those workaholic drones who kissed his wife and baby good-bye at dawn, fought the traffic all the way to the office, and spent the next twelve hours or more in a constant frenzy of phone calls, meetings, and paperwork. To make matters worse, I learned that politics in D.C. is not like politics in good old North Carolina. It's a full-contact sport where you have to watch your own back.

That lesson came on my first day at my new desk beside the door to the senator's private office. The person who sat closest to me, who had been Will's assistant, was supposed to show me the ropes, but she was unhappy about being passed over for the job I had gotten. (The Edwardses had clearly led her to believe she would get it.) Although we ended up being close friends, we had a rough start, and she won round one. She told me a bit about working with the senator and his key people and how to set the schedule and then left me to fend for myself. I could feel her smile at my back as she watched me, the upstart from North Carolina, fail miserably. I could not cope with three desk phones that seemed to ring constantly (and often simultaneously) and a stream of people who just showed up at my desk demanding time with the boss. I kept a cheat sheet on my desk, but I still had to learn a new vocabulary—what's the cloakroom?—and the meaning of the bells that kept ringing (they signaled votes on the Senate floor). While all this was going on, I experienced frequent moments of startled amazement as famous men and women rang the phone. Once John McCain called to speak to the senator, and I looked up to see him on television at the same moment.

I thought I was handling things fairly well when suddenly the door marked "Private," which led to an outside hallway, swung open with a bang and a loud voice boomed, "Edwards! How the fuck am I gonna get you elected president if I can't get you on the fuckin' telephone?"

I looked up to see Senator Edward Kennedy barreling toward me. He had some papers in one hand, and in the other he held a leash attached to a big dog with curly black hair. (Called a Portuguese water dog, the breed would become famous when Kennedy gave one to President Obama's family.)

Only Kennedy could get away with keeping a dog in the U.S. Capitol, and only Kennedy could charge through a private entrance and expect to see my boss immediately. He was stopped by a door that had been closed when Senator Edwards announced he needed to lie down on his sofa and get a bit of rest. When I told Kennedy I would get the senator for him, he asked why no one had answered the many calls he had placed to the private telephone that was one of the three on my desk.

Senator Kennedy then explained that the telephone I had been using all day to place calls was, in fact, a sort of hotline for the White House and senators. It was not to be used except in an emergency. As the door to the inner office opened and Senator Edwards appeared, I was in the middle of apologizing. Both men started to smile, and I could tell the little crisis had passed. Kennedy's face softened.

"Did you know this used to be my office?" he asked, leaning down to me, his voice taking on an almost conspiratorial tone. He then launched into a story from 1980, when he ran for president and was assigned a Secret Service detail for protection. One day while Kennedy was in his office, the agent on duty slipped away for a moment with an aide with whom he was having an affair. ("This was before it was cool to be openly gay," said Kennedy.) In the time when the agent was gone, a would-be attacker slipped into the office with a knife. "Fortunately, the agent returned in time and he tackled the guy, right here!"

Kennedy slammed his hand on my desk with a whack, which startled me and made Senator Edwards laugh. The two men then retreated to his office, where they talked politics for a while. When they emerged, Edwards said, "Hey, Andrew. Don't use that line anymore." Later, Kennedy would invite me to his "hideaway" office in the Capitol building. Tucked in nooks and crannies behind unmarked doors, these private offices are prized bits of real estate that few people ever get to visit. Kennedy's was filled with pictures of his family and one of John F. Kennedy's famous rocking chairs.

At about this time, I saw Senator Kennedy again at the Capital Grille, where he met Senator Edwards for lunch. After he asked me how I found life in Washington and I told him I barely left the office, he told me another story. "Yeah, it's not like it was when I first got here," he said. "It used to be *civilized*. The media was on our side. We'd get our work done by one o'clock and by two we were at the White House chasing women. We got the job done, and the reporters focused on the issues." He passed for dramatic effect and added, "It was *civilized*."

As much as I loved Kennedy, Bill Clinton occupied a level of professional politics that was all his own. Despite his many controversies, when he was engaged, no one had better instincts, a better command of the issues, or a better network of powerful, loyal supporters. In a town full of great egos, no one disputed this assessment. One of the most illuminating duties I performed while in Washington involved driving Senator Edwards, Senator Chris Dodd, and a couple of other Democrats to a meeting with Clinton where he allowed them to pick his brain. I waited outside, and when my charges returned and we got back on the road, they all sat in stunned silence. Clinton had been so impressive that they didn't know what to say. Finally, Dodd muttered, "I don't care how long I live. I'll never be that good."

The experience with Dodd and the others proved the value of being the guy who drove for a senator. Ironically, for someone who often served as a driver, I have an incredibly bad sense of direction, which was why I once tried to get out of driving Edwards to Andrews Air Force Base for his first ride on Air Force One. I didn't know the route and told the senator to have someone else drive, but he insisted he knew how to go. We left with just enough time to get there but got terribly lost. The Secret Service called several times, and the president finally left without us. Edwards missed his flight, and of course he said it was my fault. Within a few weeks of being in Washington, I had two strikes: the mix-up with Kennedy and the Air Force One fiasco.

Fortunately, most days didn't bring dramatic challenges or encounters with intimidating world leaders. On most days I worked from early morning until well past dinnertime, juggling phones, reviewing hundreds of requests for appointments, and playing palace guard whenever the senator decided he had had enough and just closed his door to rest. When the Senate was in session, I had to keep track of floor votes—signaled by the bells system—and make sure the senator got to the chamber on time. On occasion, this would require me to race outside to the Mall (where he might be jogging) or to the Senate gym, where a lot of members liked to hide from their staffs, the public, and lowly members of the House of Representatives, all of whom were denied access.

As much as senators may project an aura of deliberation, dignity, and decorum, the facts of life inside the world's most exclusive club are much messier. Many times, senators cast votes on the basis of a signal from a staffer or a party leader, and they have no idea about the matters being considered. Aides often control the flow of business; I once heard that the cloakroom staff—who were among the most powerful people on Capitol Hill—delayed bringing the senators to the chamber for a vote because they wanted to see the end of an episode of the TV program *24*. On several occasions I would have to chase down the senator, because he had gone for a run and refused to wear a cell phone or pager. More than once I put him in my car so he could get to the cloakroom on time. He'd stand in the doorway of the Senate in shorts or sweats to signal thumbs-up or thumbs-down to have his vote recorded.

No one talks about how rules are bent and senators cast a lot of blind votes, because the illusion of a serious legislative body at work is useful to us all. It reassures voters, who want to believe that their men and women in Washington are serious about the public's business, and it reinforces the

Senate's aura of authority, which can be a valuable thing in times of crisis. (We all want to think they are superior human beings when matters of war and peace are under consideration.) Besides, as everyone in Washington likes to say, politics is like sausage making: You really don't want to know how it's done.

For the sausage makers—elected officials, their aides, consultants, pollsters, and party hacks—the product of all the effort must include, first and foremost, getting elected and reelected. This is why first-term presidents and members of the House and Senate live in a state of continual campaigning and fund-raising. Senators spend roughly a third of their time raising money for campaigns, and if they aspire to higher office, they must consider how every vote and every public statement might affect their future.

From the moment Senator Edwards first heard he was being considered as Gore's running mate, he imagined himself as a future president and shifted his focus away from the work of the Senate. Mrs. Edwards had the same idea and was even more enthusiastic about their prospects for inhabiting the White House. They both began to read everything they could find about national politics and global issues, including the briefing materials produced by the staff. And they began to host weekly policy dinners at their mansion, where they learned from experts who understood issues, public opinion, and the quirky system that the parties use to pick nominees. The main features of this process include early straw polls, caucuses in Iowa, and the primary election in New Hampshire. Iowa and New Hampshire are two small rural states that cannot possibly reflect the will of the nation but can make or break a candidate. Iowa has a particularly arcane process that requires voters to stand in certain places to be counted for their candidate, and the horse-trading can go on all day.

Although every senator sees a future president in the mirror every morning, decorum prevents the hopefuls from formally announcing their intentions until a year or so before the caucuses. (It's just bad manners to let your giant ego show any earlier.) For this reason, precampaign planning takes place behind a curtain of secrecy that adds a little thrill for those involved. I got behind the curtain in early September 2001, when I organized a day-long strategy session at the Edwardses' Embassy Row house.

The living room at the mansion was so big that it could accommodate fifteen people, arranged in a big circle of sofas and upholstered chairs, with room to spare. The original list of attendees was actually *sixteen*, but just days before we got together, Julianna had a bitter falling-out with Mrs. Edwards. The senator publicly claimed that Julianna had resigned after an argument about record keeping, but he later told me the truth. The problem had been a personal conflict with Mrs. Edwards, as it had been with Josh. Julianna was replaced in the coming campaign by a couple of seasoned fund-raisers named Steve Jarding and Dave "Mudcat" Saunders. Mudcat was a colorful Southerner who liked to say he was going to make John Edwards the favorite of "grits-eatin', gun-totin' rednecks all over." Mrs. Edwards loved him.

I was upset about Julianna's absence but soon got lost in the excitement of the business at hand—planning a presidential campaign—and the impressive circle I had been welcomed to join. When the meeting began at ten A.M., I was seated next to Bob Shrum, a balding, middle-aged man with sloping shoulders who was one of the most experienced political consultants in the country. Shrum was famous for never having backed a winning presidential candidate, but to be fair, his man Gore had won the popular vote in 2000. Shrum had also guided dozens of people to victorious races for the House and Senate and authored some very important speeches, including Ted Kennedy's 1980 convention address, which was one of the best political addresses in American history. Our side of the room also included pollster Harrison Hickman and Erskine Bowles, a North Carolina native who had been chief of staff in the Clinton White House. Among the rest of the participants were Edwards aides, his friend Tom Girardi (the lawyer in the famous Erin Brockovich case), and, of course, Senator and Mrs. Edwards.

The senator, who wore blue jeans and a light blue button-down shirt, opened the daylong session with a three-page, single-spaced speech that he stood up to read. After thanking everyone for attending, he said, "You are all here because I think you are smart, I trust you to tell me the truth, and I need your help."

As the senator explained, we were not there to help him decide on a run for president in 2004. He was already assuming that he would run and that we would be on the team. "Each of you will make big sacrifices for me, sacrifices that Elizabeth and I can never repay," he predicted. "But you can be certain that I will work as hard as I can on the things I am responsible for." Edwards added that his immediate goals included "raising a ton of money, learning more about issues, getting to know opinion leaders and political leaders nationally, figuring out better ways to talk about these is-sues, to explain my views, and maintaining a good public image that will help whether I run for reelection or run for president."

The discussion that followed consumed the entire day. Everyone was con-cerned about a possible Gore candidacy and the repercussions of running against the Democrat who was "robbed" in 2000. The only other candidates even being discussed within the party were Joe Lieberman, Dick Gephardt, Massachusetts senator John Kerry, and Senate majority leader Tom Daschle of South Dakota. This was hardly an intimidating lineup to Edwards, and as we considered Edwards's national connections, his charisma, and his fund-raising potential, he looked more and more like a winner.

When Shrum got his chance to speak at length, he opened a notebook and ran through a series of points, touching on everything from the key elements of organizing a campaign to media strategy and policy priorities. I was blown away by the breadth of his expertise, and during a coffee break I told Hickman I was very impressed. Hickman, turning competitive, said, "Don't be impressed, Andrew. That's the same exact shit he's been saying since 1980. The same recurgitated stuff."

As lunch was served, the group worked on a long list of items that would have to be accomplished before Edwards could announce he was running. He had created a political action committee (PAC), which could be staffed to raise money, research issues, and support candidates in key states who could be helpful later. We talked about setting priorities for the senator's time in Washington, North Carolina, and around the country, and we reviewed a series of conferences where we could bring together experts in areas such as economics, foreign policy, and health care so the senator could become better informed. As a member of Senate committees that dealt with intelligence, health care, science, and commerce, he was already positioned to speak out on most of the important issues, but he needed to make himself more visible. As part of this effort, he would have to go on some fact-finding missions abroad, where he could beef up his image as a world leader. Of course, the issues didn't matter if we couldn't use them to connect with the public. Here the senator stressed "getting exposure with the people who matter." This meant national media and TV and print in places like Iowa and New Hampshire.

For me, the fellow with such a profound fear of public speaking that he remained silent all day, the meeting was a crash course in presidential politics taught by people who understood the process. For example, amateurs who think the first important races take place in Iowa and New Hampshire don't understand that the candidates fight one another first in a contest over money. Months before any votes are cast, pundits scan campaign finance reports to see who is raising the most dough. The leader in that race can pay for more staff, ads, and travel and is anointed the front-runner. At the same time, candidates take positions on issues with fund-raising in mind. If you want to get donations from oil executives, for example, it helps to be a supporter of drilling in the Alaska wilderness. Money is so important that even if you are the most brilliant candidate, political commentators will relegate you to second-class status if you are not among the top three in fund-raising. Below this level, you simply cannot compete in a national campaign.

I also learned that day that geography is not necessarily destiny when it comes to party politics. A lot of people were worried that Iowa governor Tom Vilsack might jump into the mix. If he did, he could expect to win the first voting of the season at the Iowa caucuses. Some might see this turn of events as a negative, but you could also conclude that Vilsack would take Iowa out of play for everyone, which meant that a candidate like Edwards could concentrate all his time and money on the New Hampshire primary. If he did that and won in the Granite State, he'd become the overall leader.

In nine hours, not one person said anything to discourage the senator from running. In fact, everyone who spoke had supported the idea, and they all seemed to assume they would have positions in the future campaign. I would include myself in this group, and as the senator stood up to end the day's work, I thought about being part of the team, accompanying him on campaign trips, waiting out election night returns, and celebrating victory.

Few things in adult life can match the passion and excitement of being a key player in a political campaign. During the days, weeks, and months of hard work devoted to a shared goal, people start to feel like soldiers in a battle or members of a football team driving toward a championship. You come to believe that your side stands for all that is good and the other side represents ignorance and evil. Fueled with adrenaline, ego, and hope, you work harder than you ever dreamed you could, accomplish things you never thought you could, and form bonds stronger than those of family. In the end, you get a score—the election results—that tells you whether you have won or lost. The verdict can test your nerves, but no matter how it works out, you know you were in the game—in this case, the ultimate game—and that can be deeply satisfying. Visions of the campaign danced in all our heads as the meeting at the senator's home ended, and then, as everyone stood, Erskine Bowles spoke:

"Senator, what would you tell someone who asked you, 'Why should I vote for you to be president? What makes you the most qualified candidate?'"

The room fell silent. The senator looked at Bowles with a mixture of surprise and anger, and then he struggled to answer. He said something about how his upbringing and career fighting for ordinary people against giant corporations had prepared him to lead. When this didn't come out right, he added some thoughts about health care and education and making things better for the middle class. But he offered no grand vision of America or big policy ideas, and as he struggled, I realized that in all the hours of talk, no one had said anything about what an Edwards presidency would mean for America. There had been no discussion of what he stood for. Edwards was caught off guard, but in a way Bowles had helped him by exposing how unprepared he was. The senator later told me that Bowles had made him very angry. The two men would never become close.

I drove Bowles to his hotel that night, and because traffic was bad, we wound up spending an hour in the car together. He said the senator was indeed an appealing political figure, but he had serious doubts about the timing. A 2004 bid, if it went badly, might end his chances forever. For this reason, he would advise Edwards to get more seasoning in the Senate— "actually do some good work with the opportunity he has there"—and run in 2008. He would make a better candidate then and, if he won, a better president (Bowles's experience as Clinton's chief of staff had taught him that presidential politics and the office itself were brutally demanding.) I understood his point but heard Edwards's counterargument in my head: He had a tenuous hold on his seat and might not win reelection in 2004. If North Carolina rejected him then, he wouldn't have a chance at higher office later.

By the time I dropped him off, I was convinced that Bowles had given Senator Edwards what he had asked for—his best straightforward advice. I admired his intelligence and honesty and the fact that he refused to let me help him bring his luggage and golf clubs inside. This little kindness made it easier for me to get home to see Cheri, who had once again spent the day alone and made me a well-balanced dinner that went cold on the stove.

Real estate never cured anything, but Cheri and I hoped that the tiny Watergate apartment we had bought (at a bargain price, because it was gutted) might make life a little easier. The McLean commute was adding about two hours to my workday. If we lived at the Watergate, I could spend most of that time at home with Cheri and Brody. I still had to drive, because I needed my Suburban to ferry the senator around, so mass transit was out; but it was much closer to the office. Cheri would be able to walk to shopping or even visit me for lunch. We both had these benefits in mind on the morning of September 11, 2001, the date we were supposed to close on the purchase. As usual, I needed to be at work early and spend the entire day stuck behind my desk. For this reason, we arranged to sign all the papers separately. I went to the office, did some work, and then drove to the bank so I would be there when it opened at nine A.M. Cheri would come later in the morning with Brody and drive herself home.

Shock jocks were one of my guilty pleasures back then, and I had my radio tuned to one of the local morning madness shows when the person who read the news interrupted the raunchy jokes to report that a plane had crashed into the north tower of the World Trade Center in New York City. The men on the program brushed her off with a little banter about a wayward pilot in a Cessna, but she didn't join in. She seemed to have a hunch that something more serious was going on.

In the lobby of the bank, I noticed the security guard there was watching the news—including live pictures of the World Trade Center—on a little portable TV. I went inside, found the office handling the closing, and quickly signed a stack of papers. As I walked back through the lobby, I saw that the guard's TV was still tuned to the news, only now a second plane had hit the south tower. Witnesses had begun to report that both strikes had been made by jet airliners, not prop planes, and it was starting to seem that a coordinated attack, using hijacked planes, was under way.

My schedule that day called for me to meet the senator at the Capitol building. In those times before the 9/11 attacks, a staffer with a senator's license plate could park right beside the Capitol steps, as I did that morning. As police ran mirrors under the car (for security purposes), tourists gawked into the blackened-out glass to try to see who was inside. People pulled out their cameras and asked me to roll down the window. I got out and stood on the steps beside my car, Diet Coke on ice, motor running, when the city just got quiet. Suddenly, officers were running around and people were streaming out of the building. Sirens began to wail in the distance, and someone in the crowd said the Pentagon had been bombed. (In fact, it too had been hit by a plane, and 125 people had been killed.)

The events of 9/11 have become a shared national story, and it's not necessary for me to outline here all that happened to the country that day. Like millions of Americans, I first tried to call home but discovered that the cell phone system would not work. (I heard that security officials shut down service so the terrorists could not use their phones.) I then went to the Dirksen Building, where I ran into the senator coming out of the building. I called the Capitol police and asked where I should take him. They were overwhelmed and offered to take him to a secure location, but not any of his family members. Only senators in the direct line of succession to the White House get Secret Service protection, not rookie senators. They were polite but busy. Angered, Edwards drove home alone to be with his family.

Since big symbolic buildings were obviously targets, the police evacuated the Capitol and all the congressional office buildings. The radio was already reporting that many streets and highways were being shut down, so I knew I couldn't get home. With no alternative, I jogged over to the office we used for campaign fund-raising, which was in a nondescript building that would never attract an attacker. Staffers welcomed me, and we watched the day unfold on several small TVs. We tried to make sense of what we were seeing and compare it with rumors everyone had heard about helicopters being shot down on the Mall and other possible incidents. Each of us took turns using the landlines to try to call loved ones. I quickly discovered that phone service to Greater Washington, including McLean, was still blacked out, but I was able to call family out of state. With their help, Cheri and I were able to pass messages to each other.

The cell phones never did work that day, and by late afternoon the police had yet to reopen all the roads. I walked/hitchhiked to one of the Potomac bridges, crossed to the other side, and then managed to flag down a cab that brought me home to McLean. The sun had already set, and Cheri was way past overwrought. After months of isolation, single parenting, living out of homes in two states, dinners for one, and now an attack on the Pentagon—which was close to the Watergate—she had reached a decision. She didn't want the life of the stay-at-home wife and mother supported by a Capitol Hill staffer who worked up to eighteen hours a day and weekends, too.

"Brody and I are going back to North Carolina," she told me. "You can come with us if you want to."

The expression on Cheri's face made it clear that her mind was made up. Within a few days, her car was packed and she drove back to Raleigh. We agreed that I would try to follow as soon as possible. For a few months, she lived primarily in Raleigh but occassionally visited me in Virginia. I tried to stick it out but I had to recognize that living apart so much caused too many problems. At one point, in the middle of an argument she turned to me and said, "Andrew, you're stuck with me, so you might as well get used to it." To someone whose parents had divorced, sweeter words had never been spoken.

By Thanksgiving, I knew I didn't fit in Washington—I was not cut out for that kind of politics—and needed to find a way to return to North Carolina. This is not to say there weren't some extraordinary moments for me during my Washington duty. Cheri and I got to use the senator's tickets to see a symphony at the Kennedy Center, and he insisted I use Elizabeth's ticket to sit in the visitors' gallery at President Bush's first State of the Union address following the 9/11 attack. (She was worried about a terrorist attack, and as parents the Edwardses always avoided being in the same place when they had any fear of a dangerous incident.) But the occasional symphony or special event cannot restore balance to your life. We were determined to reclaim our life in North Carolina, so we sold the place at the Watergate, and to save money I moved out of McLean and into a tiny basement apartment in the city. (It had just one little window, and that was in the bathroom.) I didn't tell anyone at work that I was fixing to leave, but I started planning and looking for the right moment to give my notice. In the meantime, I marveled at the cutthroat competition for advancement that dominates life on Capitol Hill.

I watched from afar as a staffer named Miles Lackey maneuvered to re-place chief of staff Jeff Lane. Miles made his key move at the end of the year, when he accompanied the senator on a trip abroad that included Afghanistan, where U.S. forces had just ousted the Taliban rulers who had given safe haven to al-Qaeda. Soon after their return, Lane was out and Lackey was in. At around the same time, another staffer left after a conflict with Elizabeth over the Christmas card list, which had been expanded to include many political figures in Iowa and New Hampshire. Another colleague had so many stress-related outbursts that he was required to get anger management counseling.

My unhappiness must have been pretty obvious, because eventually John Edwards noticed. I was driving him out to Dulles International Airport (National was still closed because of 9/11 security concerns), and he suddenly just said, "You don't like it up here, do you, Andrew."

"No, Senator, I really don't."

"You want to go back to North Carolina?"

"Yeah."

I didn't need to say anymore. Acting as both a friend and my boss, he said he would send me back to Raleigh immediately. My responsibilities and my salary would be split three ways between the Senate office, his re-election campaign, and his PAC, which was slowly preparing the ground for a presidential challenge. This move was the kindest thing he had ever done for me. First, it got me out of the turmoil in the D.C. office, where the senator would have five chiefs of staff in six years. Second, it put me in a position to be the person tapped to set up his presidential campaign office. Third, it returned me home, set me up to play a continuing role in his future, and allowed me to resume being a real husband and father.

Four

EDWARDS FOR PRESIDENT I

In the spring of 2002, I was one of the few people in the world who knew that Raleigh, North Carolina, was certain to become an important hub for national politics. Presidential candidates usually set up their headquarters in their home area—Jimmy Carter in Plains, Al Gore in Nashville, Bill Clinton in Little Rock—and for John Edwards this meant that a national organization would be run from the capital of the Tar Heel State. As the campaign's first employee in Raleigh, I was positioned to play an important role that would depend on the skills and contacts I had developed in the state as well as the education I had received on Capitol Hill.

God couldn't have arranged life better for me. After months of separation and unhappiness, Cheri, Brody, and I were together again. Our lakeside house was finally finished and ready for our second child, who was expected near the end of summer. I figured that now I would be able to spend more time with my wife and child—like a real father—because the senator would be traveling around the country as a presidential hopeful.

By the time I got back to North Carolina in March, Senator Edwards had already visited six states, including repeated trips to Iowa and New Hampshire, where he announced that his goal was to "make the American dream stronger than it ever has been." It was a vague theme, but it was enough for a handful of Democrats in New Hampshire, who told the national press corps that they were impressed with him. Behind the scenes, Steve Jarding and Mudcat Saunders were raising money and winning friends for the senator in unusual ways. In one of their schemes, our political action committee loaned computers to Democrats running for state offices in places like Iowa, who agreed to give them back to us at the end of the year. The arrangement helped them with the expense of campaigning, and built goodwill. When we got the machines back, they came loaded with information—e-mail lists, telephone lists, addresses—that we thought would be invaluable to us.

Supported by the money collected by Jarding and Saunders, the senator traveled from state to state, refining his pitch. At eight different Jefferson-Jackson Day dinners (banquets held to give candidates a forum), he railed against "Washington insiders" and "rich fat cats" like the disgraced executives at the bankrupt Enron Corporation, who had become symbols of the greed enabled by Washington. This kind of talk was red meat for Democrats in the hinterlands, and they ate it up.

Although I saw less of the senator during this period, he came home often enough for me to notice that he was changing. A year before, he had seemed bored and disappointed by life in the Senate. Now, with the presidency as a goal, he was focused and alert. Sure, he complained about fatigue and run-ins with people who made him uncomfortable (he still struggled to feel at ease rubbing elbows with some poor and working-class folks), but I had never seen him more energized and excited. The way he talked, I could tell that he was mastering the issues and getting to know Iowa and New Hampshire better than he knew North Carolina.

Veterans of presidential campaigns say that the early days are the easiest, and this was true for Edwards, who raced into the lead in the competition for donors and national party backers. In both New Hampshire and Iowa, he won over key political figures with his charm and audiences with his Robbins-to-Washington story. "I believe I can be the champion for regular people," he said in his standard stump speech. "My own life experience allows me to see things through their eyes. They are the people I grew up with, the people who worked with my father in the mill, the people I fought for as a lawyer."

As she accompanied him on campaign trips, Mrs. Edwards turned out to be popular, too. Unlike other political wives, she wasn't pretentious or cautious, and she openly tried to make sure the country's sexiest politician didn't get too full of himself. At one press event, she even asked the local reporters, "Have you met anyone up here who knows who he is?" In another encounter with the press, she let a writer see her stash her cell phone in her bra as she rushed out the door of her house. People, especially women voters, loved this stuff. She knew it, he knew it, and they played it to the hilt.

The national press loved it, too. *U.S. News & World Report* put Senator Edwards on its cover at the end of April and made Mrs. Edwards a big part of their story on the presidential hopefuls. A week later, *The New Yorker* made the senator the subject of a glowing profile that suggested he might be the next Bill Clinton. Writer Nicholas Lemann described Mrs. Edwards as "vibrant" and "fiercely ambitious for and protective of her husband."

In protecting the senator, Mrs. Edwards didn't shield him from her own criticism, which she offered every time she saw him perform at a rally or conduct an interview. She was the one person he trusted to give him honest feedback, which meant that when he bumbled through an appearance on *Meet the Press* in the spring of 2002, she agreed with the critics who said he looked unprepared for host Tim Russert's questions and sounded evasive in his responses. In fact, it was the worst TV performance of his career, such an awful and embarrassing display of political sidestepping that he would remember it for years with a combination of shame and anger.

Fortunately, he didn't stumble very often, and he was a quick study. Months later, he went back on national television—this time it was *Face the Nation*—and scored points with pointed attacks of Bush administration policies that had squandered a huge federal surplus in order to lavish tax cuts on the rich.

As he grew more confident, just being around John Edwards gave me the sense he was going to be the positive leader the country needed. This feeling motivated me, as did some of the early prep work—scouting locations, getting bids on phones and furnishings—for establishing a national campaign office. Because the senator was away more, it fell to me to nurture his relationship with friends, political allies, and potential donors. The work brought me into regular contact with the rich and powerful, including former ambassadors, millionaires, and billionaires.

Although I was only an aide, I was his only longtime staffer, so many of these people came to see me as a surrogate for the senator. Whenever close friends or members of the family had a question or a problem—like an inquiry from the press corps—they turned to me for help. Gradually, many of these relationships became friendly. One big donor invited my family to visit at his luxurious beach house. Another, Boyd Tinsley of the Dave Matthews Band, became a friend who came to my house for veggie burgers.

My relationship with Tinsley offers a perfect illustration of the benefits that come to a political aide thanks to fame by association. When he first called and I didn't know who he was, our senior campaign consultant Nick Baldick, who worked in Washington, told me Tinsley was rich and important. When we finally connected, Tinsley explained that he was a bit of a political junkie. We talked regularly, and Tinsley said he liked what he had seen and heard about Edwards's dedication to working people and wanted to help.

In this period, Cheri and I began rubbing elbows with people we would never have met otherwise. At every turn, it seemed, I was encountering another celebrity or walking through a doorway to an exclusive environment that I would never have seen if I weren't working for a presidential candidate. A case in point was the all-star fund-raiser I helped arrange at the start of the summer of 2002. The hosts were Reynolds Tobacco heir Smith Bagley and his wife, Elizabeth. The politically liberal Bagleys were stalwarts of the Democratic Party who, like their friends, had contributed millions of dollars to various candidates and causes. Mrs. Bagley had been rewarded, during the Clinton administration, with the ambassador's post in Portugal. Former Gore supporters, the Bagleys were leaning toward Edwards for 2004 and opened their compound on St. Simons Island, Georgia, for a gathering of national supporters, most of whom were wealthy trial lawyers.

Called Musgrove, the Bagley property covers six hundred acres in one of the richest zip codes in America. It is also one of many almost-secret sites around the country where powerful people can find seclusion and comfort while they share ideas and plans. (Allies would call it strategizing. Enemies would see sinister scheming.) Most Americans have never heard of the place, but over the years Musgrove had been the locale for dozens of exclusive conferences and meetings where national leaders discussed everything from relations with Cuba to tax policy. Before Jimmy Carter went to Washington to take the oath of office as president, he gathered his future cabinet at Musgrove.

The gathering for Senator Edwards was not about policy; rather, it concerned politics or, to be more precise, how John Edwards might become president. Strategists and consultants offered briefings on the process that led from Iowa to the nomination and dissected the strengths and weaknesses of our opponents. We talked about Senator Edwards's appeal as an outsider and a Southerner (Democrats felt they needed to break the GOP hold on the region in order to win the White House) and his populist positions.

The guests—who were often referred to as "future ambassadors"— were there because they had already shown they were willing to supply the money required to get a candidate elected. Together, the participants— between forty and fifty men and women—could claim hundreds of millions, perhaps billions, of dollars in personal wealth and connections to a network of thousands of men and women with comparable resources. Those who were trial lawyers were more than willing to pony up for Edwards because they knew him as one of their own and could expect that as a senator and a president, he would protect plaintiffs' rights and their ability to sue and win big awards.

Republicans had been attacking trial lawyers for years, claiming that lawsuits filed against corporations and individuals, especially in the health care industry, were driving up the cost of malpractice insurance and making life miserable for good, honest businesses and practitioners. They liked to call the trial lawyers "ambulance chasers" who concocted ridiculous claims that won outlandish awards from gullible juries. For their part, the lawyers brushed off the ambulance chasers as a low-rent minority and described themselves as heroes who sought justice when people were maimed or killed by faulty products and incompetent professionals. (When Edwards appeared to be the front-runner for the nomination, President Bush traveled to North Carolina to give a speech on tort reform.)

For me, the highlight of the weekend was Friday night, which began with a cocktail party where I spent a substantial amount of time chatting with Smith Bagley, who is a very tall and distinguished-looking man. My mother's father had been a foreman for Reynolds Tobacco for thirty-three years, and her mother had worked for the company as a secretary. As I stood with the man who held much of the company's fortune, I had to struggle to grasp how I had come so far and what it meant for me to be there. My mind was further boggled when we went down to the waterside for an oyster bake, which was served by an all-black waitstaff who then performed songs that could have come out of a nineteenth-century minstrel show. This kind of thing happens every once in a while in the place we liberals like to call "the New South." You get lulled into thinking that the sins of the past are long gone, and then suddenly some evidence of the old racism comes into view. It made me uncomfortable.

Later that night, I met up with the senator's former law partner, David Kirby, and a famous litigator from Biloxi named Paul Minor, who had been one of the first lawyers in the suit against tobacco companies that produced a $200 billion settlement in 1998. (Only in the New South would a lawyer who sued Big Tobacco be welcomed at the home of an heir to a cigarette fortune.) The three of us were hungry—it's hard to fill up on oysters—so we went to a local hee-haw bar. The kitchen was closed, but they let us have a pizza delivered. Kirby insisted that Minor tell me a story about the settlement, and he immediately launched into a tale that begins with a phone call he received from an attorney friend named Ron Motley.

As the story goes, Motley had begun a massive suit against the major tobacco companies (which at this point had never lost a case), alleging that the industry had knowingly hidden health risks associated with their products and a history of deceptive marketing. Recent changes in federal rules and regulations gave the litigants a fighting chance, but Motley needed $100,000 to keep his effort alive. Minor resisted at first but eventually gave him the money, although he hid the loan from his own wife. Years later, Motley called again. This time, it was the middle of the night and both of the Minors awakened as Motley was leaving a message about "that one hundred thousand dollars you gave me."

The number brought both Mr. and Mrs. Minor fully awake. Anger flashed across her face as he grabbed the phone to hear his drunken friend report that the $100,000 would soon be repaid and followed by millions more. The case had been settled, he explained, and the attorneys for the plaintiffs were going to reap fees totaling billions of dollars. After he hung up the phone, Minor explained it all to his wife, who quickly forgave him for hiding the $100,000 loan, and they jumped on the bed like little kids.

Minor told the story with the kind of matter-of-fact pride you'd hear in the voice of a former high-school star recounting his best game twenty years after the event. But instead of being a local hero, he was one of the richest lawyers in the world and I was being let into his confidence. Many of the other people I met over the weekend could match Minor when it came to power and influence. Altogether, this group donated enough money to the Edwards campaign effort to put him over $3.5 million for the year. This was much more than the amount raised by his nearest competitors, and it signaled to the national party and pundits that he was a powerful candidate.

The weekend at Musgrove gave me great stories to share with Cheri when I got home. She was entertained but never got as excited about high-flying politics as I did. She's a practical person who lives in the moment and resists getting swept up in flash and show. For her, happiness was found mostly at home, and she was satisfied to have us together again, without the pressure we felt in Washington or the round-the-clock demands that came when the senator was in town.

In many ways, the summer of 2002 was the best season of my life. For the most part I worked normal hours, which meant that I was home for dinner every night and helped put Brody to bed. Cheri and I then relaxed on our back porch, listening to music and gazing at the lake. The schedule also allowed me to run every day, which meant that my body was fit and my mind was clear. When I run, I say my prayers and let myself dream. During this period, I kept a notebook and a pen in our mailbox, so after I ran laps in our neighborhood, I could write down any ideas or flashes of insight before going inside to shower. I was so excited about the impending arrival of our next child—by this time, we knew it was a girl—that most of my notes were about baby names.

My favorite name was Grace. Cheri's favorite was Lauren. When our daughter was finally born on September 1, 2002, we named her Lauren Grace and called her by the nickname Gracie. A bit smaller and quieter than Brody, she had trouble breathing, and Cheri noticed that as she struggled to get air she made a high-pitched noise called stridor. Doctors told us the problem was not serious, but when it didn't get better and she had trouble feeding, we took her to the hospital. Only two weeks old, she stayed for several days of tests that gave us no definitive diagnosis. Worn out from the stress, Cheri asked her mother to come care for the kids while she went with me for a long weekend—half work and half fun—at the famous Pinehurst Resort.

Set for the last three days of the summer, the Pinehurst event had been the main focus of my work in the month of August. Like the event at Musgrove, the "retreat" was supposed to be an organizing and rallying point for about a hundred of the senator's key supporters from around the country. Many were "big dogs" in the nation's trial law profession, and we needed to offer some special amenities to draw them in. The resort is a golf mecca, where our guests would have eight courses to choose from, including Pinehurst #2, one of the best in the world. For those who didn't golf (and those who did), we included a concert by the band Hootie & the Blowfish, who were Edwards supporters from South Carolina. The band members donated their services but sent a list of more than two dozen requirements that included transportation, suites, free rounds of golf, five cases of beer, three fifths of Jim Beam, and "orange juice (no pulp)."

For attendees, the per-person cost for the three days, including accommodations at the Victorian-era Carolina Hotel, was about $1,200, which was hardly a consideration for the people we invited. In fact, the hotel didn't have enough fancy suites to satisfy this crowd. Almost everyone we asked agreed to come, and we had a full house for the pig roast/reception on Friday night and the lunchtime meetings held on Saturday and Sunday. At these two sessions, our backers heard from the senator and a group of experts, including two of Bill Clinton's closest advisers, Doug Sosnik and Gene Sperling. A high-energy person, Sosnik talked urgently about the public's hunger for a likable candidate who shared their values, and naturally he thought Edwards was that guy.

Sperling began with a self-deprecating story about delivering his first major policy program—for jobs creation—to Bill Clinton. In the moments before being ushered in to see the boss, he had chewed on his pen, which leaked ink all over his mouth and chin. When Sperling entered the Oval Office, President Clinton asked, "Whatcha been eatin', boy?" and political consultant James Carville, who was in the room, grinned and cackled, "What a Maalox moment, your big day, meeting the leader of the free world. What an idiot!" It was the perfect story to grab the attention of those people, who were daydreaming about helping to create the next "Bubba" like Bill Clinton.

After winning the crowd over, Sperling spoke about Edwards as a progressive whose values and Southern roots could appeal to moderates and independents. He acknowledged President Bush's strengths coming out of the September 11 attacks but noted that Bush's father had been popular after the first Iraq war and led Clinton in many early public opinion polls. The right Democrat would have a very good chance to make Bush II another one-termer, and Edwards was the right Democrat.

By the time the senator spoke, the participants had been primed to consider him presidential material, and I saw a more serious and less relaxed man than I had known before. He was clearly acting in a more careful and deliberate way, and so was Mrs. Edwards. I noticed, too, that they brought Emma Claire, who was four, and Jack, now two, into meetings and as usual allowed them to run around among the adults. Like any other little kids, they were adorable some of the time, but even when they got a bit cranky and the nanny volunteered to take them to the pool, the senator and his wife insisted they stay around. They said having the kids around would be appealing to the donors—that no president in recent times had young kids. I realized the kids were being used as props to show that the family was young and lively like, say, the Kennedys circa 1962, when Caroline was five and John Junior was two.

Of course, all politicians calculate and scheme and send messages in the way they dress and the settings they occupy. During an energy crisis, Jimmy Carter turned the heat down at the White House and put on a cardigan. In order to appear as outdoorsmen, Ronald Reagan and George W. Bush cleared brush on their ranches as though they couldn't afford to hire someone else to do it. At a time when Bill Clinton's extramarital affairs had stirred public outrage, John and Elizabeth Edwards intentionally presented themselves as a blissfully married couple and their family as a close-knit and rambunctious bunch. If it wasn't the whole truth, it was true enough, as far as I knew. And considering the fact that we were at Pinehurst to make an impression, the sight of Jack and Emma Claire running around was just one of many details in the picture.

For me, the best Pinehurst moment came late on the night of the concert, when Cheri and I were invited to hang out with the band in the complex of suites they had been given at the hotel. I walked the senator in for a brief appearance, but like most of the others who stopped by, he departed early. Eventually, it was just Cheri and me, drinking beers and trying to stump the lead singer, Darius Rucker, by naming a song he didn't know how to sing. We couldn't do it. And let me tell you, hanging out with a guy who has won two Grammy Awards while he sang and another member of the band played drums on the coffee table for a few hours was an amazing experience.

Even as it was happening, I understood that Cheri and I were privileged to have this experience, and I had the feeling of being both an insider and an outsider simultaneously. I mean, my association with the senator was the only reason we were there, rubbing elbows with powerful political figures by day and partying with Darius Rucker and the rest of the band at night. This thought made me feel grateful, but also very dependent. I knew that all of it was contingent on my continuing to do a good job for both Senator Edwards and his family.

My success at Pinehurst that weekend was confirmed by the pledges of support that were offered by the wealthy supporters who attended, their enthusiasm for the senator's candidacy, and their willingness to commit to serving as advisers and fund-raisers as we moved forward. I also got credit from the senator for making sure that every request made by a guest was promptly satisfied, whether it involved a room upgrade, a tee time, or something that required more discreet attention. At one big event the senator held during this period, I was summoned by one of the more powerful men in the room, who happened to be there with his wife. He asked me to come to his table partway through the meal and call him to the telephone. There would be no call, he explained, but he wanted me to act as if something urgent had come up.

When the time came, I performed as requested, bustling over to the man's table and whispering in his ear. He walked out of the room with me and explained that he was going to go back to the table and tell his wife that an emergency had arisen with one of his clients. She would stay for the rest of the weekend, he added. I would take him to the airport.

The ruse went off without a hitch. I brought my car around and whisked the big dog off to the nearby airport, which was about five miles from the hotel. Once we got there I took him out to his private jet, which was parked on the tarmac. Three young women, each of them wearing a great deal of makeup and very little fabric, waited for him in the plane.

"We're goin' someplace fun," he said, adding, "Wanna come?"

I said, "No thanks," and wished him a good trip. I knew there was nothing to be gained—by me, the senator, or anyone else—by my uttering a word about what I had seen. In fact, I decided that it would be best if I put it out of my mind completely. I got some help with this task as soon as our life took another dramatic turn.

In the three days we had been away, Gracie had given Cheri's mother constant worries. Despite reassurance from doctors who said her condition was not serious, she had been unable to feed well and her breathing was still labored. If anything, the high-pitched wheezing sound she made as she struggled for air was louder and more constant, and listening to it just about broke your heart. Cheri contacted a specialist she knew from work, who agreed to review the imaging done the previous week. He quickly found something the others had missed.

It turned out that a fairly large artery—it comes directly from the heart and supplies blood to the head as well as the right shoulder and arm—had developed in the wrong place and was pressing on her trachea. Between the direct pressure and the irritation of the nerves and tissues in her throat, the innominate artery was making it very difficult for her to swallow and breathe. And based on its position, this problem wasn't going to go away on its own. It was serious and life-threatening. However, we were told that surgery could correct the problem and help Gracie grow and develop normally. Like every parent faced with this kind of news, we were happy to have the medical mystery resolved but terrified by the idea of authorizing major surgery on our one-month-old daughter. But we had no choice, so on October 4 they took Gracie into the operating room and made the repair. It was by far the hardest day of my life.

As a nurse who had worked in every corner of a hospital, including the pediatric intensive care unit, Cheri knew what to expect during Gracie's recovery. As a mother, she was fiercely protective, which meant we were bound for a confrontation when we were allowed into the PICU and found alarms going off. Despite our daughter screaming out in pain, her chest sutures bulging, and her drain hanging out, no nurse was coming to help her. We found the one assigned to Gracie gabbing about movies with other nurses on her shift, and she said, "Oh yeah, I'll get some pain medicine and be right there." Twelve minutes later—yes, we counted them—she finally arrived, and as she helped Gracie settle down, she agreed that, yes, our daughter seemed to be in some distress.

The state of our health care system is a topic for another book, so it's enough to say here that I was grateful to be married to a professional who could watch over Gracie's recovery. This was especially true when she developed postoperative complications that the staff didn't want to recognize. While everyone else was marveling at the weight Gracie gained, Cheri kept asking why her heart and respiratory rates were climbing, why she hadn't passed any urine, and why she looked so puffy. They brushed her off as a nervous mother—"Oh, Mrs. Young, little Gracie is fine"—until her cardiologist and surgeon finally discovered the next day that fluid was collecting around both of Gracie's lungs. (This was the weight she was gaining.) They took Gracie to the ICU to drain some of this fluid and then sent someone from the "Risk Management Office" to calm as down. We endured scores of incidents like this that only a trained nurse like Cheri would recognize as incompetence. But after the surgery, we were thinking only about our daughter and making sure she would survive the hospital and come home to heal. (Just a few months later, the entire nation would focus on the doctor and unit that made so many critical mistakes with Gracie. A young woman named Jésica Santillán, an illegal immigrant from Mexico, died because our doctor mistakenly gave her a heart and lung transplant from a donor with an incompatible blood type.)

Although we couldn't know it at the time, the operation marked the end of the easygoing season that was the summer of 2002. Gracie's recovery would be slow, as she still struggled to eat and breathe and seemed to catch a dozen colds in the span of three months. Cheri would have to nurse her along and care for Brody, with much less help from me because the senator's push for the White House had become more intense and he had decided the national headquarters in Raleigh would open on January 1, 2003. The job of setting this up, which included finding space, furnishings, utilities, and more, was added to my ongoing duties as his North Carolina advance man, minder, and occasional proxy. I was so busy during this time—leaving early and coming home late—that a month passed before I realized that Cheri's brother had moved in with us. Every step was exciting, from my filing the articles of incorporation to the first campaign e-mail.

Campaigns on all levels are stressful, but presidential campaigns, which attract the most competitive players, can be merciless. Most workers receive little or no pay, and most have little connection to the candidate other than seeing him or her on television. You work fourteen-hour days, seven days a week, and some people actually bring pillows and blankets and sleep under their desks. The first shift starts at four A.M. as the grunts begin searching the Internet for articles about the candidate and creating digests that run to a hundred pages or more. They will spend the whole day gleaning and organizing and distributing important items. The office can start to resemble a frat house, and if you don't have protesters outside, you're doing something wrong. E-mails and phone messages came in at a rate of ten or twenty at a time. And you have to answer them all, because everything is an emergency and everything has to be done perfectly. During the few hours I slept each night, I could feel the vibrations of my cell phones in my dreams.

During this time, the senator gave a series of speeches that spelled out the positions he would take in his run for the White House. On the economy, he tried to find a place between President Bush on the right and the other Democrats on the left as he called for both steep cuts in spending and an end to tax cuts for the rich. For civil libertarians, he pledged to defend the public's privacy rights against Bush administration efforts to gather information under the cover of homeland security; and for the hawks, who were numerous in the South, he came down hard on Saddam Hussein, calling his regime in Iraq a threat to U.S. security.

Although I wasn't part of the group who set his positions, the senator still relied on me for feedback based on my understanding of everyday Democrats who would cast votes in caucuses and primaries. I told him he was on target on the budget, tax, and privacy issues but too close to George Bush when it came to Iraq. As far as I could tell, Saddam had nothing to do with the 9/11 attacks and the president was rushing toward a war that would cost far more in terms of lives and money than it would be worth in terms of our national security. With these ideas in mind, I took a risk and challenged him.

"Are you sure, Senator, that we need to move so quickly in Iraq?" I asked him. "It doesn't feel right."

My question hit a nerve, and he raised his voice with me for the first time, insisting that he had attended intelligence briefings where the administration had presented damning evidence of Saddam's work on weapons of mass destruction and of the atrocities he had committed against his own people. "Andrew, you haven't seen what I have seen. Saddam Hussein is a monster."

No one would argue that the Iraq regime was anything but a brutal dictatorship, but I did ask what purpose would be served by the United States going after this monster when there were many equally monstrous rulers scattered around the globe. The senator held to his position, which he said would probably benefit him politically, because every Democrat who runs for president must prove he is tough on national defense. I didn't change my position, either, and he would hear more of the same from Mrs. Edwards, who was more outspoken in her politics and more liberal than her husband and his key advisers.

As I watched them interact, especially when I brought him home from the airport, I could see the Edwardses were able to express strong feelings without getting upset or damaging their personal relationship. She always greeted him with a hug and a smile, and you could see she loved him and respected him. But his candidacy, like his career, was a joint project, and because he respected her intelligence and instincts, he invited her criticisms. She would tell him when he flopped while giving prepared remarks—he was terrible at reading a speech—and she read, reread, and edited every statement he issued, no matter how minor.

Elizabeth did all this work in addition to taking care of Emma Claire and Jack and supporting Cate, who was at Princeton. Because I saw how hard she was working, I didn't much mind that Mrs. Edwards called on me for help. The senator said that this assistance with his wife and family was more important than anything because it relieved some of the stress caused by his absence. As the holidays approached, I was spared the chore of taking the Christmas picture, but I got deeply involved in finding and transporting the family's main Christmas tree (they had more than one) and helping to locate certain important presents for the family.

Cheri and I argued about the time I devoted to the Edwards family, especially when I was busy doing household chores for them. She couldn't understand why I had to take on responsibility for every practical dilemma that arose in the life of the Edwards family. Time and again I told her it was necessary and would be good for our family in the long run. I apologized and explained: I didn't want to do it, but I had to. Cheri didn't buy it, no matter how many times I said it.

Cheri's point, which I refused to accept, was that I had only so much time and energy and that I was allowing the senator and his wife to take advantage of me. No one could guarantee that John Edwards would ever become president or that I would be part of his team. But that was not an outcome I would even consider. I felt that John Edwards represented my best shot at real success, and I would be a fool to give him anything less than my full effort. Since I was one of the few who had been with him since his election, I also felt a special connection, a sense of pride in helping this man go from rookie senator to presidential contender.

This all-or-nothing commitment drove me to answer every call and every request with immediate action and to approach every task with the utmost seriousness. Certain that I could do anything and everything at once, I found myself headed for Christmas with Cheri's family in Illinois with my cell phone, my BlackBerry, and a briefcase full of work. I was going to celebrate the holiday and make sure the Edwards for President office in Raleigh would be up and running on New Year's Eve, in time for its opening on the first day of 2003. (Since I had negative feelings about the holidays after my father's affair broke apart my extended family, I was actually kind of glad to have work to keep me occupied.)

The main problem I had with the office setup involved the telephones and so-called T1 high-speed Internet lines. If we were going to run a big national campaign with a major Internet presence, we needed an advanced and reliable communication system. I signed up BellSouth to handle it, but they ran into one problem after another. In Illinois, I commandeered the basement at Cheri's sister's house, turning it into an office where I sent out a stream of faxes and made hundreds of calls. While I did this work, everyone upstairs noticed my absence and started to resent that even when I was around, I seemed cranky and distracted. I overheard my skeptical mother-in-law asking what the heck I was doing down in the basement all day.

The holiday debacle in Illinois reached its lowest point as a snowstorm kicked up on Christmas Eve. I had to wait until the last minute to sign various contracts to keep them from becoming public knowledge—it was critical not to steal the thunder of the senator's announcement day. Because of this, I had to overnight signed documents for delivery on the day after Christmas. I wrote out what was needed and went out into the storm to find a FedEx office that was open, would accept a package, and would guarantee delivery on the morning of December 26. I made it with minutes to spare and considered the achievement a bit of a victory. Cheri and her family, on the other hand, watched me race around, ignoring the kids, the company, and the celebration they were enjoying, and concluded that my priorities were out of whack.

I couldn't see their point, and on the long drive home to North Carolina, I continued to defend myself. A presidential campaign is a once-in-a-lifetime opportunity, I said. I had a duty to the senator that I had to fulfill. I made the same excuses on New Year's Eve as I left the house to put the finishing touches on the office. BellSouth had finally completed its work on the phone and T1 lines, establishing consistent and reliable service at our site. The problem was, they wouldn't run the lines inside the office to serve the phones and computers on the many desks where campaign workers would sit. With no volunteers available on New Year's Eve, that task fell to me. I worked into the night, crawling on the floor to run wires and tape them down where necessary to prevent anyone from tripping the next day. I didn't get home until after midnight. It was bad enough that I missed seeing the New Year in with my wife, but I also missed a party that had taken place at my own house. By the time I got there, everyone was gone, along with the party spirit. Of course, I couldn't spend a lot of time making apologies to Cheri. I had to be up early the next morning to meet the senator and the press at his house. It was going to be a big day.

Five

PRIMARY LESSONS

The *New York Times* gets everything first. This happens because even in the Internet age, the *Times* stills sets the media agenda, especially where TV network news operations are concerned. This is why it's always a good idea to give the *Times* an early exclusive on an important story, especially if you think it might spin things your way. On the next to last day of 2002, the senator got just this kind of treatment when the nation's "paper of record" quoted unnamed sources to report that Edwards was going to announce the formation of his presidential exploratory committee—the first step toward a real campaign—and that he would be perceived by many Democrats as "the anti-Gore." As the anti-Gore, Edwards was handsome, energetic, and quick on his feet. He was also, as the *Times* said, "a more authentic Southerner who could have far more appeal in states like North Carolina, Georgia, Kentucky and the mother lode: Florida."

By letting unnamed campaign "advisers" leak the story to the *Times*, we got a flood of inquiries from other press outlets around the world. Among them were requests for live interviews from the three major networks as well as CNN. At four o'clock on the morning of January 2, the Edwardses' neighborhood was filled with production trucks from the TV networks, and the street in front of their house was lit up like a stadium set for a night game. When the senator, Mrs. Edwards, and I looked out from the window of Wade's carefully preserved bedroom on the second floor, we saw truck drivers and technicians standing outside their rigs, sipping coffee and smoking cigarettes. A few of them said hello when I later went outside to clean up so every angle visible to the TV crews looked good.

When I finished my work and went inside the house, I helped some volunteers finish clearing away furniture (much of it was piled in a neighbor's carport) so that the different networks could occupy separate rooms with cameras and lights and crews. The senator was thrilled by the prospect of all the media attention, but Mrs. Edwards paced nervously around the house. I tried to reassure her and reminded her that it was very important to just keep breathing. By the time she was called for the first interview— *Good Morning America*—she was a little less anxious than your typical deer in the headlights. Given my own fear of public speaking, I felt sympathy for her as she struggled to answer questions about her husband with both tact and openness. She got better as the morning wore on but never looked completely comfortable as she listened to the questions through an earpiece and tried to address the camera as if it were a person.

While the Edwardses were introducing themselves to America, I tried to help our press secretary, Mike Briggs, corral the growing media horde on the front lawn. The senator was scheduled to make a formal announcement and take questions at ten-thirty. At about ten-twenty, I noticed that several of the cameras were trained on a side door, where some garbage cans were lined up. Concerned they might appear in a side shot, I jogged over to move them, and as I did, Edwards emerged from the front door and the cable networks like CNN went live with the shot. I scurried to get out of view and then stood to the side as he spoke before the microphones:

> Well, good morning. Good morning to everyone. Today I filed my—the papers to set up an exploratory committee to run for president of the United States. I run for president to

be champion—to be a champion for the same people I fought for all my life, regular folks. They are people like my own family, where I was the first to go to college and my dad worked in a textile mill all of his life, or my mother's last job was working at the post office, to the people I went to school with, the people I grew up with, the families that I represented for almost two decades as a lawyer. And exactly the same group of people. They are the reason I ran for the United States Senate.

I think these people are entitled to a champion in the White House, somebody who goes to work every day seeing things through their eyes and who provides real ideas about how to make their lives better—not somebody who's thinking about insiders or looking out for insiders.

The prepared remarks belonged as much to Elizabeth Edwards as they did to the senator, and they described perfectly the man they wanted to present to the voters. Among the various archetypes found on the American political landscape, "champion of the average Joe" fit the senator best, and this was the role he would assume as he considered facing a field of potential Democratic contenders that included half a dozen men with greater experience in politics and government.

Although Edwards talked about the economy, health care, terrorism, and education, the initial questions from the press were focused more on the nuts and bolts of politics. They seemed most concerned about how much money was in the campaign account (none yet) and whether Edwards would consider running as someone else's pick for vice president if he didn't grab the nomination. (He said he was thinking only about being president.) For me, the event was a perfect example of the main problem with media coverage of politics. While voters say they want to hear about issues, and pundits complain about the lack of substance in campaigns, reporters invariably highlight the horse-race aspect of elections. I don't know if they are trying to impress people with their cynical insider perspective or they just think that issues are boring, but at the front lawn press conference, politics outweighed policy by a substantial margin.

No one in the campaign seemed surprised by the questions, and the senator was prepared for them all. In the next twenty-four hours, we would see that TV and print reporters boiled things down to the same few essential points. First, they said that in a media age a candidate's image is more important than his résumé. Next, they said that Edwards had the look of a president but would need to prove he could connect with the common man. Finally, they concluded that Edwards was at least as attractive as any of the others who would challenge George W. Bush, so he had no reason *not* to throw his hat in the ring.

Besides affirming the news media's limited interest in substance, the senator's encounters with the press that day reinforced my understanding of politics as stagecraft. Once you get the TV trucks lined up and the camera crews running around, people tend to fall into their roles. Senator Edwards was certainly aware of his opportunity, and he went to great lengths to make sure the press had all the pictures they wanted. This included coming back outside after the initial press conference to take Emma Claire and Jack for a stroll in a neighborhood nature walk called the Greenway. The kids looked like walking props to me, but no one said a word about this.

I had my own brush with fame when this happened and CNN went live with a picture that included me standing with my shirt half-untucked and a baseball cap on my head. I didn't even know I was being caught in the scene until my phone rang and I heard Cheri say, "Andrew, you're on TV!" I got myself out of the picture as fast as I could.

The way I saw it, my job was behind the scenes, and if I ever appeared in the press, it meant I had made a mistake. The big-time consultants, policy wonks, and media gurus all knew the more powerful reporters by their first names and had their phone numbers on speed dial. They played a game that involved leaking information to make themselves look good and make others look bad. After the news conference, I turned to the job of preparing for a party that would start in the early evening.

Once the press departed, I spent the afternoon making sure that cleanup crews and food servers were on schedule and trying desperately to contact the caterer, who was absent without leave. I finally got through to him and discovered that his truck had broken down and he had run into trouble finding a replacement. He reassured me that he would make it to the house before the guests, and with no other option I just accepted his apologies and told him to hurry. With the next call came another minor disaster. We had sent out a worldwide fax to the press with our new contact information. BellSouth had activated our toll-free number, but it was working in only three states.

In the middle of these two small crises, Mrs. Edwards, greatly relieved that her interviews were over, walked over to smile and ask me how things were going. Under great duress, with a BlackBerry at one ear and a cell phone at the other ear, listening to elevator music on both, I considered the consequences of telling the truth. I answered her with, "Great, Mrs. Edwards, just great."

The caterer finally appeared in a U-Haul truck about thirty minutes before the guests were scheduled to arrive. As they raced to get food and drinks set up, I noticed that the beer was warm and the finger food was cold. I prayed that nobody would get sick. Then my phone rang. It was one of the Edwardses' neighbors. He had come home from work to find that his lawn had been torn up by one of the TV trucks. I told him we would pay for repairs and dashed off a note, to be copied and placed in all the mailboxes for blocks around, telling folks to call me if their lawns had been damaged so that I could arrange for landscapers to make things right. We made good on this promise, but eventually one of the senator's neighbors made a public stink about how Edwards had shown himself to be a bad citizen by tearing up lawns.

Except for the grumpy neighbors, the response to the launch of the

campaign was remarkably positive. We saw a surge in donations and received a flood of résumés and calls from people who wanted to work with
us. I was most impressed by a young woman named Kayla Burman, who
walked through the door of the office about a week after the announcement
and asked how she could help. We were receiving hundreds of applications,
including from people with two or three Ivy League degrees, and I was
busy trying to figure out why a fax machine wouldn't work. I thanked her,
then told her to leave her résumé and wait for us to get back to her. She
promptly burst into tears.

The crying got my attention, and as she calmed down, Kayla explained
that she had driven to North Carolina from California, alone and *eighteen
years old,* in a beat-up old car, because she believed in John Edwards and
just had to do something to get him elected. Our top campaign consultant,
Nick Baldick, was in charge of the payroll, so I didn't have a paying job for
her, but I asked her to volunteer in the office. She found a free couch to crash
on for three months until we were able to pay her. By then, she had real skills
and was a valuable part of the team. And no one had more enthusiasm.

The senator had repeatedly promised me that I could have any campaign
job I wanted, but Mrs. Edwards told Cheri she was thinking about her, Brody,
and Lauren Grace when she pushed to make sure I was named operations
manager in Raleigh and didn't go on the road minding the senator as his body
man or setting up events as an advance man. She also told Cheri that she
wanted me to be in North Carolina to help with her family while the senator was traveling. In the role of operations manager, I would be responsible
for supporting the people in the field, as well as setting up and maintaining a national network of offices in key states. For the offices, I found the
cheapest space possible—in old gas stations, warehouses, even an abandoned firehouse—and arranged for phones, Internet service, computers,
and furnishings. The advance men and other traveling staff needed cell
phones, laptops, BlackBerrys, hotels, rental cars, airline tickets, and other

support, which I was supposed to supply at the lowest possible cost. With over 150 full-time employees, scores of office locations across the country, thousands of volunteers, and over $30 million in expenditures in one year, it was like setting up a small company on short notice.

Once things got going, the people who required the most support and attention were on the advance staff, which numbered about fifteen at any one time. Advance men—and they are almost all men—are a cross between community organizers and rock-and-roll roadies who trash hotel rooms and run up big room service tabs. They can turn a parking lot into a rally site and arrange for a candidate to meet key people and speak to important audiences all day long. High-energy types, they tend to have extreme personalities. Typical was a mustached former advance man for President Clinton named Sam Myers, whom we called "Senior" because he asked that we hire his son, "Junior," too. Beloved by the senator, Senior could manage an event with the creativity of the director of a feature film, and I can't think of a time when anything went wrong with an event he handled.

Another of our stars was a wild man named Marc Adelman, who spent several hundred dollars a month on cell phone calls. I liked Marc and Senior and most of the other people we sent out across the country because they worked hard, performed their duties well, and always had entertaining stories to tell when they called in. But they were also high-maintenance people who wanted to crash in the best hotels, loved room service, and tended to violate the no-smoking rules so that we had to pay expensive cleaning charges. One of our guys even hit a moose while driving a van rented by the campaign in an isolated corner of some northern state. The accident was bad enough. The fact that he had failed to check off the box requesting insurance coverage on the car rental form made it a minor disaster.

As the person responsible for both the arrangements for our people in the field and the budget to pay for everything, in a good cop/bad cop routine, I played with Nick and Sam. I was supposed to impose some discipline on these folks, which wasn't easy considering that we often changed plans on the fly and had to book travel on short notice, when the airlines and hotels charge their highest prices. The complexity of the job was mind-boggling. I mean, how do you get a handle on the cell phone budget when an organization has four hundred phones and people keep losing them?

Fortunately, in the early days of the campaign, we raced to the head of the pack in the competition for contributions, which gave us more cash to spend than anyone else. In just the first three months of 2003, the organization posted nearly $7.5 million in donations, a record that left people in the camp of the second-place candidate, John Kerry, saying, "We're impressed." The writers for the ABC News political report *The Note* went a little further with an article titled "Shock and Awe: John Edwards Sets a Blazing Pace." Senator Tom Daschle, once a viable contender, promptly dropped out of the race.

The war chest was filled by a new fund-raising team who had replaced Mudcat Saunders and Steve Jarding after the senator found out they had promised we would make sizable donations to politicians and organizations in key states. (We couldn't afford them.) The new group also employed some unorthodox techniques—according to gossip, one of them actually slept with a number of big donors—but they were obviously effective. They got a lot of help from trial lawyers like Fred M. Baron of Texas, who had become super-rich suing asbestos manufacturers and other companies on behalf of people injured by their products. A former high-school football player, Fred was extremely fit and young looking for his age, which was fifty-six. He had silver hair and a million-dollar smile, and he wore wire-rimmed glasses that made him look sort of professorial. The law firm he founded, Baron & Budd, was so big and successful that it pursued cases nationwide.

Although Fred provided invaluable connections to wealthy and powerful people, he made an even more important contribution to the campaign when he agreed to give the senator regular use of his jet. In the post-9/11 era, it's hard to overstate how important flying private is for a presidential candidate. With a private jet, you can visit four key states in one day and make it home for the night. If you fly commercial, you can only do half as many events and you won't be home at the end of the day.

Fred was often on the plane with the senator, especially for fund-raising tours, which were conducted at a breakneck pace. In one three-hour period, they might rush from drinks with a small group to two separate dinners, drinks with another crowd, and then meet privately with a major "bundler" who would gather donations worth hundreds of thousands of dollars. These trips were exhausting, and despite being around a lot of food, the senator and Fred ate so little that they'd be starving come midnight. Under the stress, Edwards sometimes got irritated when his friend pushed him to stay on schedule. Fred, who was usually a happy-go-lucky guy, was a stickler for punctuality, and because he was not intimidated by Edwards—Bill and Hillary Clinton were his close friends—he would complain every time Edwards was late for an appointment. And the senator was *almost always* late. The irritation was mutual, and after hearing a few grousing remarks from Baron, the senator took to calling him Fred A. Baron (the A stood for "asshole") whenever he talked to me about him.

I liked Fred, and his trial lawyer contacts supplied most of the low-hanging fruit—easy money—that we collected early in the campaign. Some of these fellows also got us into a little trouble with the Federal Election Commission because they tried to get around legal limits on their contributions by getting employees to donate and promising to reimburse them. These violations were resolved when the money was returned and a penalty was paid, but the effect of negative publicity around them lingered.

While Fred and the senator poured time and effort into amassing an intimidating pile of cash, an all-star group of professionals put together the machine that would be responsible for attacking the caucus and primary states. For 2004, Edwards relied on heavyweights who had previously served the presidential campaigns of Joe Biden, Bill Bradley, Al Gore, Bill Clinton, Jimmy Carter, Teddy Kennedy, and George McGovern. Senior advisers like David Axelrod of Chicago fashioned the campaign message. Consultant Nick Baldick guided the day-to-day conduct of the campaign, while Harrison Hickman handled polling. Our communications were run by David Ginsberg and press spokesperson Jennifer Palmieri, who were veterans of the Clinton White House.

The first real action in the battle came in May 2003, when nine Democrats took the stage together for a debate in South Carolina, where the senator was almost a favorite son. The only thing this session established was a sense of who the serious candidates might be, and the list included Edwards, Joe Lieberman, Dick Gephardt, Vermont governor Howard Dean, and John Kerry. Kerry and Dean, who were from states that bordered New Hampshire, were considered to be the front-runners, and they spent much of their time sniping at each other, as if it were a two-man race. After the debate, Senator Edwards announced that he was not going to run for reelection to the Senate, so that he could keep his focus on higher office. But even with this distraction removed, he found it hard to reach the voters with his message. As the months passed, it became clear that we weren't getting much traction in our effort to catch up with Kerry and Dean. Donors noticed, too, and since they were most interested in supporting the man who might actually get to the White House, we found it more difficult to talk them into writing checks.

As money became tight, I received lots of calls from field-workers who found that their campaign-issued credit cards were being rejected. (The worst moment came when the current body man, a young fellow named Hunter "Rock Star" Pruette, had his card rejected after dinner at a restaurant with the candidate himself.) On many nights I had to fax credit information to hotels at one or two in the morning so that our people could check in, and every day I engaged in a running battle to control spending. But no matter what I tried, the guys on the road were able to outfox me. For example, when I required them to double up in hotel rooms, they started listing the names of volunteers as their roommates. These people weren't actually in the rooms, but the trick allowed them to get their way in the tussle over money.

The people who work in big campaigns are all, by definition, ambitious and competitive, and they are often highly manipulative. They also fall into camps that have very different perspectives on the candidate and the future. Outside consultants, professionals hired for their expertise, may care about the cause and the Democratic Party, but they are also concerned about their reputations, bank accounts, and future work. They want to win because it's good for business. Campaigns also rely on thousands of volunteers who come and go. Most of these people never have any contact at all with the candidate. People like me, who had an established history with the candidate, hoped to continue with Edwards long into the future.

There was an odd feeling on our campaign, because very few staffers came from North Carolina and I was the only one who had worked for Edwards in the Senate. Nick Baldick, an established political pro who had had little prior contact with Edwards staffers, was hired to run the presidential campaign and given full control. (People who once ran things for Edwards in the Senate were either let go or given minor positions.) Baldick also brought in manuals left over from the Gore campaign and his own people, including an associate named John Robinson. Calling himself "J. Rob," he arrived in Raleigh driving a little Mazda Miata sports car and lugging a huge amount of bad attitude. From the moment he set himself up in the office opposite mine, he tried to intimidate me (and everyone else) by barking orders, making mocking remarks, and sending a stream of text-message requests even though I was sitting ten feet away and always available for a talk.

J. Rob didn't appreciate that besides managing all the demands of the campaign staff and the senator, I was still taking care of the personal needs of the Edwards family. Here J. Rob had something in common with my wife, Cheri, who also questioned the time I put into the care of the Edwards clan. But although I could understand the concern, I figured that as long as I didn't screw anything up, J. Rob should leave me alone.

On a particularly bad day, when J. Rob kept on sending me annoying texts about problems I was working to resolve, I answered one of his mes-

sages with a wisecrack. Incensed, he got up from behind his desk and actually walked the vast distance across the hall to my doorway and glared at
me. I was on the phone, so I covered the mouthpiece and said, "I'm on a
call."

J. Rob was not accustomed to being sloughed off. He turned on his heel,
and as he retreated into his office, he slammed the door hard enough to
shake the walls. Soon after I completed my call he came back, stood in the
doorway with his arms folded, and said, "You were sassing me."

I leaned back in my chair and said, "No. I don't think so. That's the kind
of thing a little kid does to his parents, so I wouldn't say I was sassing you."

"Well, I don't care what the fuck you call it," he shouted. "*You* work for
me, and you don't *ever* talk to me like that."

With that, he turned away and went to retrieve a gym bag so he could
change his clothes and go for a run. Now I was incensed. I got up, followed
him, and growled, "Don't ever fucking yell at me. I was here way before
you got here. I'll be here long after you are gone." Completely fired up, I
followed him to the elevator, took out my cell phone, and challenged him:
"Why don't we call the senator right now and see if he wants to fire me or
you? I've got his number. We can settle this right now."

Suddenly, J. Rob wasn't so eager to yell back. He muttered something
about calling his man Baldick, and when the elevator came, he got on it and
disappeared. I noticed afterward that he stopped yelling in my direction and
the flood of text messages slowed to a trickle. Two weeks later, Nick came to
town for a meeting with key staff, and as we sat around a table we were
asked to introduce ourselves. When it was my turn, I hesitated—as
always—owing to my fear of talking in groups. J. Rob jumped in to say,
"I'll tell you something about Andrew. He hates it when people yell at him."

Because the professionals had their own games to play—like the one
between J. Rob and me—and their long-term careers to consider, they tended
to get distracted and preferred a conservative campaign style. (Later I
would realize that some of these guys wouldn't attack an opponent in the

primaries because they were worried about getting jobs with whoever won in the end. Unfortunately, Senator Edwards listened to these consultants and followed their advice too closely, almost becoming robotic.)

Despite their flaws, they were very good at their jobs, a fact that became obvious to me when it came time for us to shift from "exploratory" status to a genuine presidential campaign. First they arranged for an informal "announcement" on Jon Stewart's program, *The Daily Show*, which would appeal to younger voters. Then they put together an event for the big formal announcement. The main event would be held in Robbins in front of the old textile mill, which had been shut down and stood as a massive brick emblem of the troubles in small-town America.

The plan called for the Edwardses to spend the night before the event at his parents' home. Wallace, his father, and Bobbi, his mother, were salt-of-the-earth types who were so kind that they sent us baby gifts, food when Gracie had surgery, and cakes for our kids' birthdays. Mrs. Edwards did not enjoy spending time with them. When I arrived at their house in Raleigh to drive them to Robbins, it was six P.M., but she was far from ready, and she was arguing with the senator. (They didn't seem to care if I stood there while they shouted.) We didn't get out of the city until around eight o'clock, and on the way she said she wanted some strong cold medicine to take so she would be sleepy and ready for bed as soon as we arrived. I had to stop at three different stores but finally got what she wanted. As we pulled up to the house in Robbins, she was so out of it that the senator walked her to a bedroom, where she escaped for the night.

The next morning, the senator and I went for a run at four-thirty so his head would be clear enough to handle a string of live morning show interviews. Along the way, we passed his old high school and the mural of astronaut Charles Brady. As a youth, John Edwards had been the "golden boy" in his family and in his town. Sometimes I wondered if he had been loved too much back then and somehow got the idea that the rules might not apply to him the way they did to everyone else. I knew for certain that he was his mother's favorite and that she had almost never disciplined him.

"Johnny just never made any trouble," she would say, and in her mind this was true.

Bobbi had breakfast for us when we returned, and as we ate he called her "Mama" and referred to his father as "Daddy," sounding very much like the fine Southern boy he was. After we ate and showered, he said, "Hey, Andrew, let's go check things out." We got in the Suburban and, after getting lost, which was hard to do in such a small town, found our way to the factory. As we drove, the senator asked me what I imagined his old classmates might think of him. It astonished me to hear that at a moment like this, when he was about to announce a run for president of the United States, he was thinking back to the kids he knew in school. But I hid my surprise and said, "They're proud of you. I'm sure of it."

The big abandoned mill had been draped in red, white, and blue to serve as a backdrop for a metal platform that faced a parking lot, where a crowd of several hundred people had already staked out their places. Music blared from the sound system, and TV crews were busy setting up their cameras. Clearly, our campaign crew would deliver the excitement they had promised.

Back at the house, the senator, his parents, and Mrs. Edwards sat for TV interviews, and then we all left for the mill site. When we got there, two thousand people, including busloads from hundreds of miles away, cheered the senator as if he were Elvis. His big applause lines addressed the failures of the Bush administration and his promise to halt government's neglect of working-class people. The biggest cheers came when he talked of growing up in Robbins and said, "I promise to fight for you." At the end, his campaign theme song, "Small Town" by John Mellencamp, poured from the loudspeakers.

The song matched the candidate's biography, which was at the center of his message. Edwards insisted that he was not, as his opponents might say, a rich, inexperienced guy with oversize ambition. Instead, he was a son of small-town America with the strength and independence, thanks to his self-made wealth, to stand against the entrenched political power brokers.

For audiences who might hear him only once or twice, the way the candidate harped on small-town America in his appearances probably rang true, but for the staff of the campaign, who heard the words *small town* hundreds of times a day, the phrase and the song became more than a little irritating. When staff people gathered to watch him in a televised debate or speech, they often played a drinking game that required every player to drink a shot of something strong whenever the words "small town" or "I'm the son of a millworker" came out of his mouth. On a typical night, people would be howling drunk after half an hour.

Although this theme struck a chord with some voters and amused his aides and advisers, it was no substitute for a well-defined platform of ideas, and Edwards was criticized for a lack of substance. By November, polls showed him running a distant third or fourth, and both the press and political experts were saying he had a "gravitas" problem, meaning he seemed too young and inexperienced. When I caught him on television in this period, I detected little of the energy and passion I had seen at the Ocean Creek Inn and throughout his Senate campaign. That man was gone, replaced by a robot that looked like John Edwards but spoke like a man reading a briefing paper.

On many nights, my phone would ring and I would hear the senator on the other end. Sometimes he sounded petty and irritated by ordinary events. He especially hated making appearances at state fairs, where "fat rednecks try to shove food down my face. I know I'm the people's senator, but do I have to hang out with them?" He sometimes called in the middle of a televised event. He'd say, "Hey, Andrew, I'm on TV talking to you. Turn it on." He would then put on a serious face, pretending to talk about something important, and we would chat about basketball. When he asked, I also gave him some Ambien tablets from my own prescription, so that he could get to sleep on nights when he was just too wound up. These little conspiracies, which reminded him of the times we had spent together on the road, brought us closer together. And when, in these unguarded moments, he asked for my evaluation of the campaign, I didn't hold back. I told him that friends, family, and longtime supporters were telling me that the John Edwards they knew had disappeared. They wanted him to speak more forcefully about the needs of working people and issues like health care and how the insurance companies were running amok. I was very critical of the "inside the Washington Beltway" people and told him they were overthinking things. "Go with your gut instincts," I said.

With Christmas approaching, I was more involved with the preparations at the Edwards home than I was with my own family. While Cheri did the shopping and decorating at our house, many of the toys that needed my attention sat in boxes, but I put together an electric-powered toy Jeep for Jack, which I adorned with campaign stickers. I am sure that Cheri resented the time I gave to the Edwards family, but I was fully committed to the "never say no" work ethic. Cheri tried to understand.

When I picked Senator Edwards up at the Raleigh airport around this time, he was happy to be back in North Carolina but miserable about the state of his campaign. "Andrew, I am really sick of this shit," he said wearily. "I'm not going to go down like this. I'm going to start being me. What the fuck do I have to lose?" As the third or fourth man in a race that had boiled down to six contenders, the senator had nothing to lose and everything to gain by a change in approach. I told him to start loosening up. He looked out the window at that familiar landscape and nodded in agreement.

Days later, I switched on CNN to see Tucker Carlson and Paul Begala, who hosted the political talk show *Crossfire* at the time, reporting from New Hampshire. They had bumped into Senator Edwards as he came out of a restaurant in Manchester, and he'd instantly agreed to walk with them to the network's bus and conduct an impromptu interview. Snow flurries came down and the TV guys protected themselves with heavy coats, while the senator, who wore only a light jacket, bustled along as if he had all the energy and time in the world and couldn't feel the blustery cold.

As they walked, Edwards said he had been hearing from voters who were worried about health care, especially the power of insurance companies and "the lack of any cost controls on prescription drugs, adding, "They're very suspicious about it." Carlson, a conservative, wondered aloud if Edwards might depict President Bush as "a big spender" when it came to health care and win some support from conservative voters. While Begala laughed at the notion, the senator picked up on it.

"Yes, I think that's correct. You're right about that."

By this point in the broadcast, the three men had reached the CNN bus and Begala invited the senator aboard. He took a look at the vehicle, called the *CNN Election Express*, and blurted out, "Oh, cool bus!" It was an unguarded little remark, and it made him seem sincere, like the guy I used to know. Watching this series of unscripted moments, I shouted at the TV, "Dude, there you are! Welcome back, man!"

As they took their places in a little studio inside the bus, Begala and Carlson seemed thrilled. They told Edwards he was the first candidate ever to visit and then began asking about his previous experiences in life. This gave him a chance to attack George Bush's policies at length and to talk about growing up in a small town and having experiences most Americans might find familiar. Then Carlson played right into his hands, offering up observations about how Howard Dean (like John Kerry) came from extreme wealth. The senator then went on to explain that Dean was never going to grab the nomination, and he made a reasonable argument for how he could actually win it.

"What will happen is what always happens in these multicandidate races. There are going to be huge changes between now and the New Hampshire primary, the Iowa caucuses, the South Carolina primary. Voters are going to start to focus on who their candidate should be. And they're going to care about a lot of things. And one of the things is . . . who, in fact, can compete with George Bush everywhere, who will be the best candidate for the Democratic Party."

Not long after this encounter, the senator called to catch up. When I told him I was delighted by his encounter with Begala and Carlson, he said the moment had revived him. "I saw those guys and just thought, Fuck it. I'm going to do and say what I want." The result had given him a sense that if he could continue to present himself with genuine emotion and reached enough voters, especially in Iowa, he might just win the nomination.

With the heightened commitment came a new message, devised with the help of consultant David Axelrod. Edwards began to talk about "two Americas," one where everyday people played by the rules but were buffeted by powerful forces beyond their control, the other populated by a wealthy and influential minority who wielded too much power and influence, especially in Washington. Following Axelrod's advice, the senator emphasized hope for the future and resisted personal attacks on his opponents. He also tried to adjust his image a bit to address the complaint that he looked too boyish.

For the next month, the senator pushed hard and made steady headway. When Al Gore endorsed Dean, Edwards brushed it off with a wisecrack about how the Republicans have "coronations" but Democrats have elections. In both New Hampshire and Iowa, he discovered die-hard supporters, and polls showed he was rising in popularity as voters began to narrow their choices. The change was slow, however, and a week before the Iowa caucuses he was still in fourth place, almost twenty points behind Dean, according to one poll. That Sunday, he got some encouragement when he appeared on ABC and George Stephanopolous noted that a quarter of Iowa voters were still undecided, "and they like you." Stephanopolous then played a video clip of a voter who said his one concern about Edwards was that he was a little too green.

"I've heard it all my life," replied the senator. Then he talked in a way I had heard many times before, recalling how he was never expected to graduate from college or law school, and he wasn't supposed to make it in his career as an attorney or as a candidate for United States Senate. At each step he had surprised people (and himself) by not just succeeding, but excelling. "My job is to convince them with my passion, my energy, that I can get this done."

Unlike other candidates, Edwards promised Iowans he would never raise taxes on the middle class and that he would help everyone who qualified go to college, no matter their income. He raced around the state talking about hope, and as he had when he ran against Faircloth, he refused to be baited into attacking his rivals. "Cynics do not build this country, optimists build this country," he repeated to crowds that were growing larger every day. By midweek, Howard Dean was sniping at him by name in his TV commercials, and he had earned the endorsement of the state's most important paper, the *Des Moines Register*. The front-page article was titled "John Edwards, Your Time Is Now." This endorsement was so important that the senator called me at one-thirty in the morning, saying, "Andrew, this is huge." Then he had me connect him by phone with his parents. The next day, John Kerry began attacking Edwards with snide remarks about his youthfulness, saying he was probably "in diapers" in 1969 when Kerry served in Vietnam.

In the brief exchanges we had on the phone during this push, Edwards sounded to me like a preacher at a revival meeting where everyone was catching the spirit and wanted to come to Jesus. Hoarse and exhausted, he was thrilled by the way people responded to his attacks on Bush and his optimistic message about a future with a Democrat in the White House. He understood that caucus participants were far more committed to the success of the party than people who voted in primaries and that they didn't want to see their own guys shred one another. For this reason, he avoided making harsh attacks on his opponents. Grassroots Democrats seemed to appreciate his restraint. "We're getting through, Andrew," he crowed. "We really are."

When the caucuses finally met, Edwards surged from fourth place with 11 percent to second place at about 32 percent. Unfortunately, John Kerry, who had also made a furious final week crusade, finished five points ahead and came out the clear winner. Howard Dean, who once seemed unbeatable, fell to below 20 percent and was then captured by TV cameras making a speech that included a strange-sounding victory howl that was instantly dubbed the "Dean scream" and subjected to endless mockery by pundits, comedians, and Internet commentators.

Inside the Edwards campaign, we knew that with another week's time we could have passed Kerry and won Iowa. Instead, the Massachusetts senator with the long résumé and extremely sober demeanor got most of the press attention as the campaign shifted to New Hampshire. Kerry, who like Dean lived in a neighboring state, had a huge advantage over us, and we had only a week to try to close the gap. To make matters worse, we were running out of money faster than we were running out of time. As the senator dashed around the state, he discovered the crowds were smaller than they had been in Iowa, but we couldn't afford to buy enough advertising to reach them through the media. On election day Kerry scored his second win, Dean made a comeback to claim second, and Edwards finished a distant fourth, just behind General Wesley Clark.

With his early wins, the fund-raising tide also turned toward Kerry, as donors who were eager to be with the winner rushed to show their support prior to March 2—called Super Tuesday—when ten states from Vermont to California would hold primaries. In Raleigh, I juggled money to keep Edwards on the road, and the staff was pared back. The senator's mood and the feeling in our offices turned dark as it seemed that barring some disaster, Kerry was going to run away with the nomination.

Although it's wrong to wish bad fortune on someone else, a feeling of hope rippled through the campaign when the Internet site DrudgeReport .com—run by a mudslinger called Matt Drudge—posted a story suggesting Kerry had had an affair with a tall, twenty-seven-year-old blond news reporter. We had heard similar rumors and innuendo for months and began following the story with so much intensity that another Web site measured the Internet traffic and announced that we had checked DrudgeReport.com a thousand times. When this got out, John Robinson went around the office telling people to cut it out. We were making ourselves look bad.

Soon after the supposed affair was reported, Alexandra Polier, who was supposedly Kerry's paramour, stepped forward to say the story was a lie. I'd like to believe she told the truth, but in politics you never know. True or not, her statement killed the best chance we had at overcoming Kerry. In the last week before Super Tuesday, some commentators said the senator was keeping up the fight only to position himself to be the vice presidential candidate on a Kerry ticket and was therefore being too easy on him. Then Edwards took some swipes at the front-runner, trying to depict him as a Washington insider. It didn't work. Kerry won every Super Tuesday state, except for Dean's Vermont, by big margins. To our credit, Edwards finished second in all nine of those states and grabbed 41 percent of the Democrats in Georgia, the one state in the Deep South.

The talk of Edwards joining a Kerry campaign as the vice presidential nominee, which began even before Super Tuesday, flared for a moment after he decided to withdraw from the presidential campaign. (One of our supporters actually waved a handmade Kerry-Edwards sign at the gathering in Raleigh, where the senator announced his decision.) E. J. Dionne of *The Washington Post* said that Edwards had actually gained a great deal in his losing campaign and had positioned himself as a favorite in the veep sweepstakes. (Dionne complained, however, that Edwards had failed to challenge Kerry in a way that would toughen him up for the fight with Bush.) But while the pundits pointed to Edwards's appeal and potential, not one of them mentioned the challenge the senator faced coming to terms with his loss—the first major defeat in his entire life—and figuring out what he would do next without an office to serve as his platform.

When he returned to North Carolina, we went to a postcampaign gathering that the headquarters crew threw in a local brew pub. (Remarkable as it may seem, some of these devoted workers would be meeting John and Elizabeth in the flesh for the first time ever.) I knew that the Edwardses, especially Elizabeth, were sore about the advice they had been given—and accepted—until his "fuck it" moment in Manchester, so I was wary of how things would go at this event. The senator was fairly upbeat and appreciative. Elizabeth was not. At one point I saw that Kayla, who had come from California to volunteer, was crying. Nick Baldick, a big, hulking tough guy, stood alone looking very upset. It struck me that I would be the only one kept on salary, while he, J. Rob, and the rest had just become unemployed. I went over to console him and said, "Nick, you did a great job. The best you could." He nodded and then with a little catch in his voice said, "Thanks, Andrew. I wish Elizabeth shared that thought."

Six

MICKEY MOUSE AND
JOHN KERRY

After John Kerry had the 2004 Democratic presidential nomination wrapped up, the *Dallas Morning News* published an article
citing all the reasons he should ask John Edwards to join the
ticket. The arguments revolved around three main points. The first was
that Edwards had proven himself in the primaries to be a disciplined and
exciting campaigner. Second, "his private life, finances and pre-political
career [had] all have been vetted" when he was considered to be Al Gore's
partner in 2000. And third was his Southernness: He had the accent, the
regional base, and the charm to balance Kerry's persona, which was colder
than a New England winter.

Although it's generally bad form to be seen vying for the running mate's
spot, especially when you are still in contention in the primaries, Edwards
had started sending signals that he was open to an offer even before Super
Tuesday. Using go-betweens like Bob Shrum, Harrison Hickman, and South
Carolina congressman James Clyburn, he made sure Kerry understood his
strength as a fund-raiser, communicator, and effective campaigner. Polling
showed he was far more popular than Dick Gephardt, who we believed was
Kerry's personal favorite, and no one looked better on television. As part of a
charm offensive aimed at getting Kerry's attention, Edwards agreed to be

featured in the March 8 *People* magazine. The article highlighted a telling comment from a female voter who said, "He's real, and he's easy to look at." (This comment was tame compared with the words women whispered in Edwards's ears or wrote on notes they pressed into his hand at public appearances. I knew this because I had been with him in the past when he rebuffed advances from women and a few men, which seemed to come whenever we were in public.) Altogether, Edwards seemed to provide the perfect balance for Kerry. In fact, the only negative where a Kerry-Edwards ticket was concerned was that the two guys didn't like each other very much.

When we talked about him, the senator complained that Kerry, despite his long-winded, professorial demeanor, "just wasn't all that smart." The man seemed well-informed, he added, like someone "who had read *The New York Times* every day for twenty years," but he wasn't a creative person or even a good problem solver. He also found Kerry to be aloof and far too aristocratic in his bearing to succeed as the leader of a party that looks for major support from unions, African Americans, and people in big cities. During the primaries, Kerry had been the opponent our side most loved to hate. Our political strategist Jim Andrews, who I swore cussed and smoked in his sleep, used to bellow, "We just can't let this motherfuckin' blue blood get in the White House."

The resentment toward Kerry had been heartfelt, and it had come from the top of our organization, but when it appeared that the two teams might join forces, my boss tried to see the advantages. When Edwards met with the head of Kerry's search committee, Jim Johnson, he stressed how they had complementary strengths, and whenever we talked about it, he focused on the idea that we would *both* move our families into the vice president's mansion and that after eight years as Kerry's second, he would spend eight more in the White House. He talked often about our kids growing up together in Washington. (I liked this idea, too, and when Gus Gusler, lawyer for Hootie & the Blowfish, teased me and asked me what I charged for "delivering groceries," I replied, "Sixteen years in the White House." He laughed and said, "I would, too.")

As Edwards saw it, Al Gore had squandered the opportunity Clinton had handed him. He said he wasn't going to make the same mistake.

We had these conversations in my Suburban, at his home, and on the occasions when we took our kids out for some fun. During the spring of 2004, our two families grew as close as they would ever be. Jack and Emma Claire came to our house regularly, sometimes with their nanny, Heather North, and they would play for hours on end. Sometimes I'd take the whole gang out on the lake in our motorboat. I don't think four kids ever had more fun.

In late spring, when the Edwardses were in Washington, they walked from their home to Kerry's house for what could only be called job interviews. Kerry brought the senator to one part of the house, and his wife, billionaire heiress Teresa Heinz, took Elizabeth to another. (For political purposes, she called herself Teresa Heinz Kerry, but she never adopted this name legally.) As I heard it from Elizabeth and John, these meetings went terribly. Teresa asked Elizabeth if she would pursue any particular causes as the vice president's wife. When she began to talk about education, Teresa cut her off and began talking about the education foundation she supported with millions of dollars. Elizabeth told me the same thing happened when she brought up a school computer lab the Edwardses established at Broughton High and Teresa acted like "she owned IBM." They spent perhaps five or ten minutes together, and then Teresa left Elizabeth alone to search out her husband.

According to Bob Shrum, the two senators also struggled to get along. In an attempt to establish some intimacy, Edwards told Kerry he wanted to tell him a story no one else knew. He then told him about embracing Wade's body in the medical examiner's office. Kerry was stunned and put off, because Edwards had actually shared the same tale with him once before.

When I saw him after this meeting, Senator Edwards said nothing about the Wade story but confessed that he had serious doubts about whether Kerry would make a good president. The Edwardses both called John and

Teresa "complete assholes," and the senator concluded that their shared wealth, power, and privilege had left them out of touch with ordinary reality. He said, "Andrew, I'm rich, but they are ludicrously rich. How can he possibly be the leader of the Democratic Party? I bet he doesn't know the price of milk." (Mrs. Edwards always made sure her husband knew the price of milk, as well as gasoline, just in case someone asked.)

Of course, these personal feelings didn't affect the senator's professional ambitions or his public statements. All through the spring, he helped the Kerry campaign in any way they asked, even flying to the ends of the earth—okay, Fargo, North Dakota—to give a rousing speech on the nominee's behalf. Inside the Democratic Party, support for a Kerry-Edwards ticket began to build. Kerry still had other candidates on his list, and while he labored over the choice, Senator Edwards invited my family to join his at Disney World, and he paid for the trip. The group would include little Jack and Emma Claire, plus the Edwardses' twenty-two-year-old daughter, Cate, and the Young family of four. Or four and a half, since Cheri was eight months pregnant.

The summer high in Orlando averages about ninety degrees. The humidity generally hovers around 75 percent, and it rains every other day. These conditions would be hard enough on anyone hauling kids around the Magic Kingdom, but our group was further challenged by the fact that Mrs. Edwards was recovering from an abdominal operation (she still had a surgical drain in her belly) and Cheri was pregnant. In retrospect, I would guess that we mounted this expedition primarily so the world would know the Edwardses were at the most American vacation spot of all if the call came for him to be vice president.

To be fair, John and Elizabeth did not expect that he would be chosen, and the vacation was a thrill for the kids. A terrific father, the senator took Emma Claire and Jack on the flying teacups, allowed himself to look as silly as possible aboard the Dumbo ride, and endured the cloying melody of "It's a Small World (After All)" as many times as they wanted. The experience was a little more difficult for Mrs. Edwards, who tended to have an inflexible concept of fun and was never able to relax like her husband. Instead, she seemed to get preconceived notions about what an experience should be and then tried to force everyone to play certain roles so the picture looked as she had imagined it would. For example, when we saw Peter Pan she had the kids listen as she told the entire story when all they really wanted to do was rush to see the young woman dressed up as the character.

The characters were a huge hit with the kids, and the Edwardses chose to pay for VIP treatment, which meant we had a tour guide—her name was Tracey—who drove us from the hotel to the theme park in a van and then stayed with us to make sure we got to the front of every line and got into the better restaurants on the property. Tracey saw our group at its best and its worst. One morning as she collected us at our hotel, Mrs. Edwards noticed something had been left behind with the senator, who was still in their room. I happened to be talking to him via cell phone, so when she tried to reach him she couldn't. When she found out what was happening, she actually cussed me out in front of my family and people who stood nearby. I just took it, which made me feel humiliated. When the senator finally appeared, he discovered a stony silence in the van. Eventually, Cate spoke up and asked Mrs. Edwards to apologize. To her credit, she did. But I was reminded of all the times Cheri questioned how the Edwardses treated me and thought her concern was valid.

Mrs. Edwards was especially tense that morning because she and the senator were starting to think that he would not get the call to be vice president. That night, we had dinner at Chef Mickey's, where the kids got to meet a gang of Disney characters. As we walked into the place, Brody saw Mickey Mouse and ran over to see him, with Emma Claire and Jack following right behind. The senator and I chased down the kids, and then I went to our table and took a moment to check my phone. It showed six or seven missed calls, all from the same number in Washington, D.C.

The messages were from Mary Beth Cahill, a major figure in the Massachusetts Democratic Party who was John Kerry's campaign manager.

After leaving one of the messages, she had handed the phone to Kerry, who said, "Hey, John, this is John Kerry. I'm hoping to speak with you as soon as we can."

As I finished listening to the messages, the senator appeared with the kids and I told him what was going on. His eyes got wide, and I asked if he wanted to go back to the hotel and return the call. He said he'd prefer to do it right away and asked me to find a private place where he might use the phone. I had performed this duty for him countless times, and it's remarkable to see how people always respond positively when they are told that a prominent person needs a private place to conduct important business. In this case, the manager of Chef Mickey's cleared out a little outdoor smoking spot for employees and we sat there at a table, with amusement park rides in the background and lights starting to come on all around us.

When we reached her, Mary Beth didn't put Kerry on the phone and was evasive about the purpose of the call. All she wanted to say was that Kerry was inviting Edwards to a meeting in Washington and wanted him to fly up the next evening. They then engaged in a little debate over whether he would travel in a private jet or fly commercial. He wanted the campaign to send a jet so he could avoid public attention and because the gesture would signal their respect for a family man interrupting his vacation. She wanted him to head for Orlando International Airport and hop a commercial flight to save the campaign money. (I suspect she also feared that if they sent a jet, it would indicate that Edwards was already the chosen one.) They agreed that he would try to get to Washington, but they left the transportation issue up in the air, so to speak.

When we returned to the table inside Chef Mickey's, Mrs. Edwards was bursting with curiosity. The senator explained what had transpired with the calls but emphasized that Mary Beth had not told him anything about the reason for the invitation. For all he knew, Kerry wanted to reject him in a face-to-face meeting. Mrs. Edwards insisted that the senator go to Washington as requested, even if it meant spending a few hours on a commercial flight.

The buzz about the call continued until we returned to the hotel, where Cheri went to the Edwardses' suite with Elizabeth, and the senator and I took the kids down to the pool to swim and watch the nightly Disney fireworks show. We ordered some drinks, and after his third or fourth glass of wine, he got a little louder and more pessimistic about his prospects. Almost certain he wouldn't get the nod, he said, "Andrew, this is bullshit. Unless they send me a jet, I'm not going. He's fucking with me, he's yanking my chain. I've been in the Senate with him for four years, why does he need to meet with me?"

Worried that the senator was speaking too loudly poolside, I went to pay the bar bill. When I turned around, he and the kids were gone. I assumed they had returned to the room, so I went upstairs. They weren't there. Mrs. Edwards lost her temper and screamed at me, "Andrew, you know how irresponsible he is. You can't leave him alone with four kids."

She called security and we all searched the hotel. I went back to the pool area, where I saw him and he asked, "What's going on?" He was carrying a bunch of clothes and there were four buck-naked kids trailing behind him. He explained that he had taken them to a little beach for a moonlight swim in a pond where big signs warned, DO NOT SWIM. ALLIGATORS.

In the morning, with the families set to spend the day at the Animal Kingdom theme park, Jim Johnson, Kerry's lead scout in the hunt for a running mate, called a little after eight o'clock. He said he wanted to go over the issues that Kerry was considering as he settled on his choice. His first concern had to do with whether his vice president was serious about the work of governing. The second was long-term loyalty. (Kerry wanted a guarantee that if they lost, Edwards would not run against him for the presidential nomination in 2008.) The third and final concern was about Edwards's stand on the issues. Kerry wanted to make sure that his partner at the top of the ticket would present a united front with him.

It sounded to me as if the Kerry team was giving Edwards a chance to get the answers right. With visions of life in the vice president's mansion in my head, I urged him to go see Kerry even if he had to take a bus. I was surprised when he wouldn't be moved on the private jet issue and surprised again when they actually gave in to his demand. We spent the morning at the Animal Kingdom, where several rides take you through pretend wilderness settings around the world. After lunch with the families at the Rainforest Cafe, I accompanied the senator back to the hotel for a change of clothes, then drove him to the private airport. He was excited but also irritated to be called back for what seemed like another job interview. When we got to the airfield, we drove to a small jet that was waiting with its engines running so the cabin could be air-conditioned. The senator went up the steps, stopped at the door, and gave me a wave before ducking inside. I noticed that he looked nervous.

Only John Kerry and John Edwards can say for certain what happened in their meeting later that day. I know that Edwards stopped first at his house and went for a jog. The get-together was held at the home of Madeleine Albright, secretary of state under Clinton, and Edwards was driven there in a town car rented in my name. The windows were so heavily tinted, no one could see him. According to Edwards, who filled me in, Senator Kerry was friendlier than he had been before and impressed that Edwards had interrupted his vacation to have the meeting and that he was heading back to Orlando that same night so he could be with his family.

It's hard to imagine John Kerry having a relaxed conversation about something as ordinary as Walt Disney World, but according to Edwards, when he told him that he'd spent the morning at the Animal Kingdom, Kerry's eyes lit up and he said he had loved visiting the park with his daughters. During the rest of the time they spent together, they discussed the upcoming campaign, which would be both a referendum on George Bush and a chance for the Democrats to present some new ideas, and the overall political landscape. Kerry did ask Edwards whether, in the event that they lost, he would challenge him in the 2008 primaries. Edwards proudly told me he let Kerry think a challenge was unlikely but in lawyerly fashion left himself an out.

Besides impressing Kerry with his commitment to family, Edwards believed he scored big points when he was told that both Dick Gephardt and Senator Bob Graham had said they would be able to accomplish more as vice president because they were experienced in the ways of Washington. Edwards didn't make any counterclaims for himself or try to criticize these other contenders. Instead, he noted that people with their skills and extensive experience would be perfect picks to serve in somewhat lesser jobs in a Kerry-Edwards administration.

I heard all about this when I went to the airport near Disney World to meet the jet that brought Edwards back that night. While I waited outside the private terminal, I watched a couple of maintenance workers who were hanging around for this one last arrival, playing cards, smoking cigarettes, and reveling in the fact that they were getting paid overtime. The jet finally landed at 12:50 A.M., and as the senator came inside, I could see he had relaxed with a little wine. He introduced himself to the card players (as if they really cared who he might be) and then said, "Man, I gotta piss." (The senator was irked that the jet was too small to have a decent toilet.)

Once we got in the car, Edwards refused to tell me what had happened until I assured him that everyone he had left behind had enjoyed themselves during the day. Once I'd done this, he told me about the car with the tinted windows, Albright's house, Kerry's interest in the Animal Kingdom, and the substance of the conversation. He thought it was ridiculous that Kerry had asked him to promise he wouldn't run in 2008 but considered the rest of the meeting a terrific success. Kerry had stopped just short of offering him the job, but before the session was over he'd shown Edwards a mock-up of a Kerry-Edwards campaign logo: red, white, and blue, with an American flag.

It was about two o'clock when we got to the hotel. We went upstairs together, and as we split to go to our rooms we exchanged a victorious high five, like a couple of UNC ballplayers celebrating a three-pointer. The next day, the national press was reporting that John Kerry had conducted a secret meeting with the person leading the contest to join the ticket. Several commentators noted that since John Edwards was at Walt Disney World with his family, he was almost certainly out of the running. But one source, ABC's *The Note*, offered a hint by posting the mileage from Washington, D.C., to Disney World. I never figured out how they knew and why they didn't follow up on it.

Several days passed while Kerry made his final pick. The Youngs and the Edwardses went home to North Carolina, and at both houses the phones rang continuously. For four days, I couldn't say anything as friends, colleagues, neighbors, and members of the press called to ask questions and share rumors, the most persistent being the idea that the only one on the Kerry team opposed to Edwards was Teresa Heinz Kerry. Gradually, her resistance was overcome (or set aside), and by the Fourth of July, Edwards seemed to be in the lead, according to everyone we spoke to.

On that day, I accompanied the senator on his annual "Beach Walk," which was really just a stroll along the ocean with stops to talk to voters and their families. In private moments, we discussed where we might hold the first Kerry-Edwards rally in North Carolina and decided we could get the biggest crowd in Raleigh. Robbins was now way too small.

Two days later, in the early morning hours, deliverymen working from trucks that stopped at newsstands throughout the New York region hurled onto the sidewalk bound stacks of the day's *New York Post*. On the cover was a big photo of Dick Gephardt and John Kerry below the headline KERRY'S CHOICE.

In Raleigh, my phone rang at about six A.M. A friend whose father was a bigwig in the national Republican Party practically shouted into the phone, "Congratulations!" He then explained that his father had received word that Edwards was on the ticket. The source was completely reliable, he said, and the *New York Post* was as wrong as the *Chicago Daily Tribune* had been with its DEWEY DEFEATS TRUMAN screamer in 1948. The Republicans must have had a very good line into the Kerry operation, because I called Senator Edwards immediately and heard that he was still waiting to hear the news.

I got off the phone with the senator in order to keep his line open and practically shook with anticipation. Although the senator was the focus of the decision, and no one outside my immediate circle even knew I would be affected, I felt as though the rest of my life depended on what John Kerry was thinking. Desperate for information, I called Fred Whitfield, a friend of mine who just happened to be Dick Gephardt's neighbor in Washington. (A close friend of Michael Jordan's, Whitfield was then an executive with the Washington Wizards basketball team.) Whitfield said that Gephardt was in town and some media folks were camped out by his door. But the mood in this crowd was not positive. This suggested that the *Post* was wrong and Edwards was in.

While I had talked with Fred, Kerry had finally phoned Edwards to ask him to be on the ticket. The match was made, and the senator immediately called the hotel where Elizabeth was staying. Ironically, she was in the washroom and didn't get to the phone before it went to voice mail. I then got through to the senator, and he told me, "It's good, Andrew, I'll call you back in a second." After he finally spoke to her, he dialed me right back and said, "We're in, Andrew, and we're going to win it."

Mrs. Edwards flew home immediately, and the family called on me to come help them pack to leave for the Heinz farm outside Pittsburgh. The mood at their house was high, and while the senator and I talked in the library, he said, "Andrew, isn't this great? We're going to do it. We're really going to do it."

In an unguarded moment, I tried to joke with the senator by saying, "Yeah, but it's too bad that Kerry is such an asshole."

In an instant, the rapport between us disappeared. The senator called out to his wife, "Did you hear that, Elizabeth? Andrew thinks Kerry's an asshole." I was suddenly flushed with embarrassment, and though I couldn't hear her reply, I'm sure it was a scolding remark. The senator went into another room, and although the chill soon thawed, I had been taught a lesson. Everyone in the Edwards camp now approved of John Kerry, and this would be our attitude for the foreseeable future.

I was willing to go along, but I was unable to stop noticing the things about the Kerrys that struck me as odd. For example, when the Kerry and Edwards families got together for their first photo op at the Heinz family farm, Teresa took it upon herself to reach over and try to pull little Jack's thumb out of his mouth. Of course, this was the moment when the photographers started clicking and it was the picture published in many leading papers. Soon enough, commentators in the *Times* and on National Public Radio were asking, What business was it of hers to handle a nervous four-year-old who was someone else's kid?

The family summit at the ninety-acre farm was followed by a four-day campaign swing that would end on Saturday in Raleigh. They traveled on a Boeing 757 that was decorated with the Kerry-Edwards logo and were met by big crowds in four states. (The senator had come a long way from the days when I drove him around the state with a Velcro-backed U.S. Senate seal.) While they rallied the faithful, I raced around the Edwards home to prepare it for a crew from the CBS News program *60 Minutes* (they were going to tape interviews in the living room) and for the Kerrys to stay overnight.

The Edwardses were not meticulous housekeepers, and I was hard-pressed to chase down all the dust bunnies, empty Diet Coke cans, and throw out old newspapers and magazines that cluttered the place. Once again I had to move furniture out so that TV cameras and lights could be positioned, and I had to make sure that the balky air-conditioning system was in good order and the kitchen was stocked for both families and the media crews.

Just like many VIPs I had worked with, the Kerrys sent their preferences ahead. According to the list, Teresa would eat either grilled salmon with steamed vegetables or one of two types of salad: Cobb or chicken Caesar. John Kerry wanted Boost energy drinks (strawberry or vanilla) and a dinner of roast chicken, meat loaf, or pot roast. They both requested chocolate cake and only one kind of wine—Kendall Jackson Sauvignon Blanc. I made sure every item on the list—including peanut butter and strawberry preserves—was in the kitchen. Following Mrs. Edwards's orders, I also hired a chef to stand by and prepare whatever anyone wanted.

The main event for the North Carolina visit was an afternoon rally at North Carolina State University that drew more than twenty-five thousand people. It was to be the largest political rally the state had ever seen and would raise the hope that Edwards might actually give the Democrats a chance to win North Carolina for the first time since 1976. While en route, the senator called to ask me to send a sport coat to the airport. I ignored the request because it was ninety-plus degrees and I was extremely busy.

The rally became a love fest, with Edwards shouting, "He's with me!" and Kerry asking if the Tar Heels would mind lending the nation Edwards's services for eight or maybe sixteen years. At many points in the rally, the huge crowd roared its approval. One of these moments arrived when Chuck Berry's "Johnny B. Goode" rang out of the sound system. After the song, Teresa Heinz Kerry took the microphone and assured folks that "these Johnnies will be good if Elizabeth and I have anything to do with it." Later, she explained that she and Mrs. Edwards would protect their husbands from those who would "inflate their egos or try to destroy them."

I know about what happened at the rally only because I saw bits of it on television. I was at the senator's house, making sure all would be ready when they arrived to talk with Lesley Stahl of *60 Minutes*. I thought I had considered every potential problem when I called an air-conditioning guy to make sure the balky cooling system would hold up. Then I started to hear a noise that sounded like chirping in the chimney for the living room fireplace. A bird had somehow found its way inside. After I made a racket and the bird stayed put, I placed a frantic call to an exterminator—the company was called Critter Gitter—who agreed that it was an emergency and came right over.

With a strong flashlight, the exterminator spotted a nest of baby birds and then gave me the bad news. They were members of an endangered species. This meant he had to follow specific procedures to ensure the birds' safety. I believed what he said, but as politically incorrect as it may sound, I didn't care what he did to get rid of this feathered nuisance. "Just get them out of there as fast as you can," I told him, and then I left the room so I wouldn't have to watch. To this day, I can't tell you what he did, but it worked. And fast.

As the exterminator was leaving, the Secret Service came through the house to make one last security sweep. I forgot to tell them the AC guy was in the crawl space. He jumped out of his skin when he saw the bomb dogs and had to explain why he was there. The Secret Service declared the house safe even though they were not happy with the condition of the chef. While I was running around, he had downed a couple of beers.

When the candidates arrived, the Kerrys looked at the house with obvious disdain. Though the plan had called for them to spend the night, they made it clear they would not. Senator Edwards, obviously in a bad mood, complained to me that I had forgotten to send his sport coat to the big rally, which meant he couldn't make a show of peeling it off in front of the crowd and saying, "It's great to be back home." Kerry found everything the cook had made inedible, and the Secret Service drove his body man to a Boston Market store for replacement food. Teresa, who was nervous about the *60 Minutes* appearance, drank a glass of wine. Loosened up, she then paced around the house and clomped up and down the wooden staircase, making so much noise that the field producer had to holler, "Cut!" several times during Stahl's interview of the candidates in the next room.

Seated side by side, Kerry and Edwards grinned like a couple of guys who were having fun, and I believed they were. The hostility they may have felt seemed to have been submerged in their pursuit of a mutual goal, and they insisted that they were comfortable with their roles and their agenda. When Stahl pressed him with questions about their relationship, Senator Edwards reduced the issue to a matter of commitment. "At the end of the day, all the words in the world will not make up for one thing," he said. "You have to have trust. I trust him."

After a break to get people arranged, the candidates' wives joined the interview. As I watched from the back of the room, I marveled at how far Mrs. Edwards had come. I knew she was uncomfortable, but she looked composed and she spoke without hesitating. Stahl was most interested in how these women saw their roles, and Mrs. Edwards accurately described herself as the person who would tell her husband the truth when others would not, and would provide a sort of ballast to keep him stable. To have someone who will play this role is "a very good thing," she said.

Like Mrs. Edwards, who had always tried, in her way, to help her husband maintain his balance, I would be assuming a role similar to the one I had played since I volunteered for his campaign. I tried to make things run smoothly for the senator and to fix problems as soon as they arose. My immediate concern was the upcoming national convention in Boston. The senator asked me to be responsible for the care of his family and friends. While other people might get frazzled by logistics and dealing with emergencies, it came easily to me.

At the convention, Mrs. Edwards gave me a tough problem to solve when she left a dozen or so messages on my cell phone explaining that she had left the outfit she intended to wear when her husband accepted his nomination at a dry cleaner's back in Raleigh. I knew that the last flight to Boston left Raleigh-Durham International Airport in less than an hour. With a few quick calls, I managed to get someone to race to the cleaner's, pick up the outfit, and take it to the airport, where my contact with American Airlines got it on the flight. Mrs. Edwards was thrilled when her clothes arrived just a few hours after she'd informed me they were missing. (She also insisted I remove two women from a list of VIP guests from North Carolina, though I wasn't told why they had to be cut.)

The following day, I had to get the senator's friend and former law partner David Kirby from his law office in Raleigh to the arena where the convention was held in just over three hours. (He was stuck in an arbitration and feared he was going to miss his best friend's nomination.) This task involved pulling strings with friends at the airline, who parked his car for him and held the flight. When he landed at the airport, he saw himself on TV in an interview I had set up the day before. The police escorted him from Logan International Airport to the Fleet Center arena. Kirby arrived grinning and flabbergasted. "Damn, the only person you need to know in this world is Andrew Young," he told people in the senator's box. "Fuck John Edwards. It's Andrew who gets things done."

I appreciated Kirby's praise, but for me the real reward came in just attending a historic political event where future leaders emerged. This was where Barack Obama gave the speech that made him famous. The speech was electrifying, and minutes after Obama left the podium, I brought Kirby's daughter to take a picture with him. Although Senator Edwards had told me Obama was lacking in substance, I could see he was a brilliant person with a level of confidence similar to what I saw in Edwards. He was far more appealing than John Kerry.

As far as the average television viewer could tell, Kerry and Edwards were a closely bonded team and the convention was a celebration of their shared vision for the country. But I was close enough to the senator at this time to hear what was on his mind, and after less than one month into his partnership with John Kerry, I could tell it was starting to come apart. He wasn't ready to start calling him names again, but he was frustrated because Kerry wouldn't listen to his advice and had insulated himself with too many advisers. (At one point, he had more foreign policy aides than President Bush had in the White House.) A typical example of the way the men were diverging arose as Edwards was preparing his acceptance speech, which would be his first extensive address to a national audience. For six years, the senator had been calling on people to embrace a heartfelt hope for the future. More than any other word, hope was at the core of his politics.

Hope was not exactly an original theme. Jesse Jackson had made his name with speeches in which he implored the country to "keep hope alive." However, it is a reliable and positive message. Unfortunately, Kerry's staff insisted that the refrain in Senator Edwards's speech be built on the word *help,* as in "Help is on the way." The difference is not as small as it may seem. "Hope" allows people to imagine solving problems on their own. "Help" suggests a handout, which can deprive a person of his or her dignity. Edwards stood his ground and got to use the theme he wanted.

When the time came, and Edwards stood before a sea of flag-waving partisans and the major networks all beamed his image and voice across the nation and the world, the senator did his duty by praising John Kerry and then rocked the house with a series of declarations that each ended with the promise "Hope is on the way."

The speech was a hit with everyone except John Kerry's top people. Afterward when I ran into Julianna Smoot, she said, "You picked the right horse," and told me, "You deserve everything you get." She asked me to pass word to the senator that she hoped he would call her. He never did.

The next night, Kerry stuck to his choice of "Help is on the way," and while the delegates gave him all the noise you could ask for, the speech did not wind up on anyone's list of best American political addresses. In contrast, Barack Obama's brilliant keynote address, which challenged the idea that Americans were hopelessly divided, marked a historic moment. It was the one performance that every analyst gave a top grade, and more than anyone knew, it revealed the future of American politics.

Coming out of the convention, the Kerry-Edwards team had a significant lead over Bush-Cheney, but by the time the GOP had their convention and their allies began their well-funded attacks—remember the "swift boaters"?—it became obvious that it would be difficult to unseat the incumbent. Kerry's decision-making style—slow, even dithering in response to the lies coming from the far right—frustrated Edwards, and he told me he suspected he was being sent to make low-impact appearances in out-of-the-way spots because Kerry was afraid of being upstaged. So much for trust.

Presidential candidates handpick staff for their running mate long before the candidate is even selected. As a result, Edwards had only two of his loyalists with him during the 2004 run. As often happens, tension arises between the vice presidential nominee—who's supposed to be a lapdog—and the people serving the person at the top of the ticket. This dynamic was in full force on a weekend when I joined Edwards at his beach house. Except for the presence of the Secret Service guys, the weekend recalled the time we had spent together in years past, and we talked more football than politics. But when we did discuss the campaign, Edwards bragged about how he had won a minor victory by getting Peter Scher, whom Kerry had picked to be his chief of staff, to "go native." By this he meant that Scher had come over to his side of things in some dispute with Kerry.

Candidates never recover the time and energy wasted on distractions in a campaign, so it's always best to keep them out of intramural battles over issues like staff loyalty and to control any personal issues that might flare into controversies that would draw attention from important issues. During the 2004 campaign, the senator's younger brother, Blake, a good ol' boy who reminded me of the actor John Goodman, began telephoning the lawyer Wade Byrd, who was a big political contributor. Blake wanted help with what he said was a serious problem. With Roger Clinton and Billy Carter in mind, Senator Edwards asked me to find out what was going on and resolve it.

It turned out that Blake had a history of arrests for driving under the influence and had had his license suspended in Colorado. He had contacted Wade Byrd in hopes of getting his license back and perhaps having the charges removed from his record. But as I quickly discovered, this was not even a remote possibility. Instead, as authorities in Colorado indicated, Blake was wanted for failing to appear on a decade-old charge of driving while intoxicated. The press learned of the warrant for Blake's arrest and descended on the little house he shared with his longtime girlfriend, Debbie, in the town of Fuquay-Varina, North Carolina, which the senator had bought for them.

While Blake and Debbie hid behind their locked front door, Mrs. Edwards reacted angrily when the press called the campaign. "How could he do this?" she asked, as if Blake had gotten drunk and taken to the road in a deliberate attempt to derail his brother's ambitions. The senator was more relaxed in his response. He issued a statement that said he understood that Blake had committed serious crimes but that he was now taking responsibility and that he loved him.

The senator asked me to visit Blake and Debbie to reassure them, and help them network their way to the best lawyer available, who could try to delay the proceeding in Colorado until after the election. Eventually, we found someone who promised to do just that. The main challenge in this process would be to help Blake with the anxiety he felt about the case and getting him to Colorado. Although his crimes had been dangerous, Blake hadn't hurt anyone, and the man I knew was truly remorseful and frightened about what he faced. I did my best to reassure him, and when the time came for him to appear in court in Colorado, I picked him up at his house at five A.M. so he could catch an early-morning flight and avoid the press. I've never seen a more forlorn person than he was as I dropped him at the terminal, but the outcome of the hearing was a reprieve: The judge delayed sentencing until January. Until then, Blake was a free man and the press would leave him alone.

It may come as a shock to the obsessive, twenty-four-hour-a-day crusaders who work in presidential campaigns, but life goes on for people who live away from the frenzy of cross-country tours, press conferences, and debates. On August 11, 2004, the Kerry-Edwards team was arguing with George Bush about health care. You might say I was involved with the same issue, but in a far more personal way, supporting Cheri in the delivery room as our third child, a boy we named Cooper, came into the world.

Before he was born, doctors had told us the odds were against Cooper having the kind of congenital anomaly that made Gracie's first months of life so difficult. When he showed some of the same signs of distress, but in a milder form, we asked to have him checked out anyway. Incredibly, we went through many of the same problems we had getting Gracie diagnosed until we confirmed that lightning sometimes strikes twice. Cooper did have an almost identical problem, and while we didn't have to address it immediately, surgery would be required.

Informed by our previous experience, we decided to find the best surgeons for the job. I turned to a logical source, a famous malpractice attorney named Tom Demetrio, who helped us narrow the choice to Children's Hospital in Boston. The doctors wanted to give Cooper some time to grow stronger, so we scheduled the procedure for late November. Cheri would keep a close eye on him until then. I would go back into the frenzy of the campaign, which, thanks to the swift boaters, became one of the nastiest in modern times.

By the end of September, everyone in the campaign assumed the race would be neck and neck to the finish. The war in Iraq occupied much of the candidates' time and attention, but they also traded jabs related to character, and who might be better suited to the job of leading the free world. Occasionally, a gaffe or minor mistake gave comedians something to squawk about and distracted everyone from the substance of the campaign. For our side, one of the worst came when John Kerry insisted on going windsurfing in the waters of Nantucket.

Hard as it may be to accept, Kerry's hobby had actually been the subject of intense conversation inside the campaign, and it was widely agreed that it was the kind of activity many Americans would view as effete and unpresidential—what if he fell off?—and it would be better if he just gave it up until after the election. Despite warnings, Kerry just couldn't resist. On a day off he spent in Nantucket, he put on a bathing suit, grabbed a pair of gloves, and took to the water atop what looked like a surfboard with a sail. The image of Kerry tacking back and forth reminded everyone of the opposition charge that he was a "flip-flopper" who couldn't stick to a position and prompted Jay Leno to say, "Even his hobby depends on which way the wind blows."

Fortunately, the first presidential debate came about ten days after the windsurfing exhibition and shifted the conversation away from the water. Kerry seemed to outpoint Bush in the first of the three presidential events, but the result was so close that it put more pressure on Edwards to score a knockout in the one encounter he would have with Vice President Cheney, the Darth Vader of Washington. Of course, Cheney also faced similar pressure, as Republicans said he needed to stomp Edwards in order to seize the momentum for his side.

The Republicans seemed most concerned about Senator Edwards's telegenic looks and his ability to work a room. Standing next to Edwards, Cheney would look like a stooped old man. However, Kerry's people gave away some of this advantage in the negotiations over the debate format when they agreed that Cheney and Edwards would be seated at a table for the entire ninety minutes. (The Republicans said they were concerned about how standing would affect Cheney's heart.) Presumably the Democrats received something in return from the Bush side, but I never heard what it was.

When the date of the debate arrived, I escorted the senator's parents to Cleveland and brought them to the site at Case Western Reserve University. During the event, I was positioned a few yards from the stage. I like to believe it helped him to see my friendly face. He performed about as well as could be expected, limiting the points Cheney scored against John Kerry and steering the discussion toward the deception the White House had practiced to get the nation into the Iraq war. The vice president went to great lengths to sell the country on his extensive experience in government, which stretched back more than thirty years. Edwards came back with a perfect retort, saying, "Mr. Vice President, I don't think the country can take four more years of this kind of experience." However, his performance was not flawless. At one point he brought up Cheney's lesbian daughter, and this would be viewed by many as a cheap shot.

On my scorecard, Cheney failed to get the big victory he needed and Senator Edwards prevailed, as he showed he was equal to the job of vice president. The instant polls done that night found similar sentiments among viewers, but as time passed, the Karl Rove Republican spin machine shaped opinion and more people began to say that Cheney had won because he didn't collapse when confronted by Edwards's superior communication skills. This is how the scoring often proceeds with debates. First impressions are followed by endless nitpicking, and before you know it, the partisan analysis matters more than what actually happened during the debate itself. In the case of Edwards vs. Cheney, the only certain conclusion you might reach is that very few voters were moved out of their preestablished groupings, which found them divided almost evenly between the parties.

Unfortunately, Americans were so hardened in their positions that as election night grew close, everyone realized that we were fighting over a tiny number of voters—a few hundred thousand in each of a handful of "swing" states—who might actually be undecided. Kerry's campaign team decided that Edwards could serve them best by making a series of national TV appearances, and he performed perfectly on shows ranging from *The View* to *The Tonight Show with Jay Leno*. Leno and Edwards liked each other. The host told the audience he loved the oft-told story about how every year Edwards took Elizabeth to Wendy's for hamburgers to celebrate their anniversary. He said that any man who could get away with that deserved to be elected.

Between the national TV shows and the debate, Edwards was seen by well over 100 million TV viewers in the span of a week. But when he suggested the campaign let him make a bigger effort to woo voters in the South, especially in North Carolina, Kerry's people balked. Despite polls showing Democrats had the best chance there in decades, they refused to buy any television ads in the Tar Heel State. Instead, they focused their spending on the Midwest and sent the senator to out-of-the-way places like Latrobe, Pennsylvania, and Waterloo, Iowa. Edwards was furious about this.

For reasons that were never explained, the advisers and managers at the top of the campaign developed a surprising amount of confidence in the final weeks and, to our surprise, held back more than $14 million that could have been spent on advertising and get-out-the-vote efforts in Ohio and Florida. Although we kept hearing concern, even worry, in the voices of friends, Kerry operatives talked to the press about the combination of states that would get them to the magic number of 270 electoral college votes. In every winning scenario, either Ohio or Florida was painted blue for a Democratic Party victory.

The campaign ended in Boston. On election day I flew into Logan with the senator's family and friends and checked in at the Copley Plaza. (Cheri came with me to soak up the moment.) The weather was dreary, but the hotel was so alive with press and security people that it felt as though we had arrived at the center of the universe. Everywhere we turned we bumped into someone we knew, and our conversations were filled with a mixture of relief, hope, and gratitude. As Cheri and I sat at lunch with the Edwards family, the senator's sister, Kathy, said, "You're closer to him than anyone, Andrew, and if he's elected, he's going to need you even more." His parents said they agreed, and it made me feel good.

Kathy was part of a large group I shepherded on a day that included an afternoon aboard an amphibious tourist craft operated by an outfit called Boston Duck Tours, which took us around to historic sites and to the Charles River and Boston Harbor. (The senator's mother, Bobbi, got a chance to drive the "duck.") All the while, I was receiving text-message reports on exit polls that were very promising for our side. As I gave them updates, Bobbi and Wallace seemed overwhelmed by the thought that their son might win the second-highest office in the country. We couldn't be sure of the outcome, of course, but by the end of the afternoon, as Cheri and I went to the hotel to dress for dinner, we were almost convinced that the Kerry-Edwards team had won.

Our minds were changed as we gathered at the Palm restaurant for the last supper of the campaign. Although some in the friends and family group clung to the hope that we had received better "inside" information, the television reported that Bush was likely to hold on to the White House. As I checked in with people high in the campaign, they stopped talking about their new offices in the West Wing and started to sound very pessimistic. Eventually they stopped answering their phones, and with their voice-mail files full, I couldn't even leave a message.

After dinner, Cheri and I went back to the Copley Plaza with the senator's family and got on the elevator with the folk trio Peter, Paul and Mary. Upstairs, we headed to the senator's VIP area, where we ran into the actor Matt Dillon, model Christie Brinkley, and *Seinfeld* creator Larry David. By the time the polls started to close, we were almost sure we had lost, so although the place was filled with the sounds of phones ringing, people talking, and TVs blaring, the atmosphere was still fairly somber. We heard lots of reports of minority voters—our voters—being blocked from the polls.

The count and the media coverage reminded me of 2000, when I had sat in the senator's living room and irregularities cast doubt on the legitimacy of the election, especially in Florida. This time the center of controversy was Ohio, where, we heard, people in mostly Democratic wards were having a difficult time with long lines and officials who challenged seemingly valid voter registrations. Although some newscasters called the election for Bush, at midnight Kerry conducted a conference call from his house with about fifty advisers and Senator Edwards and concluded that the race was so close, he couldn't concede.

Even though he had problems with Kerry, Edwards saw the election as a battle of good versus evil and truly believed the country would be hurt by four more years of Bush-Cheney. Although he was concerned about all the people who were standing in the rain at the Kerry-Edwards rally site in Boston Common, the Bush-Gore fiasco of 2000 had made him deeply suspicious of the vote-counting process. Kerry continued to hold out, and at about three o'clock in the morning he sent Edwards to the Common to speak. (Many people thought it was strange that Kerry didn't address the crowd himself.)

The diehards who stood in the rain on that cold November night numbered in the thousands. Many had on Red Sox caps, worn like emblems of their tremendous patience, which had been rewarded just days before when their beloved team had finally won the World Series after eighty-six years. They had seen Tom Brokaw and Wolf Blitzer declare Bush reelected on the big TV screens set up near the stage but remained waiting faithfully to hear from their candidates. When Edwards appeared, they cheered so loudly that his parents called from the hotel to ask me if the Democrats had actually won. Of course they had not, but I thought that the roar confirmed that the wrong guy had been at the top of the ticket. "We've waited four years for this victory," he said. "We can wait one more night."

By morning, when it seemed they had lost Ohio by about one hundred thousand votes, Edwards spoke to Kerry and could tell he was devastated. Although Edwards thought he should wait and perhaps contest the Ohio result, Kerry soon conceded to Bush via a phone call and then scheduled a public appearance for ten-thirty at historic Faneuil Hall. While he waited for this event, the senator asked me to find his parents and bring them to his suite. When I brought Wallace and Bobbi to the room, I could see that something other than the election was going on. The senator told his parents and then told me that they thought Mrs. Edwards had cancer.

At Faneuil Hall, Senator and Mrs. Edwards seemed untroubled, smiling for the audience and applauding as John Kerry thanked them for their hard work and friendship. She had seen a doctor four days earlier and with his support delayed further tests so they could continue the campaign. As soon as the event ended, they went to see a specialist at Massachusetts General Hospital, who performed a biopsy that confirmed the cancer was present and showed it had spread in a way that was extremely serious.

As public figures who had made their life experience part of their political appeal to the nation, the Edwardses didn't wait to tell the world about their crisis. Their statements to the press, and background provided by aides, helped reporters present them as bravely soldiering on—Mrs. Edwards went to a dozen events after she learned she might have cancer—for the good of her husband, the Democratic Party, and the country. Ironically enough, the news of Mrs. Edwards's diagnosis appeared in the press at the same time the media was filled with analysis of the election and articles predicting the senator's political future. Although he was widely regarded as the Democrat most likely to challenge Hillary Clinton for the 2008 presidential nomination, he downplayed his prospects, noting that for the foreseeable future he would be focused on his wife's health. I felt a chill when he talked privately about how her cancer affected his chances for attaining a higher office.

Cheri and I returned to Boston two weeks later, bringing Cooper to Children's Hospital for his surgery. While doctors in North Carolina wanted to employ the same technique they had used on Gracie, the surgeon in Boston was a specialist who used three tiny incisions and high-tech instruments to make the repair. Cooper's recovery was quick. In a week we were home, and within a month he was pain-free and growing like a weed. Although we faced an uncertain future in the aftermath of the election, our family was healthy and together for the holidays.

Just after New Year's, I drove down to Fuquay-Varina to pick up the senator's brother, Blake, and drive him to the airport for a flight to Colorado, where he would surrender to the Arapahoe County sheriff and begin serving a sixty-day sentence in the county jail. His plane departed at seven A.M., so I had to fetch him at about four-thirty. He lumbered out of the house looking dejected and scared. The drive was tense and awkward, and our conversation was punctuated by his apologies. Blake was worried about how his problems reflected on his brother and how he had upset Mrs. Edwards. "Man, Elizabeth must be pissed," he said.

As I said good-bye to Blake at the airport, I tried to encourage him by saying that everyone makes mistakes and that he would soon be home again. He asked me to make sure that the senator wrote to him while he was in jail. I got out of the car, gave him a hug, and thought it was bizarre that no one in his family had come to see him off. I passed along Blake's request several times, but I heard the senator never called or wrote him while he was in jail.

Seven

IT'S GOOD TO BE KING

The silence that falls after a losing political campaign is almost total, like the quiet inside an abandoned mine. The senator said, "There's no other business to compare it with. Based on how people vote, you go from almost leading the free world to not having a job in twenty-four hours." A few media types might call for help with their postmortem stories, but after a day or two you no longer hear from the thousands of people who a week earlier jammed the phone lines with advice, requests, and offers of support.

After John Kerry and John Edwards lost, they didn't even call each other very much. In fact, they lost touch in a matter of weeks as Kerry prepared to return to the United States Senate and Edwards turned his attention to his wife's health and his own uncertain future.

Mrs. Edwards's prognosis seemed dire. Her cancer was aggressive, and by the time it was discovered it had already moved beyond the duct where it started and into surrounding tissue. When this occurs the cancer can spread almost anywhere in the body, and the best treatment is an all-out assault with chemotherapy and radiation. It was a grueling regimen that took about six months to complete. During this time the senator divided his attention between her, their children, and his own struggle to get past his defeat and set a course for his political future. During a week when Elizabeth was between treatments and strong enough to be alone, the senator and I went together to Figure Eight Island, where we could rest and brainstorm.

The Edwards beach house sits on the Intracoastal Waterway, with a commanding view of the water. During our first few days, the senator spent much of his time walking on the beach and reading through a stack of books by or about Bobby Kennedy. Calls from political supporters brought the suggestion that he run for chair of the Democratic National Committee, and if he'd been interested in this kind of nuts-and-bolts party work, he could have had the job. However, he rejected the idea because he didn't see how he could run for president from the DNC position, and he was probably right. When Howard Dean announced he wanted the job, he more or less accepted the end of his own desire to occupy the Oval Office.

Aside from occasional chats with his cronies, the senator's main contact with the outside world during this beach retreat came from Elizabeth, whom he called about half a dozen times a day. I was impressed by their friendship and how he valued her input. Sometimes she'd ask to speak to me so that I could give her a report on his spirits. More than once she said, "I'm glad he's with you, Andrew. It makes me feel safer."

At night we would go to Wilmington, where restaurants that bustled with business in the summer were mostly empty and quiet. Although he sometimes seemed plagued by doubts about his campaigns for the White House, he also made arguments about why he had done it and even why he should try again. Invariably, the rationale would come down to his concern "for people who can't help themselves" who needed him to be their champion, their white knight.

In all these conversations, the senator noted that Elizabeth was certain that he should mount another campaign, whether she was sick or not. During this time he admired her determination, but I noticed that he also complained more about her mood swings and demanding nature. Toward the end of the campaign, she had started picking fights with him as he was leaving for a flight or about to go onstage for some event, not caring how it might make him late or affect his performance. Often these arguments were about staffers she didn't trust (she didn't trust most of the senator's aides) or about something he said or did that she didn't like. "Sometimes I think she's crazy," he said.

We drank a little more than usual during this week, and as the wine took hold, the senator invariably talked about the tragedy of his son Wade's death, going over the details as if repeating them might release some of the pain. On the day it happened, Wade's companion, who survived virtually unscathed, had called friends in the neighborhood, who knew about it before the Edwardses. The senator told me about how the police came to their home and Elizabeth knew what was happening even before they spoke. She screamed, "Tell me he's okay! Tell me he's okay!" When they hesitated, she collapsed on the floor. One of the officers turned to Edwards and said, "I'm sorry, sir. Your son was killed instantly in a wreck."

As he told this story, the combination of emotion and wine filled the senator's eyes with tears. He said, "This is just between you and me, okay?" and then continued. The most poignant moment would come when he recalled that when he went to the medical examiner's office to identify Wade, he actually climbed onto the table where he had been laid out so that he could embrace him one last time. This was the same story he told John Kerry, but unlike Kerry, I didn't judge Edwards for repeating it. I know that people have to tell their tales of grief over and over again, so I didn't mind. I hoped the process would help him recover his energy and optimism, and by the time our retreat was over, it seemed he had.

Despite the obstacles he might face, John Edwards believed he would occupy the Oval Office in January 2009. To get there, he would need some way to remain in public life and maintain an organization that could provide the base for a run at the nomination. I would continue to work for him as a sort of personal assistant, which meant I accepted some very unusual assignments. One required me to make good on a promise that Elizabeth made to a young woman who asked her for help getting trained to drive trucks.

Elizabeth had said she would help. I wound up driving the woman, who had been Wade's friend at school, more than an hour each way, at least a dozen times, so she could get to class. These round-trips always started before dawn.

I was not happy serving as a chauffeur so that Mrs. Edwards could fulfill a personal pledge of charity, but I did it because I believed in John Edwards and wanted to be part of his long-term effort to win the White House. No out-of-office Democrat had won the nomination in modern times. But there were some advantages to being freed from the Senate. He wouldn't be forced into voting on legislation related to issues like abortion and gay marriage that Republicans crafted in order to paint Democrats as lacking commonsense or morality. Freed from this trap, he could present himself as a person of faith, who held moral Christian views, and this was critical to him being elected president. We began the effort by creating two organizations: a PAC called the One America Committee and an institute at the University of North Carolina called the Center on Poverty, Work and Opportunity.

The PAC, which was named by Mrs. Edwards, would fund a small staff in Washington and pay for the senator's travels and other expenses. The antipoverty center would support research and education and host conferences that would bring together experts on jobs, education, housing, health care, and other issues that would become the core of the senator's 2008 campaign. He would draw only a modest stipend from this organization, but he did ask me to try to get the university to grant him certain benefits—tickets and parking for basketball games, for example—in exchange for lending his name and presence to the school. He didn't receive these wish-list items, but he did get a beautiful office to share with his wife. However, she never actually worked there, and on the rare occasions when he was at the center, he did mostly political work, including fundraising.

In choosing a populist, antipoverty focus, Senator and Mrs. Edwards threw out the advice of prominent consultants like Bob Shrum and

David Axelrod, whom they blamed for the timid Kerry-Edwards campaign that failed in 2004. They were determined to run the next campaign themselves and as they saw fit, and they thought it didn't matter if poverty was not a popular cause with a majority of Americans. They believed that people just wanted to see that a candidate stood for something important, as had Ronald Reagan and Jesse Helms, and was strong in his resolve. (You might not agree with them, but you knew what they stood for.) They also thought that the issue would appeal to the small number of intensely political folks, especially labor leaders, who participate in the Iowa caucuses and can give a contender the momentum to win the nomination.

Edwards dreamed of getting more political legitimacy from an independent grassroots movement that would demand that he run for president. Since no one in the country was actually building such a movement, he explored the idea of creating one, on the Internet, but in a way that he could deny having anything to do with it. I attended a meeting with the senator, Mrs. Edwards, and a consultant named Zack Exley, who they hoped might pull off this trick. (Exley had been a major force in the online efforts of the liberal activist organization called MoveOn.org.) It was a giddy session, with lots of excitement about how they could start an online petition to make it seem as if thousands, if not millions, of people were begging Edwards to run. However, in the end, the Edwardses decided Exley wanted to have too much influence on the campaign. The senator would have to find support the old-fashioned way, by meeting people face-to-face and winning them over.

Once the plan was set, the Edwardses embarked on a schedule of visits to homeless shelters, union halls, universities, and other places where he gave speeches and joined forums that allowed him to remain in the public eye. He used his appearances to test ideas for his platform. One of his favorites was a College for Everyone program that would fund the first year of study for poor students willing to work ten hours a week. When he wanted to test the idea in a pilot demonstration, I raised a million dollars to fund a College for Everyone trial in Greene County, a poor community in eastern North Carolina.

Money is the fuel that runs every think tank, every political action committee, and, for that matter, every aide to an out-of-office politician. I worked hard to fuel-up all three of the Edwards organizations, raising more than $4 million, which freed him from having to spend much time on the phone asking for cash. Sometimes the hardest part of this job involved getting the senator and Mrs. Edwards to participate. For example, when I recruited a Chapel Hill businessman named Michael Cucchiara, one favor he asked for in return for his donation was that I get tickets for his wife to see *The Oprah Winfrey Show*. He also asked for dinner with the Edwardses.

As everyone knows, *Oprah* tickets were a tough get, but I managed to score some through her friend Gayle King. Cheri went to the show with Mrs. Cucchiara. She received a video camera from Oprah, who gave them to audience members willing to film themselves doing something positive in their communities. Cheri raised $30,000 for soldiers at Fort Bragg.

Getting the Edwardses to drive across town for dinner with the Cucchiaras was much harder than finagling the tickets to *Oprah*. I finally had to pitch a fit to get them to do it. Despite this kind of resistance, I helped to get the three Edwards organizations rolling and then maintained them with a flow of cash. Fred Baron purchased a jet, which he remodeled according to the senator's specifications and then gave to him to use.

While most of his expenses and staff were covered by the money I raised, and favors from supporters like Fred, Senator Edwards wanted to continue to generate personal income as a matter of both financial security and pride. His political contacts and experience made him an attractive commodity for influence- and information-based operations like law firms, lobbying outfits, management consultants, and investment houses. Always alert to opportunity, he went to the industry with the most money—finance—and got a part-time gig with a hedge fund called Fortress Financial for a salary of roughly $500,000 per year.

As he did with the poverty center, the senator put very little time into his Fortress job, but it allowed him to become an investor in exclusive funds generally closed to newcomers. He put $16 million into Fortress, which before the economic collapse of 2008 used a variety of creative and controversial schemes to deliver high rates of return. If you think that hiring on with a hedge fund that avoided taxes by incorporating offshore accounts conflicted with Edwards's political concerns about "two Americas," rich and poor, you aren't alone. The irony wasn't lost on his critics, and they would eventually catch up to him; but before they did, he would profit handsomely. He added to this income by making speeches about poverty, some of which netted him up to $55,000 apiece. One of these appearances was in the United Arab Emirates, where he was accompanied by a new body man, Josh Brumberger, who later told me that the service at the seven-star luxury hotel in Dubai was "the kind of attention Edwards always wanted."

With his need for a political base and personal income met, the senator next turned attention to his home and his appearance. Using my name to register under, he checked into a hospital for extensive dental work and plastic surgery to remove a mole from his upper lip. The new teeth were susceptible to stains, so after he got them he switched from Diet Coke to Diet Sprite and diet orange soda. Still holding to the routine, I bought these drinks by the caseload and had them waiting whenever I met him with the car, but at this time I also began a quiet exercise in rebellion by making sure the left armrest for his seat was always lowered when he got in. It may seem like a small thing, but he preferred to have it raised so he could move around in the seat. I put it down and smiled to myself whenever an annoyed look flashed across his face before he pushed it up. I also took silent pleasure in waiting for the moment he would demonstrate that he had become truly spoiled rotten by voicing a complaint about this tiny inconvenience.

The senator got lots of opportunities to complain to me during this time because I was his only North Carolina–based aide, and he needed to be home as much as possible as Mrs. Edwards planned the construction of her dream house in Chapel Hill. The process began when they put their house in Washington up for sale and bought more than a hundred acres to accommodate a sprawling house, as well as a barnlike athletic building housing a basketball court, racquetball court, exercise room, and indoor swimming pool along with living quarters. Emma Claire and Jack got adjoining tree houses, complete with working windows, measuring more than one thousand square feet each. Mrs. Edwards, who added rooms for Christmas ornaments and gift wrapping to the plans, had found inspiration for this project at John and Teresa Heinz Kerry's estate in Pennsylvania, which is a beautiful collection of rambling old structures set amid rolling farmland.

As the Edwardses' lifestyle became ever more extravagant, I began to feel incredulous. His big issue was poverty, but he was flying around in a private jet, building a gigantic estate, drawing big checks from a hedge fund, and booking speeches for tens of thousands of dollars apiece. In frustration, I once said to Mrs. Edwards, the architect, and the builder, "The press is going to eat him alive on this." They laughed and dismissed my concerns. The guy who once drove a beat-up Buick for appearances' sake told me it was impossible for him to cut back on the house because his wife was sick with cancer and it was her dream.

As the employee who never said no to the senator and Mrs. Edwards, I simply accepted extra assignments related to the new house. One of the first required me to drive a rented truck to Washington, D.C., where I struggled to back it down the narrow alleyway behind their house. The entire Washington campaign staff had come on Mrs. Edwards's order to load stuff she couldn't trust to a moving company. I drove back the same day, and after finishing in the early hours of the morning, instead of thanks, I received a grilling about buying beer and pizza for the volunteers who met me to unload.

In time I would realize that my relationship with the Edwardses had grown so close, so familiar, that they felt comfortable asking me to do anything they might imagine, and without expressing much gratitude. During the construction of the mansion, I became Mrs. Edwards's assistant and informal project manager in charge of chasing down the architect, harassing contractors, and keeping track of appliances, flooring, and other essentials. I helped pick out and purchase most of the furnishings and devoted days to pushing stuff around until it was all positioned perfectly.

Fortunately, when you are working for a presidential candidate, you don't have to call a 1-800 number to get service. Instead, you call the CEO of the phone company or electric utility and get immediate attention. This power was especially helpful as I worked through to-do lists written by Mrs. Edwards for me and other PAC employees. These were many pages long and required us to set up everything from the room designed for the sole purpose of wrapping Christmas presents to outfitting a project area with arts-and-crafts supplies.

A few problems were beyond even the Edwardses' power and influence. When the fellow who lived across the street from the Edwardses put up a RUDY GIULIANI FOR PRESIDENT sign, I even posed as a real-estate speculator to see if his land was available. (Elizabeth was also bothered by the "slummy" buildings and auto repair shop the owner, Monty Johnson, kept on the land.) Monty's asking price—more than $1 million—was so high, she decided she would just put up with the irritation of seeing Rudy's name every time she left the house. She often joked about burning down an abandoned house that was on the property.

I, meanwhile, resented having to deal with her neighbor and all the other extra work related to the house, especially the more menial labor. However, I didn't say anything because these assignments all seemed to flow out of a relationship that was far more complex and personal than the usual employee-employer arrangement. I believed I would work for the Edwardses for many years to come, and to make my commute easier, I began pushing for us to move closer to their house. Cheri resisted when I suggested building our own new place but eventually agreed. I felt confident taking on the expense because I was making a very good salary, which I expected would grow whether the senator was elected president or not. We bought some land and we hired the same architect and builder that the Edwardses had and began a misadventure similar to the plot of the 1986 movie *The Money Pit*.

Of course, as this all happened I couldn't see that I had allowed myself to be trapped in the Edwardses' orbit. Cheri worried about how entangled my life (and hers) had become with theirs, and though she tried to be supportive, it was a source of conflict in our marriage. However, when she tried to talk to me all I heard was that she objected to the amount of time I put into my job, time that could have been spent with my family. I didn't understand her other major point, which was that I had come to identify too closely with the Edwardses at the expense of my own priorities and hopes. After so many years, I no longer saw them clearly. In fact, I was willing to imagine they had positive qualities they didn't actually possess and overlook their flaws and mistakes, because I needed them to succeed.

Of course, once you allow someone to get away with being pushy, they become only more demanding, and this is what happened with Mrs. Edwards. The clearest illustration of this truth came on Thanksgiving weekend 2005, when I bought the turkey her family would eat for the holiday, left it in the refrigerator, and tried to enjoy the long weekend with my family. On Saturday I was with about twenty members of my family and had turned off my cell phone so I could enjoy the holiday. When I turned it back on, I discovered eight or nine voice mails about a flood at the Edwards home. In one of them, Mrs. Edwards accused me of leaving the water on and causing the flood. In fact, the hose that supplied water to a washing machine had broken and Wade's room was flooded. Senator Edwards said he and his wife would meet me at the house, where neighbors, a cleanup company, and the fire department were on hand. When I arrived, I found the senator and his wife in the backyard, spreading things out to dry. Noting that his wife was distraught, he asked me to take charge so they could leave.

The plumbing disaster at that house occupied much of my time for several months. First I had to clear out the soaked furnishings and property—everything from rugs to a baseball card collection—and dry whatever might be dried. I then had to have hundreds of items put in storage along with household goods that would be packed away pending the family's move to the mansion under construction. Between the mess and the valuables such as Lladró figurines that were supposedly damaged in the move, I devoted hundreds of hours to physical labor, managing contractors, and haggling with insurance firms. Mrs. Edwards was initially very pleased with all this work, but this episode would come back to haunt me years later.

Gratitude was often in short supply with the Edwardses, as was empathy. When I was working with the senator, I accepted that he would always be the center of attention, but even when we were alone and I was supposedly "off duty," he would never express much interest in me, which was a change from our early days. Now he was focused on politics to the exclusion of everything else. Sometimes I would tease him by saying, "Okay, now let's talk about you!" but even this joke failed to make him less self-centered.

I trained myself to ignore his self-centeredness and overlook incidents where he seemed hypocritical—remember when Kerry stopped being an asshole?—and refused to notice when things he said or did made no sense or conflicted with the image he wanted to project. When he flirted repeatedly with a young waitress in Wrightsville Beach, I forced the memory of it out of my head. When I heard about him having extramarital affairs, I refused to believe the stories. And when he arranged for the campaign to pay a hundred thousand dollars for a video project to a woman with almost no experience, I didn't let myself ask the questions that needed to be asked. Instead, I listened as Josh Brumberger told me to put this mysterious person, named Rielle Hunter, a woman the senator had met in a bar, on the payroll. It was a strange request because the senator knew I wasn't in charge of the payroll, but I promised to relay it because he was the boss.

The senator first met Rielle in early 2006 when he was in New York during a cross-country speaking tour with actor Danny Glover on behalf of hotel workers who wanted his help at union rallies. As she eventually told me herself, she saw Edwards in the lounge of the Regency, a five-star hotel on Park Avenue. A tall, slender blonde with blue eyes and a warm smile, Rielle was the kind of woman who moved comfortably in a place like the Regency lounge, where at any given time half the tables are occupied by big-money power brokers and celebrities. Her sense of ease in such settings had been acquired over time, as she had tried to climb the social ladder in the world's most important city. As I heard it, she moved like someone who was practiced at identifying rich men, married or not, and connecting with them—at least temporarily.

Born Lisa Druck and raised in Ocala, Florida, she had dropped out of college and moved to New York City in her early twenties. Drawn to the cocaine-fueled fast life enjoyed by young artists, writers, and fashion models, she quickly earned a reputation as a sexually liberated party girl. She briefly dated the writer Jay McInerney (*Bright Lights, Big City*) and inspired the repulsive character Alison Poole, who appears in two of his books. In 1991, she married attorney Alexander Hunter and changed her name to Rielle Hunter. (This new name allowed her to escape the shame associated with her infamous father, who had participated in a horse-killing insurance scam.) Rielle did a little acting, produced a short film, and in 2002 appeared on a TV game show. She had studied Eastern and New Age religion for years, seeking some special understanding of her place in this world and whatever lies beyond. By the time she saw John Edwards, she had lived much of her life on the edge of glamour, wealth, and enlightenment but was, at forty-one, divorced, unemployed, and living rent-free with a friend in New Jersey named Margaret "Mimi" Hockman.

According to Rielle, when she first saw John Edwards, she noticed "an aura" of energy floating over him. When she made eye contact with the senator, she knew their destinies were intertwined, and that she had been sent to Earth to serve him. His "old soul" had known her "old soul" in a previous life, she said. She asked him if he was the candidate she had seen on television. After he identified himself, she said, "You're so hot, but on television that doesn't come through. You seem distant. I can help you with that."

Rielle said that Edwards gave off an "energy" that told her he could be a powerful force for peace and progress, like Martin Luther King Jr. She decided immediately that she would devote herself to helping him reach this potential. This assistance would begin later, after she arranged to bump into him on the sidewalk, where she would flirt some more.

As Rielle later told Cheri and me, she recognized that the senator was married and her attraction was mixed with a feeling that he was somehow "dangerous." But when he gave her one of the key cards for his room, she waited a few minutes and then followed him upstairs. Inside the room, they sat for a while on separate beds (she was trying to play hard to get). Rielle said he got her to come over to the bed where he was relaxing by saying, "Hey, c'mere and watch some TV with me."

I first encountered Rielle Hunter in the flesh at Dulles International Airport, outside Washington, when I met a plane bringing the senator in for a meeting I had arranged with a donor who would become one of his most important supporters. Rielle was with him as they walked into the baggage claim area, and when I went to grab the senator's luggage, he said, "No, Andrew, help Rielle with hers."

He introduced her to me as a filmmaker who was going to make brief documentaries—called "webisodes"—that would air on the Internet and bypass the media to connect the senator directly to voters. The idea fit perfectly into Edwards's desire to make his campaign the first to take full advantage of the World Wide Web. Although he hardly ever used a computer himself—I never saw him send an e-mail or surf the Web—he understood that this approach would appeal to younger voters and wealthy backers in Silicon Valley, North Carolina's Research Triangle, and other centers of innovation. He also understood the Web's potential for raising campaign donations, dollar by dollar, from vast numbers of people.

On that day at the airport, Rielle and I weren't in each other's company for more than a few minutes, as she took her bag and went off on her own. But something in the way the senator looked at her, or maybe it was the way she looked at him, made me decide I wouldn't say a word about her to the senator during the hour-long drive to a district of estates and

Thoroughbred horse farms called Upperville in Virginia. I needed him to focus on the person we were going to visit and the opportunity she represented.

At ninety-five years of age, Rachel Lambert "Bunny" Mellon, whose deceased husband, Paul, was the son of the great banker Andrew Mellon, was one of the richest women in the world, but her public profile was so low that few Americans outside of high society knew of her. In fact, when she contacted our 2004 campaign to offer her help, no one recognized her name or followed up on her offer. Nevertheless, Bunny spent large sums buying pro-Edwards newspaper ads on her own.

In 2006, Bunny contacted me with the assistance of her close friend Bryan Huffman, a decorator whose sister had been in my law school class at Wake Forest. When Mrs. Mellon reached me on my cell phone, I was driving home for the night, so I pulled into the parking lot of a McDonald's and listened carefully. She told me that she was terrified by the imperial rule of George Bush and Dick Cheney at home and abroad—war, torture, bullying allies—and was sure that John Edwards could be the great president who would save the country from ruin.

As I recalled for the senator, Mrs. Mellon had sent her private jet—a Dessault Falcon capable of transatlantic flights—to bring Bryan and me from Raleigh to the mile-long private airstrip at her estate. (The interior of the jet was decorated with paintings from the National Gallery of Art, to which she was a major donor.) When we arrived, one of her staff drove me past statues of Paul Mellon's four greatest horses, including Sea Hero, a Kentucky Derby winner.

Mrs. Mellon was the last of a dying breed, the closest thing to royalty in America. As a child she played in the White House, and as a woman she dined with kings and queens. But I was impressed to discover that she lived in a relatively small, graceful home in a secluded spot, where she welcomed us with Bloody Marys, lunch, and fascinating stories of her relationships with John F. Kennedy and Jacqueline Kennedy (later Jacqueline Onassis). In the Camelot years, Bunny had redesigned the Rose Garden, aided the decoration of the White House, and mentored Jackie in art and fashion. She was Caroline Kennedy's godmother.

Remarkably, the senator had actually resisted going to meet Mrs. Mellon, and he had come only because I had insisted. Now, as we drove through Upperville and his jaw dropped at the sight of the houses, he said, "Shit, Andrew, these people have real money," and was glad he'd said yes. (The senator often gawked at the homes, offices, airplanes, and similar signs of wealth displayed by others. He would also ask me if the people he met were "rich like me" or "really, really rich.")

After we were admitted to the Mellon property by an armed guard, we drove past a North Carolina flag and EDWARDS FOR PRESIDENT signs that Bunny had set out to welcome us. I reminded the senator that she had already offered at least a million dollars on her commitment to see him elected president "and save the world."

In the few hours we spent with Bunny, who was warm and unpretentious, she concluded that John Edwards was the best of John and Robert Kennedy combined. She said he had JFK's intelligence and wit and RFK's intensity and drive. She also bonded with the senator based on the loss of his son Wade and her daughter Eliza's terrible auto accident, which had left her profoundly brain-damaged and bedridden. Bunny took the senator into Eliza's room, where they sat together for a while.

Before we left, she assured the senator that his PACs would soon receive the first of two $1 million donations.

"Have Andrew stay in touch," she told him. "We're going to do whatever it takes to make you president."

With a laugh, Bunny recalled her late husband, a staunch Republican, and added, "Paul is going to roll over in his grave." (Later, I would learn that Paul had kept a mistress through much of their marriage, something that hurt Bunny but which she accepted as such a common practice for powerful men that it was hardly worth noting.)

As we drove out of Upperville, the senator was high with excitement. Aside from trial lawyers like Fred Baron, he had no backers ready to make the kind of unconditional commitment Bunny had made. Others asked for more in return than they gave.

I was happy because Bunny and I had established a very good rapport. For the next few years she would call me regularly and I would send her video and news clips almost every day. She would work with me and Bryan to help her "beloved senator save America." Eventually, "whatever it takes" would amount to more than $6 million.

When someone like Bunny Mellon invites you to her guarded estate, declares you superior to John F. Kennedy, and makes a multimillion-dollar commitment to see you elected president, it has an effect. Ever since he ran for the Senate in 1998, John Edwards had experienced similar encounters on a regular basis, and by 2006 he had evolved into a man who was absolutely certain he should be the leader of the free world. This change had also been aided by countless people who added their ambition to his because they hoped to get carried into the White House with him. I count myself in this group, along with various other professionals and Mrs. Edwards.

Committed to her political ideology, Elizabeth Edwards was even more excited about addressing the country's serious problems—in health care, foreign policy, and economics—than the senator himself. And when she talked about living in the White House with him, it was with the assumption that she would remain his closest confidante and adviser. Mrs. Edwards showed plenty of ego as she made these plans, but she had the brains and courage to back up her dreams. These qualities saw her through her cancer treatment, which came with all the terrible side effects—hair loss, anemia, insomnia, terrible pain, and nausea—and I admired her bravery. Despite her outbursts and the times when her demands seemed excessive, I loved her and prayed for her to recover. I also admired her strength, which got her to her computer keyboard day after day to work on a book about her life, including her battle with cancer. It was to be called *Saving Graces*, and I was honored to be among the half dozen people she thanked in its pages for making the book possible.

The opportunity to tell her story, and a big-money contract from a major publisher, came because Mrs. Edwards (like her husband) was a visible and popular public person. In presenting herself to the voters through the media, she had played up the elements that appealed to the majority of Americans—her roles as mother, wife, and advocate for things that mattered to families—and played down her career as an attorney and the role she had in helping to direct her husband's campaigns. She also showed herself to be flawed in ways that might endear her to people. She struggled with her weight, ran herself ragged dealing with the demands of her life, and was guided by commonsense values.

Compared with political wives like Teresa Heinz Kerry, Hillary Clinton, and even Laura Bush, Elizabeth Edwards presented a more approachable and warmly human persona to the world. In private she was sometimes these things, but she was also fiercely ambitious and determined to advance herself. Because she got help from people like me and the nanny, Heather North, who lived with her husband, Jed, in an apartment over the garage, she had the kind of support for her writing that others just don't get. She poured herself into the work, especially during early 2006, and even made frequent overnight trips related to this project and others.

When Elizabeth was away, Emma Claire and Jack were tended to by the senator and Heather North. Heather saw as much of the family as I did, and we became friends as we talked—shared war stories, really—about the care and feeding of folks who considered themselves "the First Family in waiting." She set firmer limits than I did on the time she gave to the Edwardses, and this caused some friction between her and Elizabeth. But Heather's job was safe, because when she was on duty she was completely reliable, Jack and Emma Claire loved her, and she loved them back with a consistency that made them feel safe and secure. She was a perfect fill-in mom.

Heather was so much like a third parent that when Jack was upset and couldn't find his mother or father, he naturally ran to her. In the fall of

2006, this happened in the middle of the night when Elizabeth was away and Jack went to his parents' room hoping to get a reassuring snuggle from his father. He found the bed empty and then ran to awaken Heather. She took him by the hand to look for his dad and found he was gone. Somehow she managed to get Jack to go back to sleep, and in the morning the senator was back in the house to make breakfast and see the kids off to school.

My phone rang at nine A.M. On the other end of the line, Heather sounded worried, angry, and confused as she reported that the senator had gone missing in the night along with one of the family cars. (This was the first of several incidents like this.)

I didn't lie when I told her I didn't know where he might have been, but I did try to offer the most innocent explanation. He must have been unable to sleep and driven someplace where he could take a run.

How, then, Heather asked, would I explain the hotel key card from the Courtyard by Marriott hotel that she had found on a kitchen counter?

I couldn't explain the card, except to say that perhaps he had gotten tired and just checked in someplace. I knew this was a lame explanation, but I did manage to calm her down, and since Mrs. Edwards was on her way home, she agreed to throw away the card and stay quiet, at least in the short term. As I told her I would look into things, I felt a sinking feeling in my stomach, as if a long-dreaded crisis were at hand. I also found myself recalling little incidents that should have given me pause in the past but that I had chosen to ignore.

On the campaign trail, I had seen that the senator occasionally pocketed notes from eager women he met at an event rather than hand them to me for disposal. I had also received calls from other staffers who said that the senator had begun to request that they stay on different floors, away from him, whenever they were booked into a hotel for the night. On the hundred-county tour, there were many nights when he would go out for "jogs" at two o'clock in the morning. I hadn't been concerned about those episodes because I believed he was faithful to his wife.

My worries and Heather's report came spilling out that morning as I told Cheri about Heather's phone call. A committed skeptic when it came to John Edwards, she was not surprised that he might be sneaking around, but she was upset about the threat an affair posed to his family. For all her flaws, Elizabeth was an essentially good person. Jack and Emma Claire were great kids who adored their dad. These concerns dominated Cheri's reaction. But in a moment, when she was able to set them aside and offer a witty observation or two, she said she was shocked that the key card was from an inexpensive hotel and equally surprised by the identity of the woman I suspected was his mistress. For a man who could have his pick from among thousands of women who had literally thrown themselves at him, Rielle Hunter was, in my eyes and Cheri's, a strange if not dangerous choice.

I could have confronted Senator Edwards immediately, but I didn't. For one thing, the prospect of challenging one of the nation's great trial lawyers without more evidence than I possessed seemed futile. For another, I thought—or rather hoped—that whatever he was doing amounted to a brief fling that would end soon and never be discovered. Despite his complaints about her, he loved Elizabeth and his children, and I knew he wouldn't want to hurt them. I thought he would understand that an affair, if made public, would ruin him politically and personally. Cheri and Heather and I decided to keep our mouths shut in the hope that with a little time, he would realize that he had too much at stake to continue.

In the meantime, the senator was more affectionate toward his wife and our friendship was never closer. In part, this was due to the fact that I was raising extraordinary amounts of money for his various causes, and this made him respect me more. My confidence was climbing, but I never ceased to support the senator in any way he asked. When his son Jack needed surgery—not a major operation, but still serious—he wanted me to go with him to the hospital. After the operation, when he knew everything was okay, he left Mrs. Edwards with Jack and came to tell me the news. I suggested he call his parents, which he did, and when that call ended, I asked him if he wanted to call anyone else. I expected him to dial up family and friends. He noted that he had some time and a quiet place to work, and it seemed like a good idea to call some of his more important donors. "Andrew, it will mean something for me to call them from here," he said. "It'll make them feel important."

I thought Edwards's idea was strange, especially since like most candidates, the senator didn't enjoy fund-raising. (Actually, he hated many of the chores one must perform to gain office and did them reluctantly.) To make it easier on him, we sometimes parked a couple of staffers at his house with cell phones and let them dial down a list of bigwigs until they got someone who was willing to wait, on hold, for the candidate to come on the line. He would walk around into his library and in front of the massive fireplace, chatting away about some big interview or event, and then he'd offer an anecdote that was "just between you and me."

When he got a donation, he'd hang up and say, "Shit, they love me— they would do anything for me. Make sure we follow up on that one! Who's next?" If someone else kept him on the line too long, he would roll his eyes, look at me with a sarcastic face and a half grin, point at the phone, shrug, and mouth to me, "Ass kisser." If he hung up without getting a commitment, he would say, "What the hell—why are they wasting my time? I'm going to be president. I don't have time for this shit. Everyone wants to give me advice. I don't want advice. I want their money."

As the summer of 2006 began, both of the Edwardses had taken on an overwhelming amount of work. He was campaigning full-time. She was working with the editors for her book and planning a nationwide media and signing tour that would start at the end of September. Together, they were taking responsibility for all the major decisions related to the presidential campaign. As part of this effort, the senator joined the Wake-Up Wal-Mart tour, which was sponsored by a union that was pressuring the company to improve its pay and benefits. The tour was conducted from a brightly painted bus and brought politicians and celebrities to towns and cities across the country. They spoke about Wal-Mart's employment practices and called on the company to buy more American-made products. For John Edwards, the tour offered a chance to connect with local politicians and voters who might come to his side in the primaries, but it also provided settings where his speeches and other performances could be captured by his new videographer, Rielle Hunter.

Having used part of her first check to buy a camera, Rielle joined the senator as he flew to and from events on a jet provided by his friend Fred Baron. The five-minute film she made about the Wal-Mart tour, called *The Golden Rule*, opens with Boyd Tinsley singing, "When you look into the mirror, do you like what's lookin' at you?" It shows the senator making speeches about the misdeeds of the world's largest retailer—"It's about responsibility and basic human morality"—and signing autographs, and it ends with outtakes, including Edwards sharing an inside joke with Rielle and saying, "Very graceful, camera girl."

In another webisode, Rielle caught Josh Brumberger as he sat inside Fred Baron's jet and filled out forms for a trip to China. (He actually never went.) The camera focused on him and he said, "I never know what to put for 'Occupation.' Perhaps I should put 'His bitch.'" This little scene was still available on the Internet at the end of 2009.

By the middle of the summer, Camera Girl was booked to accompany the senator on many of his trips, and I soon had an idea of what was going on between them. The senator would often tell me his cell phone battery was dead, ask to use my phone, and dial her number. (In fact, Mrs. Edwards had a habit of checking his calling history, and he didn't want her to see Rielle's number.) They would talk about the campaign and politics, but their long conversations included too many "I miss you"s to be considered strictly business.

Rielle also developed the habit of telephoning me directly to ask about the senator's schedule, to offer critiques of his performances on television, and to ask for favors. In one case, she requested backstage passes to a Dave Matthews concert in New York City. I got them for her and later heard that she had practically tackled Matthews when she saw him. A member of the band's staff called me and asked, "What's up with this Rielle chick?" and told me she had "weirded out" everyone backstage.

A dramatic person who seemed to act before thinking, Rielle worried me for many reasons. She was flashy and loud, and she acted as though every man she met wanted her. I was worried that she might do something to make her relationship with the senator public. And I was also concerned about how she might affect important relationships, like the one between the senator and members of the band. It's hard to overstate the value of having rock-star friends. I once organized a special trip to a Dave Matthews concert, with backstage access included, to reward a busload of big Edwards donors. (To show off, the senator also had the group meet him at the airport to see his new jet.) The experience of hanging out with a presidential candidate and musicians who made thousands of fans scream for two hours was enough to persuade one fellow to give $2 million to "combat poverty." I didn't want to lose access to that kind of star power because of Rielle Hunter.

With the risk she posed in mind, I told the senator about Rielle's behavior at the New York event and watched him carefully when he reacted. He seemed most concerned that she had offended Dave Matthews and promised to speak to her about it. The fact that she may have been flirting so aggressively with another man did bother him, but I would later learn that he and Rielle had agreed to an "open" relationship. They were free to do whatever they wanted with whomever they wanted, just as long as they were honest with each other. I soon found out that they told each other everything about their sexual histories and behaviors. To my embarassment, they also told me far too much about their sexual activities.

Whenever Rielle called me, she tried to talk explicitly about her relationship with the senator. For obvious reasons, she couldn't talk about these things with anyone else, so I figured I was serving as a sort of safety valve, letting her blow off steam. When the details about specific sexual acts, love bites, or the condition of her vagina got too graphic, I cut her off, but my attempts to set limits on Rielle were only partly effective. She was a bright person who loved to talk, and she tried hard to get close to people by sharing her spiritual insights—including her predictions of the future—and her opinions. Senator Edwards listened when she discussed his campaign performances. (She was right about how he sometimes "switched off" and came across at half power.) He also fed off her devotion, since she promised to do anything he asked because he was destined to be world leader. I wasn't surprised when I heard that she would accompany him to Uganda on a trip that would add a little foreign policy exposure to his résumé.

As the trip approached, it fell to me to arrange for the senator to get the required vaccines at the last possible moment. Rielle was in town, so when I told him he was up against a deadline, he invited her to go with him to a walk-in clinic. I didn't like this, because folks in the rather gossipy community of Chapel Hill would see them together. To make matters worse, the senator's parents were due for a lunch visit, so he just told them to meet us at the clinic.

The scene, as Bobbi and Wallace Edwards came upon it, found their son hidden away in the doctor's private office with a younger woman who was not his wife. They sat side by side chatting playfully, like a couple preparing to go away on their honeymoon. Unlike the nurse who attended the senator and Rielle, who looked at them incredulously as she did her work, Bobbi and Wallace didn't seem to notice anything was strange. I went to a nearby deli to get sandwiches, and we all ate together. When we finished, Wallace and Bobbi wished their son well in Africa and went home.

The Africa tour was sponsored by the International Rescue Committee, which was trying to address a humanitarian crisis caused by a civil war that had displaced more than one million people. Rielle filmed Edwards, clad in khaki pants and a Tar Heel blue T-shirt, inspecting refugee camps and listening as groups of children greeted him with songs. On video he looked like the great white leader who had come to save the country. Later he and Rielle would tell me that during this trip, when they spent every night together, he said "I love you" to her for the first time.

When the senator and Rielle returned to the United States, he stumbled into the house exhausted, brought his luggage into the huge dressing room where he kept his wardrobe, undressed, and then flopped into bed. At some point a secret cell phone he had left in his suitcase began to ring. Mrs. Edwards heard it, found it, and, noting a number from a New York City area code, answered.

Without hearing a "Hello," Rielle Hunter launched into a romantic monologue about how much she missed the man who was supposed to answer the phone. In her defense, this particular phone had been purchased by Rielle for the sole use of John Edwards, and she was the only person who had the number. Still, unless she intended to force some kind of showdown, Rielle's blurted professions of love and adoration were a big mistake.

After ending the call, Mrs. Edwards, carrying the phone in her hand, went to the senator and demanded to know what was going on. He confessed to having had a one-night stand but didn't say with whom. For some reason, she accepted this explanation but demanded he return the call and, as she watched, end the relationship. He did as he was told, but as soon as he was able, he telephoned Rielle again to tell her what had happened and reassured her that they were still in a relationship.

The senator explained all of this to me soon after it happened. We were alone backstage at an event, and as often happened, the conversation got around to the fact that he was unhappy in his marriage. He said that Mrs. Edwards was being overly demanding, obsessive, even "crazy." But he also said that he would never seek a divorce. For one thing, he still loved Elizabeth in certain ways. And he believed that his wife was more popular with many voters than he was and that if he left her, he might as well forget ever becoming president. (I cringed when he said this.) When I thought about how it would look if he divorced a wife of almost thirty years, who had lost a child in a car wreck and was living with cancer, I had to agree with him about the political impact. And since becoming president was his single driving ambition, it was never going to happen.

When Mrs. Edwards left Chapel Hill to start her book tour, the senator brought Rielle to his home, where she met Jack and Emma Claire and even interviewed them briefly while holding a video camera to capture their replies. (She also interviewed Edwards's parents, who were there that afternoon.) When I went to the house to see him, I discovered her sitting in the living room curled up in a chair like a cat, with her shoes and socks off. She wore blue jeans and had a colorful scarf around her neck and sunglasses perched atop her head.

The mood in the house was relaxed and upbeat. Instead of the news blaring out of various TVs, which Elizabeth kept tuned to C-SPAN. I heard music playing. I noticed because the senator had told me he had stopped listening to music when Wade died, and I had seen him turn off music whenever it was playing. We went on a run together, following our usual route past a cow pasture full of mooing heifers and waving to neighbors who hailed us from their front porches. While we were gone, Rielle napped in Cate's room.

That evening, we ate take-out ribs from a place called Nantucket Grill and sat on the senator's back porch, a huge space covered by a sturdy roof. The group included me, the nanny, Heather, and her husband, Jed, the senator, his kids, and Rielle, who talked excitedly about everything from national politics to astrology. She said she had been a spiritual teacher and that she believed the future was foretold by the stars. Rielle took great pleasure in noting that John Edwards's future was limitless, and every once in a while she punctuated her observations about him with a laugh and the line "It's good to be king."

As the wine flowed and Heather put the kids to bed, the senator and Rielle became more comfortable touching each other and dropped the pretense that they weren't involved. At one point, they started musing about how the house seemed like a happy place with Elizabeth and her "negative energy" removed. Rielle talked about living in the mansion once Mrs. Edwards was out of the way. A new family would be formed, the senator said, after he and Rielle married on some rooftop in Manhattan with a celebration that would include music from Dave Matthews. As Rielle listened to the senator spin this fantasy, she smiled like a little kid who had gotten her way.

As the night wore on, clouds rolled in, followed by thunder and lightning and the heaviest rain I had ever seen. Protected and dry under the roof, we watched the water come down in sheets, and in a quiet moment the senator said, "This is the way it should be—no stress, no fighting."

"It's good to be king," said Rielle.

I left the house during the downpour, shaken by everything I had seen and heard. As I turned the key in my Suburban and flipped on the wipers, my once-bright future seemed to be in peril.

The next time I spoke to Rielle, she happily told me that she had spent that night in the Edwardses' bed and slept in while the senator made breakfast for the kids and then drove them to school. She said that when he returned, he got into bed and they "made love."

Eight

MEN BEHAVING VERY BADLY

I had my own problems.

While the senator had been in Africa, Cheri and I had tried to celebrate our wedding anniversary. Our occasional lifesaver ("babysitter" doesn't do her justice), Melissa Geertsma, came to care for the three kids while we got dressed and went to a nice restaurant. We ordered wine and food, but at a moment when we might have marveled at how far we had come together in life, we talked instead about my twenty-four-hour-a-day devotion to the Edwards family and my scheme for moving us out of Raleigh and into a house in the woods at the end of a long dirt road.

We had already purchased the land from an Edwards donor and friend named Tim Toben, and I was ready to put the house on Lake Wheeler up for sale. Cheri loved this house, the church we attended, the preschool where our kids were enrolled, and the friends who lived nearby. She dreaded packing up everything and moving a two-year-old, a four-year-old, and a five-year-old to a temporary home we would occupy while the house in the woods was constructed. I was motivated by the good offer we had for the house we were selling and the prospect of eliminating a tiresome commute. The move would require us to take on a much bigger mortgage, and though I was finally earning a very good salary and getting some respect from the powers-that-be in national politics, Cheri knew I was not guaranteed a position over the long term. We were dependent on John and Elizabeth Edwards for our income and health insurance, and these people had not shown themselves to be paragons of stability, especially since the arrival of Rielle Hunter.

Cheri was right. I was wrong. But I wasn't going to admit it that night. Instead, I said what I always said—"John Edwards is going to be president one day"—and reminded her that I had been right about him so far. Cheri had heard this before and didn't want to hear it again on our anniversary. True to our style, we didn't shout or bark at each other but instead seethed with emotion. With both of us feeling too upset to eat, we asked to have our food boxed to take home. The wine was on the table, so I finished it, and when the boxes came we left. The argument got worse during the forty-five-minute ride home.

Having eaten next to nothing during the day and consumed just wine and a little bread at dinner, I was not exercising good judgment when I got behind the wheel of the car. We made it home safely, but in the privacy of our house, Cheri and I went from seething to an open argument. I couldn't hear all of her resentment for my devotion to the Edwardses and her fear that I trusted them too much. I wasn't sensitive to how she felt about Rielle Hunter and the idea that my boss, who was supposed to be one of the "good guys," was apparently cheating on his wife. All I heard was that she was criticizing me for how I did my job, the same job that supported our family. In the heat of the moment, I stormed out.

What happened next holds a special place in the little Hall of Shame that occupies a corner of my heart. While I was essentially driving nowhere, I looked in the rearview mirror and saw flashing lights. I pulled over (again into a McDonald's parking lot), and my heart sank as the police car slid in behind me. Part of me was glad I had been stopped before something worse had happened. (I was still under the effects of the wine I'd had at dinner.) But I also knew immediately that an arrest for driving under the influence could hurt me and my position with Senator Edwards, especially if it got into the press. Panicked, I refused to take a Breathalyzer test. The police officer, who could tell I had been drinking, put me in handcuffs and took me to a police station I knew well from having visited with Senator Edwards during our hundred-county tour.

From the first words I exchanged with the officer who arrested me to the moment a judge released me to take a taxi home, I refused to cooperate beyond giving the police and court officials the barest information about my identity. When asked about my employer, I mentioned the names of the organizations that paid me, not John Edwards. In the end, as the process led to my release, I became completely sober and terrified about my future.

At home I found Cheri sick with worry and anger, but she quickly grasped the seriousness of what we faced, namely the loss of my reputation and, quite possibly, my job and health insurance for our family. With my DWI arrest, every other concern faded in importance as we tried to protect our financial foundation.

The practical problems that befall anyone stupid enough to drive under the influence in North Carolina are more than enough to teach an important lesson. First, you automatically lose your driver's license, which rendered me unable to work. The courts also require you to attend frequent alcohol awareness meetings (much like sessions of Alcoholics Anonymous), and you face even more punishment, including possible jail time, once you go before a judge.

With the help of Cheri and her brother, who lived nearby, I managed to get to the meetings, and I had to hire an assistant to help me get around for work. However, I still had to deal with the damage the arrest might do to my reputation and relationship with the Edwardses. I agonized for a few days, feeling the way I used to in my shameful twenties. Finally, I followed the advice I got from Wade Byrd and David Kirby and picked up the phone to call the Edwardses. Cheri sat beside me and listened as Mrs. Edwards answered, and I decided to begin by telling her what had happened. Her response confirmed all the good feelings I had ever felt for her.

"Andrew, you are family," she said. "You don't worry about this. John will call you in a few minutes. It's going to be all right."

The senator, who had been exercising on a treadmill when I phoned, called me about half an hour later. This time I was alone on our back porch. After I laid out the story and told him I was worried about my future with him, the senator's voice dropped into a reassuring tone as he insisted that everyone faltered at some point, and he would not abandon me. "We've all done something like this, Andrew. I have. I know you feel like the lowest person on earth right now, but I love you. You are like a brother to me." I felt as if a great weight had been lifted off my heart.

Words like "love" and "family" make you feel a powerful bond, one that suggests an us-against-the-world kind of loyalty that is very comforting at times when you feel threatened. But this bond can also be a trap. When I told them about the drunk driving arrest, which the press did not report at the time, I handed the senator and Mrs. Edwards a bit of information about myself that I wanted to hide. It gave them a type of leverage that matched whatever power I held through my knowledge of the senator's relationship with Rielle and of Elizabeth's more unattractive qualities: ambition, haughtiness, impatience.

Although we never actually spoke of it this way, years of intimacy had brought us to a point where we were all forced to ignore certain truths and devote ourselves to the shared goal of putting John Edwards in the White House. If this sounds to you like the unspoken pact that binds members of the Mafia, you are correct. Mob loyalty is based on fear, and with the crisis around my arrest, the basis for my loyalty to John Edwards was shifted from hope for a better future to an almost desperate dread of being exposed and losing my livelihood.

The similarities with the Mafia go beyond mutual blackmail. Like the Mob, the Edwards clan was willing to "whack" those who got out of line. A prime example of this ruthlessness arose as I was dealing with my DWI issue. A staffer who had developed deep suspicions about Rielle Hunter during the trip to Africa had taken his concern to Nick Baldick, who was still running operations for the senator. The aide, Josh Brumberger, was one of several people who had spoken to me about Rielle, but unlike the others, he wasn't satisfied with my evasive reassurances. Soon after Brumberger talked to Nick, the senator brought him into the American Airlines Admirals Club at LaGuardia Airport and suggested he leave the Edwards team. Edwards made sure that Josh would remain discreet by arranging for him to have a job at Fortress Financial, but his dismissal sent a signal to everyone in the inner circle of the campaign.

The sudden disappearance of Josh Brumberger made me even more concerned about my future and the senator's judgment. He should have taken Josh's questions as a warning about the dangers of indiscretion, but he did not. In the fall of 2006, he and Mrs. Edwards traveled extensively to promote themselves (she for her book, he for the White House), and the senator saw Rielle and spoke to her by phone as often as he could.

Although he had not formally declared, the senator had been operating as a candidate for the 2008 Democratic Party nomination ever since the 2004 defeat. He faced two main opponents in Hillary Clinton and Barack Obama, who were similarly undeclared but already campaigning. (Iowa governor Tom Vilsack and Ohio representative Dennis Kucinich were declared candidates, but they were not given much of a chance to win.) Some analysts would say that Clinton and Obama enjoyed an advantage in their offices, which gave them credibility with voters. They also received an inordinate amount of press coverage because of the historic prospect of a woman or a black man reaching the White House.

The senator's personal finances were secure. He had raised a political war chest and he had a private jet at his beck and call. He began devoting all his attention to building relationships across the country, devising strategy, and putting people into key jobs. All the campaigns were performing this task. Hillary Clinton had her husband, the most experienced politician on the planet, as her top adviser. Barack Obama loaded his staff with extremely talented former Edwards loyalists like Julianna Smoot and David Axelrod. Abandoning the practice they followed in 2004, when they tapped highly experienced professionals, Senator and Mrs. Edwards chose a host of relative newcomers. Shrum and Baldick were gone, replaced by malleable young people. Our new chief of staff, Kathleen McGlynn, had been Mrs. Edwards's scheduler and director of "special affairs" for the clothier Kenneth Cole. Jonathan Prince, a speechwriter for Clinton, ran the campaign day to day. Josh Brumberger was replaced by John Davis, a pale, mild-mannered Midwesterner who had been hired because of his contacts in Iowa.

As the new body man, Davis would be in charge of the senator's care and feeding whenever he left North Carolina. This meant keeping him on schedule, shepherding him to and from events, and traveling by his side. Like most new staff members, he turned to me, as the senator's longest-serving and closest aide, whenever he ran into an issue he couldn't resolve or needed answers to questions he couldn't ask the senator directly.

Recently married to a sweet young woman whom he obviously adored, Davis was a fairly proper and morally conservative guy who rarely swore or raised his voice or got overly excited. He was also smart and started calling me with questions about Rielle Hunter almost immediately after he took to the road with the senator. When I couldn't give him satisfying answers, he pressed me harder. Finally, on a night when he was staying in North Carolina, I went to the hotel where he was staying (the same Courtyard by Marriott that issued the key card discovered by Heather) and sat with him and one of the senator's top political advisers, David Medina. (Medina would eventually become First Lady Michelle Obama's deputy chief of staff.)

As John and David worked their way through a supply of beer (I abstained because of my DWI), the conversation became more animated and John slowly grasped what was going on between the senator and Rielle. He also became quite profane, which I would discover was something that happened on the rare occasions when he drank.

After Medina left, he said, "C'mon, Andrew. You don't think he could be so fuckin' stupid as to think he can get away with it, do you?"

It was a good question, and the only answer was that the senator obviously *did* think he could get away with it. And why wouldn't he? For all of his life he had been told he was special, and every year brought him ever more adulation. He had wealth, fame, and a younger woman who called him "the king" and promised to do whatever he wanted her to do at any time.

For John Davis, who cared deeply about the issues and had come to the campaign as a true believer, the more important matter was, in my mind, protecting himself. My sense of commitment to John Edwards was becoming frayed, and I was not excited about working on a campaign for another year. Here I could offer some solid counsel. I told him that his best chance of avoiding trouble was to remain loyal to the senator, not Mrs. Edwards. (I suspected that some of the staff were actually more attached to her and may have been feeding her information about Rielle.) In the short term, I told him, "try to make his life as simple as possible." In the long term, his goal should be to anticipate the boss's needs so that he wouldn't even have to ask. It's like being the best friend of the quarterback in high school. You protect him even if that means helping him get away with stuff.

As I explained the facts of life to John, I recalled similar conversations with Edwards's body men Hunter Pruette and Josh Brumberger, and the warnings I had received from Julianna Smoot and Will Austin when I took the job in D.C. I felt as if I was forcing him to abandon the idealism that had brought him to the Edwards campaign and to recognize the dark side of politics. Everyone thinks politics is dirty, but I was starting to think it was disgusting. You do it because you hope that the good you accomplish outweighs the excesses that accompany the pursuit of power. That's how you justify it to yourself morally. But the burden of secrets and the loss of innocence—and this included my own loss of innocence—is always painful.

When I left John, I felt sorry for him. I felt even worse a few days later when I tried to remind the senator to be careful about letting too many people in on his secrets. Edwards said that he believed firing Josh had sent an effective message to everyone who might go public with information about Rielle. And where John Davis was concerned, he said, "Don't worry about him, Andrew, he's one of us." The next morning, Heather North, the nanny, called and said the senator "was gone again last night."

With a single phrase, the senator had declared that John Davis was trustworthy. Remarkably, the senator assumed that everyone, including old friends who had known him and Mrs. Edwards for decades, would simply go along. I can think of no other explanation for his decision to continue seeing Rielle and to bring her into even more public settings.

In November, after the trip to Africa, the cell phone mishap, and Josh's removal, the senator headed for Asheville and a weekend conference of the North Carolina Academy of Trial Lawyers. (I went with him, as did John Davis.) When Rielle called from New Jersey, Edwards decided that it would be just fine if she joined the party at the Grove Park Inn. She flew in from Newark and found her way to the local campus of the University of North Carolina, where the senator was winding up a visit with students and faculty. At first she went into her Camera Girl routine, hauling out her equipment so she could capture the moment on tape, but I had to tell her she couldn't do campaign work at an event sponsored by the UNC poverty center, so she put the camera away.

As we left the university to meet the lawyers at the inn, the senator beamed at Rielle like a lovesick teenager. He was thrilled that she had come and would spend the night with him at such a romantic hotel. Although a local staffer asked him to ride in her car so she could brief him on the next event, he insisted on riding with me and Rielle. The staffer glared at me. I rolled my eyes as if to say, *What can I do? He's the boss.*

Later, at the hotel, we met his old friends Wade Byrd and David Kirby, who had been his original political backers and closest friends but had recently begun to feel neglected by him. Although he would give a brief talk to the academy on how he intended to protect trial lawyers from Republican-backed tort "reforms" that would hinder lawsuits, the senator's main goal for this overnight visit was to heal these relationships. As he turned on the charm, I could see his old friends begin to forgive him.

When dinnertime arrived, Edwards made the move that would signal that his friends were on the "inside" and everyone else was "outside." Instead of attending the formal dinner where annual awards would be presented— "Andrew, I don't want to sit through that shit"—he asked me to arrange something private at a local restaurant, where he could sit with Kirby, Byrd, and a few others. His host, my former boss and the head of the academy, responded angrily to this insult, but Edwards didn't care. As we drove away, he was completely unaffected by how he had disappointed the crowd back at the inn, but he was annoyed by one thing: The car we piled into was too small, and Rielle wound up sitting on my lap for the short ride. She told me later that he didn't like the sight of her sitting on my lap.

At the restaurant, the senator split up the party: John Davis and Rielle and I stayed in the bar to eat, while he went into the dining room with his lawyer friends. The senator often asked for privacy when he was with political or personal contacts, so John and I were accustomed to this kind of treatment. But Rielle hadn't been in this situation before and resented it. She fumed and complained all through the meal, and when we got back to the hotel, she made it clear she wasn't going to be hidden away.

The rest of the evening was spent drinking until Rielle, Edwards, David Kirby, and I were quite intoxicated. (I wasn't driving.) At some point the senator declared, "I need to be around some people," and we all went to the hotel bar, where he could soak up a little attention from the other guests. When he had had enough love, he began to ask about Wade Byrd, who had long before retired to his room.

"Where's the Byrdman?" he kept asking me. "Let's go get him."

Byrd had checked into the Gatsby suite, which was reached via a private lobby. Outside the door, the furnishings included a table and chairs with an oversized chess set. After pounding on Byrd's door to no avail, the senator sat at the table and moved some pieces around. For the next half hour or so, we all loitered outside the suite while the senator moved pawns and rooks and knights and repeatedly wandered back to the door to pound away. Byrd never did come out, but I got a pretty good idea of how John Edwards may have acted on party nights in his college days.

When we finally concluded that Wade Byrd wasn't going to show, we all went back to Senator Edwards's suite. Within a few minutes, Rielle and the senator were cuddling on the couch. Feeling worse than awkward, Kirby and I left. Kirby was flabbergasted.

"What the hell is going on?" he asked when we were alone.

All I said in response was, "Mr. Kirby, you know him better than I do."

That night, Rielle would have eventually retreated to her own room, because the senator couldn't take the risk of her falling asleep and reflexively answering the phone if it rang. (Once when he had answered the phone in this kind of situation, Rielle got angry and bit him on the lip. The wound was difficult for him to explain.) Mrs. Edwards had begun to call her husband at all hours of the night just to make sure he was where he was supposed to be. In time, she would also develop protocols that campaign staffers were required to use so that groupies wouldn't be able to find him in hotels. Her orders were that callers who asked for her husband would have to mention the name of a designated staffer before being put through. On the rare occasions when she called and the senator didn't answer, she immediately requested that hotel security get the body man to go into the room to see if he was all right. This would happen at least half a dozen times to my knowledge, but it always turned out that Senator Edwards was alone and had simply slept through the ringing.

Because Mrs. Edwards was watching the senator closely, Rielle purchased a new cell phone we came to call "the Batphone," which she gave to him so they could stay in touch. Whenever this phone was discussed, Rielle and the senator hummed the theme song from the old *Batman* TV show. I often held the phone for him, to keep it secret from Mrs. Edwards, or arranged for three-way calls on his regular phone to keep Rielle's number off his calling record.

Friends and staffers who had to deal with Elizabeth Edwards's suspicions and saw signs of his infidelity tried not to think about the issue. I believe that David Kirby and I avoided having a frank conversation about the senator and Rielle because if we said out loud what we were thinking, we might have to deal with it directly. Also, we were powerless to do much about it.

The senator and Rielle made it difficult for me to ignore the affair, because he let me see them kiss and I had heard Rielle recount their sexual exploits and pledge her love. But he always used the lawyer's trick of speaking in code so he could claim "plausible deniability" if it was ever needed. She would say she loved him and spoke so loudly that I could hear her on the phone. He would say only, "Me too." And if she asked him if he missed her, he would say, "That's correct"—pronouncing it "cohhhhhh-rect"—but never, "I miss you."

I thought this practice was ridiculous, especially since we often talked about Rielle, but the senator would keep it up for months to come. Similarly, Mrs. Edwards chose to limit the questions she asked, because looking the other way could delay a confrontation and give the senator a chance to change his behavior. Of course, there was no intellectual trick that would help any of us with the feelings we had about the senator's betrayal. I was disappointed and worried by what I was seeing. Mrs. Edwards, who had heard another woman expressing her love and lust on a strange cell phone, was hurt and angry. As Christmas approached—the first in their new mansion—she expressed her emotion by becoming more demanding and impatient with me as I tried to help her make everything perfect, from the arrangements for a tree to the presents.

The tree part was relatively easy, because Mrs. Edwards referred me to a local dealer who specialized in premium trees, which were delivered and set up in your home. As so often happened, since they were afraid of being cheated because of their fame and wealth, the Edwardses had me negotiate. I got a good discount on the asking price for a twelve-foot Douglas fir but still had to explain to her why it was so expensive. Next came the presents and one of the most unlikely, but painful, fiascoes of my long association with the Edwards family.

It all started with the Sony Corporation's diabolically clever marketing plan for its PlayStation 3 gaming system, which was scheduled for release on November 17. Sony had generated an avalanche of publicity about the game and its features but had manufactured only a limited supply. Like almost every other boy in America, Jack Edwards wanted one. On November 15, I stocked my Suburban with Diet Coke, beef jerky, and green peppers (Mrs. Edwards was on a diet) and went to pick her up at the airport. She arrived exhausted and crabby from her book tour and medical treatments. I told her to relax and we'd get her home quickly. After she caught her breath, she said, "Andrew, do you have a sleeping bag I can borrow tonight?"

I went along, asking why she would possibly need a sleeping bag, and she explained that she intended to camp out in front of a store so she would be among the first in line on the day the Sony gaming system became available. The idea of a middle-aged, cancer-stricken, "First-Lady-in-waiting" huddling in the dark on a sidewalk for hours on end was ridiculous. I told her I would investigate the options and come up with a better solution.

The assistant I had hired as a driver heard me talk about the PlayStation problem and volunteered to jump in. I was extremely busy setting up the 2008 campaign, which had to be ready January 1, and gratefully accepted his offer. He promptly rang up the nearest Wal-Mart store and talked his way to the manager of the electronics department. He left a voice mail dropping the senator's name and discussed the availability of the new Sony system. The next day, as shoppers all over the country waited in line to plunk down their Christmas savings for the toy, Wal-Mart issued a press release that said Senator John Edwards, a vocal spokesman for the Wake-Up Wal-Mart campaign, had tried to jump to the front "while the rest of America's working families are waiting patiently in line."

With Wal-Mart's press release came a flurry of inquiries from reporters across the country. Forced to respond, Senator Edwards explained that a new volunteer who was unaware of the Wal-Mart controversy had made the mistake of using his name in an overeager effort to get one of the gaming consoles. "He was not aware," said the senator, "that Wal-Mart doesn't provide health insurance or decent pay for many of its employees or of my efforts to change the way Wal-Mart treats its employees."

If you subscribe to the belief that "all publicity is good publicity," the PlayStation 3 blowup was a bonanza. With the campaign kickoff six weeks away, Senator Edwards was in the middle of a media blitz. In the previous week, he had appeared on *Good Morning America*, *The Charlie Rose Show*, *The Daily Show with Jon Stewart*, *Late Show with David Letterman*, and *Meet the Press*. When Wal-Mart went after him, the senator used the attack to draw attention to his critique of the company's employment practices. Most of the news outlets that went with the story referred to the Wake-Up Wal-Mart campaign, so I tried to convince myself that the reporting was balanced. Mrs. Edwards did not agree. Having worked hard to cultivate a "plain folks" public image, she believed nationwide publicity about John Edwards trying to jump the line at Wal-Mart was a disaster. She sent me an e-mail headed "This is what can happen" and wrote: "This is what can happen when we ask for special treatment. We cannot ever ask for special treatment. Ever."

Below her note, she pasted a bunch of articles from newspapers and Web sites, all of which made fun of Edwards. A typical one said, "There are two Americas, one for rich people who can bypass the line, one for poor folks who can't."

For the next few weeks, Elizabeth searched for these items on the Internet and sent them to me by the dozens. They arrived on my BlackBerry on weekdays and weekends, in the middle of the night, and over the holidays as I drove with my wife and kids to visit with family in Illinois. Although I apologized, explained what had happened, and took responsibility, nothing seemed to satisfy her. She was certain that I had told my assistant to throw around the senator's name, which I had not.

As the negative comments continued in the blogosphere, she sent me an angry note, the key sentence of which was written in capital letters: "I HAVE A LOT OF TROUBLE WITH YOUR APOLOGIES WHEN COMBINED WITH YOUR OWN BENIGN DESCRIPTION OF YOUR ROLE." When another apology from me didn't work, Mrs. Edwards switched from expressing her anger to trying to make me feel ashamed. On December 4, she wrote: "I noticed that although you have steered clear of me, you are bringing John home tomorrow. Think of that as an opportunity to be completely honest . . . not to complain that I am being too harsh on you. In my view, you are not harsh enough on yourself."

At some point, even a good soldier gets angry at the brass, and after weeks of her harangues I got angry. I printed out many of the e-mails I had received from her and brought them with me to the airport on a day when I was meeting the senator. Once he got in the car, I showed them to him and then told him I'd resign if necessary. When I finished, the senator recalled previous talks we had had about Mrs. Edwards, their marriage, and their difficulties. He said, "Andrew, this is fucking harassment. Don't worry about this. And you're not quitting." The e-mails about the PlayStation 3 stopped that evening.

On the day after Christmas, Mrs. Edwards wrote to tell me to make sure the Christmas tree supplier would come to collect the big Douglas fir at eight-fifteen on the morning of December 29. "Also," she added, "the kids loved their presents—thank you!"

While Mrs. Edwards, and much of America, spent the quiet days before the start of the New Year cleaning up wrapping paper and putting away ornaments, Senator Edwards jetted off to New Orleans, where dead trees and hurricane-ravaged homes in the Lower Ninth Ward would serve as the backdrop for a speech announcing the start of his presidential campaign. (Two weeks earlier, Joe Klein of *Time* magazine had heralded Edwards as the front-runner, with a two-to-one lead in the polls over Hillary Clinton, his nearest competitor.) Although he still mentioned the "two Americas," rich and poor, most of what Edwards said in New Orleans focused on the Bush administration's post-Katrina failures, his call for withdrawing troops from Iraq, and proposals for dealing with global warming and America's dependence on foreign oil.

The policy ideas were almost standard-issue Democratic talking points, but as any campaign expert would tell you, the words the senator spoke were not as important as the staging and images he hoped the media would transmit. He appeared in jeans and shirtsleeves, and between the muddy yard, the boarded-up windows, and the fallen tree, the scene around him all but screamed "disaster area." A casual glance at the picture would have left you with the impression that a strong leader had come to New Orleans and was about to take charge and make things better.

The event attracted lots of press attention, which you can see in the video shot by Rielle Hunter, who accompanied the senator to New Orleans while Mrs. Edwards stayed home. Wearing tight-fitting jeans, a dark fleece top, a jester-style knit cap, and a big pink scarf, Rielle flitted between the senator and the hordes of journalists and camera operators, presumably documenting the moment as the official campaign filmmaker. If anyone in the press saw something unusual in the way Rielle interacted with Edwards, it wasn't reported. But Rielle had awakened that morning in the senator's room at the luxurious Loews hotel, where, she later told me, she "felt just like his First Lady."

Rielle continued to play First Lady as she spent the next few days traveling to campaign events. In Iowa, where he was leading in the polls, he signaled his Internet savvy by conducting a town hall with online participants around the world. He went from there to New Hampshire, where people noticed he had accented his shirtsleeves wardrobe with a plastic "Save Darfur" wristband, and then to Nevada and finally South Carolina. Big crowds greeted the senator and Rielle at rallies in each of these early-voting states. At his last stop, before flying home, they were met by an adoring crowd of more than a thousand people.

At some point after they left the South Carolina rally, the would-be president and the wannabe First Lady began a premature celebration. The senator had one last appearance to make, a late-afternoon address in the central square of Southern Village, a planned community organized around the shops and restaurants on the square. Our national headquarters was on the second floor of a building that overlooked the retail area. Outfitted with an amphitheater and lights, the square was the perfect backdrop for a rally.

As crowds gathered at Southern Village, I went to the airport to meet the senator and Rielle as they arrived on Fred's jet. They got into my Suburban and shared sips from a plastic water bottle filled with Sauvignon Blanc. As we approached the square, we saw thousands of people gathered in front of a bandstand. Flags fluttered behind the stage. High-powered projectors threw images of stars onto the buildings. Disney couldn't have done a better job.

Knowing that Mrs. Edwards would be waiting for him, the senator had me drop him in a parking garage, where he could take an elevator upstairs. Before he got out, he leaned over to me and said, "Don't let Rielle get close to Elizabeth."

I then parked and walked to the office with Rielle. To say that everyone noticed Rielle as we walked into the busy campaign office would be an understatement. With sunglasses perched on her bleached blond hair, tight designer jeans, and a black sweater, she looked like she was taking a meeting in Hollywood, not attending a rally in North Carolina. Everyone else was dressed in more businesslike clothes and had the pale, drawn look of exhaustion that comes with working for a presidential campaign. Eyes followed her as she turned toward the restroom, and just before she reached the door, it swung open and Elizabeth Edwards came out.

For a moment, the two women were face-to-face. Rielle knew instantly that she was staring at John Edwards's wife. Mrs. Edwards glanced past her, caught my eye, and quickly realized that this must be "the other woman." A look of pain flashed across her face, but as she turned to go look for her husband, that pain seemed to turn to anger.

Out on the square, the Del McCoury Band struck up some trademark bluegrass and entertained the crowd gathered to celebrate the start of the campaign. Away from view, Elizabeth Edwards confronted her husband about the glowing blond woman who had obviously arrived with him from the road. However, they couldn't discuss the issue at length because people were all around and they were about to go onstage.

When the Edwardses finally emerged from their private backstage hell, Mrs. Edwards looked stricken. At center stage, political consultant Mudcat Saunders, veteran of the 2004 campaign, took the microphone and declared himself a "redneck from Virginia Tech, a Hokie who is a recovering alcoholic." He offered a little testimony about his struggle with alcoholism and how John and Elizabeth Edwards had given him a second chance. Eventually, he worked his way to an introduction of "the next president of the United States," and the senator instantly transformed his demeanor and walked forward to accept the acclaim of thousands. (Both of the Edwardses had this ability to shift instantaneously from private rage or anguish to public benevolence, and I had seen it so many times that I no longer took much notice.)

The hour was late, and the weather was cold. Edwards's brief talk covered health care, the war in Iraq, global warming, and the need for change in Washington. He finished with a call for everyone to roll up their sleeves, dig into their pockets, and wear out some shoe leather to win an election that "isn't about me," said the senator, "but is about all of us."

As he finished and the cheering reached a crescendo, no one who looked at the scene could have guessed that the senator's marriage was coming apart at the seams because his wife had just stumbled upon his mistress, who stood mere yards away. All anyone in the crowd knew was that by announcing early, John Edwards had landed the first punch in the fight for the nomination. Conventional wisdom held that Hillary Clinton was such a polarizing figure that she could never win a general election. Barack Obama was so little known that he seemed to be positioning himself to take the second seat on the ticket, as candidate for vice president of a future White House run. This left John Edwards as the logical and likely choice.

That night, I drove the Edwardses home in silence. The next day, I picked up the senator at his house for another drive to the airport. When he settled into his seat, he said, "What the hell was Mudcat talking about last night?" It was a nice icebreaker, and we both laughed. Then he told me that all the previous night, Mrs. Edwards had shouted, cried, and refused to stop until the senator told her about Rielle and promised to fire her. (I knew something about this because Heather, the nanny, had phoned me to say she was concerned about the arguing and how it was affecting Jack and Emma Claire.)

What I wouldn't find out for many months was that the senator had told Elizabeth that although he had indulged in a "one-night" fling with Rielle, in recent weeks she had become *my* mistress! And that's why we were together as we arrived at Southern Village.

Nine

CLOWN NIGHT AT THE
GOLDEN CORRAL

I f you're not from the South, where these places seem to be on every other corner, the first thing to know about the Golden Corral buffet is the price. Our family of five could eat there for about thirty dollars. The second thing is clown night. Once a week, the management at our local corral brought in a clown to work the dining room. With the kids gaping at his makeup and big rubber shoes and occupied with balloon animals, the clown gave weary mothers and fathers a chance to breathe.

On a clown night in early 2007, Cheri and I balanced the nutritional hazards of turning our kids loose on a pile of fried and sugary food against our need for a little stress relief and decided the rewards outweighed the risk. After we worked our way through the line and found a table, my cell phone began to ring. A check of the screen told me the call was from Mrs. Edwards. All I had to do was show it to Cheri, and she just sighed with acceptance and glanced toward the door, which let me know I could take it outside.

I answered the phone as I walked through the dining room, past the clown and tables filled with families like mine. The first words I heard were, "Hey, Andrew, how are you? How are the kids?"

The pleasant opening made me wary. She hadn't been nice to me since the PlayStation 3 conflict. She told me the refrigerator at the new house had been acting up, and I thought that perhaps she wanted me to call the repairman again. But as I stepped outside onto the sidewalk and leaned against the wall, her tone changed abruptly. She said that she and the senator had been discussing Rielle Hunter and that while she believed she knew the entire story, she wanted to clear up a few details with me.

Once I agreed to talk, Mrs. Edwards turned from friendly to prosecutorial. The interrogation began with questions about Rielle's visits to her home. She knew that Rielle had been there to interview the senator's parents and the children, but she had spent hours reviewing the tape handed over when Rielle was fired and couldn't find the stuff shot at her house. This only made her more suspicious, and she wanted to know how many other times I had helped this "other woman" invade her sanctuary, to sit on her furniture and enjoy her food and drink.

As my mind raced, I couldn't think of any other time I may have transported Rielle to the estate, but the shock of being questioned made me feel uncertain and confused. Whenever the senator was home, I might bring half a dozen parties a day to see him. Rielle could have been in one of those groups. But I didn't think this had happened more than once, and I told her so.

"Andrew," she replied, "I *know* you are lying."

Here she was acting like a detective, using the old technique of suggesting she possessed some kind of incriminating evidence when in fact she did not. It worked a little, making me scour my memory for something I may have forgotten. But then I got a little angry. After all I had done for the Edwards family, I didn't deserve to be pushed into a triangular drama with the senator and his wife. (He should be answering those questions, not me.) When I stood my ground, she applied one last bit of pressure: "And I have Heather standing here beside me. I know you are lying to me, and if you don't tell the truth to me, I'll have John fire you." When I repeated my answer, insisting I was telling her the truth, she abruptly hung up the phone.

The call gave me something to discuss with Cheri when I got back to the table. She was accustomed to hearing about my difficulties with the

Edwardses and had grown bored with their complaints about household problems like broken refrigerators. However, Rielle Hunter had introduced a new level of drama and danger into the Edwards saga, which made any scene involving her far more compelling. At the table, we agreed that Mrs. Edwards's investigation was not over and that Rielle was not going to go away. Of course, we didn't know that Mrs. Edwards believed I had become Rielle's lover after her husband saw the error of his ways.

After dinner, we went home and I decided to get on the treadmill to work off some of the mashed potatoes I'd eaten. I was still angry when our home phone rang. I checked the caller ID and answered because it was Mrs. Edwards again. Cheri, who had glanced at a phone in another room and knew who was on the line, came to listen to my side of the conversation. It was a good move, because this was one of the few times that my end of an exchange with Elizabeth Edwards was worth hearing.

She began by saying that she thought I hadn't been given a full opportunity to "tell the truth" and now she was willing to listen. After I asked whether she wanted the truth or "what you want to hear," she opted for the straight story and I launched into a minor diatribe.

"Mrs. Edwards, I love you like a big sister, and I love your husband like a big brother," I continued, "and after ten years of me working for you, for you to treat me like this is wrong, utterly wrong."

She was not impressed. As far as she was concerned, the real issue was her "thirty-year marriage" and not "about you working for us" as a staff person. "Andrew, you are *not* family. You *work* for us. Nothing more. You get paid for all you do."

For a decade, I had heard the senator and Mrs. Edwards use that word— "staff"—to dismiss certain people as if they were interchangeable parts. Hearing it used to describe me was too much. "I don't do the things I do because I get paid," I answered. "I've changed your kids' diapers. I helped your parents move twice. That's not what a staff person does. You take advantage of people. You chew them up and spit them out. I've done everything in my power to help you and your family because I believe in you and your goals."

My resistance and anger only made her come on stronger. She said that her husband wore "blinders" when he looked at me, not noticing that I had worked my way into a tight relationship with the family so I could exploit them. "Andrew, you hold us close so you can advance yourself."

"What do I get for changing your kids' diapers?" I asked. "What do I get out of helping your parents move?"

After telling me that household chores were part of my job, Mrs. Edwards said I had "thirty seconds to tell the truth" or I would be fired. This time I was the one who ended the call. As I clicked off the phone, I turned to see Cheri staring in amazement. "Fuck her," I said. "It looks like I no longer work for the Edwardses."

"Yeah, right," said Cheri. She didn't believe they would let me go.

Later I thought about the commitment we had made to build a new house (I had really forced that decision on her) and about our kids and their needs, like health insurance. Then the senator called to ask about my argument with his wife. "Did you just yell at Elizabeth?" he asked. I told him I had and explained why. He laughed in amazement and then asked, "You said that to Elizabeth?" He then told me how the storm had developed.

According to the senator, once Rielle was dismissed, Elizabeth demanded that campaign manager Jonathan Prince gather all the videos Rielle had shot. She then locked herself in her crafts room to review them hour by hour, and then day by day, coming out only to use the bathroom and/or fetch a Diet Coke. She interrogated Heather, who told her about Rielle interviewing Jack and Emma Claire at the mansion. She knew that if all of the work had been turned over, she should be able to see this footage. None of it was in the collection she received. In fact, she saw nothing at all from the house, not even the interviews Rielle did with Wallace and Bobbi Edwards. Knowing that Rielle had held out this material made her furious, and she pored over the videos again and again, devoting days to the work, believing she saw things that suggested that a great deal of potentially incriminating evidence had been withheld.

During this time, Mrs. Edwards also focused on me in her effort to track down information about Rielle, including her phone number. She left me a voice mail saying, "Andrew, I am tired of playing games with you. I want every single number, every single person. And if you DARE, you can call John."

As the senator discussed all of this with me, I could imagine his wife scanning for clues and then shaking with rage as she confronted him. Now I understood her fury. He said, "Let me take care of Elizabeth," and he repeated that he needed me and would be terribly hurt if I walked away at the start of his big push for the White House.

What he didn't say was that I was the only person in the world who knew everything about Rielle Hunter and his marriage, and he needed me to keep the charade going. The knowledge made me the one friend he would open his heart to and the one person besides Rielle who could hurt him the most. Years of service had also earned me a place as his most trusted adviser, and at the time no one was able to raise more money for him from big donors.

Taken together, everything I could do for John Edwards and everything I knew about him made him more loyal to me—a rare switch in roles—than he had ever been. I could hear a hint of desperation in his voice, and I knew that if I stayed working for his political action committee, I would be able to stop doing domestic chores at his house and enjoy more autonomy at work than I had ever known. I agreed to stay on. And from that day forward, my status changed. In the campaign office, people began making fewer demands on me, but they also began to shun me. I found out this happened because Mrs. Edwards had called many of the people I worked with and informed them that I wasn't to be trusted or included. I was soon banned from the house I had helped them build, and she stopped letting her children play with mine.

Elizabeth Edwards was able to control what happened at our office because for all intents and purposes she was the manager of the campaign. She set the strategy, determined the senator's political positions, approved the schedule, and made all the key hires. (In most cases, she picked people with little or no experience.) There was a philosophy behind this approach. She and the senator believed that they were smarter than the big-time consultants and that they were going to pioneer a new kind of campaign that would use the Internet in a huge way. Instead of old speechwriters and pollsters, they focused on hiring the hottest Web gurus they could find. (The key one was Matthew Gross, who had been a big influence on Howard Dean's 2004 campaign.) Elizabeth was right about the World Wide Web, but as far as I could tell she was wrong about the way she used these fellows. She told them what to do and then second-guessed them. They were afraid to discuss issues with her because of her temper.

Ironically, the Web guys were very competent in their specialty and would have delivered the innovations Elizabeth wanted had they been managed properly. Similarly, the majority of the players who filled out the 2008 Edwards roster were smart and effective despite their inexperience. But in her rush to bypass so-called party hacks, Mrs. Edwards had failed to bring in people with real passion for John Edwards and for the issues at the core of his campaign. In 2004, we may have been a bit behind the curve when it came to technology, but we were deeply committed to the cause, and Nick Baldick was an assertive and effective manager. This time around, we had no strong manager and seemed to be reactive instead of proactive.

John Edwards, however, was far improved as a candidate, willing to outwork everyone in the field and burning with real intensity. Everyone else felt the desire to win and harbored hope for a victory but made the effort as if it were a job instead of a crusade. I still recognized that John Edwards was a charismatic campaigner and that he was right about the issues. But my enthusiasm was flagging, and I was being shunted aside. I used the freedom I enjoyed to set my own agenda and schedule, and to focus on raising money from donors. I was able to enjoy my family more, and pay attention to our dream house project.

The acreage Cheri and I had purchased on a forested hilltop in Chapel Hill represented a dream come true for me. Before any construction started, we got a camper and set it up on the site so we could enjoy weekends in the woods with the kids. On Super Bowl Sunday 2007, we held a big party where we set up a television outside, made a big bonfire, and laughed and hollered into the night. That party was more fun than I could recall having in a long time, and the vision of our home—all stone, glass, and natural wood—rising among the pines gave me a powerful sense of optimism about the future.

Visits to the land became even more important for me and the rest of the family after we moved out of Lake Wheeler and into a rental in Southern Village. The new place was painted such an odd shade of violet that the kids took to calling it "the purple mansion," and everything about the move was painful. For one thing, it required us to adjust to living in a space less than half the size of our old place. For another, when the time came to make the transfer, I was busy with the campaign and unable to drive because of the DWI conviction. Cheri's mom and dad came from Illinois to lend a hand, and they did it all without me. At one point, her mom was so angry about this that she literally turned her back on me. I couldn't blame her, really; I was fed up with me, too.

The cramped space, the circumstances of the move, and the ugly paint weren't the only reasons for our urge to flee for the trailer on the hilltop whenever we could. The previous occupants of the mansion had been pet lovers, and soon after we settled in and turned on the heat, we discovered that the whole place smelled of cat pee. Constant cleaning and deodorizing helped, but the scent never really went away. You would have wanted to escape, too. Our cat Pepper certainly did. A rambunctious boy we had adopted in 1999, he went outside as much as possible, and on a fateful night soon after we moved in, he was killed by a car. I found his body along a busy highway and rushed to dispose of it before the kids saw him.

Cheri and the kids spent far more time in the purple mansion than I did, because every day I walked over to the Southern Village town square office to work. This convenience was in contrast with the demands the move made on Cheri. The kids remained in their school in Raleigh, and she drove them back and forth for three months. She also brought them there for sports after school and visits with friends. She must have felt as though she spent her life on the road.

My workdays were devoted to chasing donations, fielding calls from the senator, and solving certain problems. Once, when he was on the road, he called sounding very upset and explained that he had lost the Outward Bound pin that Wade had received before he died. (Edwards had worn it to public events since 1998.) Many staff members dropped what they were doing to search in every vehicle or room he had occupied in the last twenty-four hours. When they failed to find it, we bought a new one from the organization, but it was a new design and did not resemble Wade's pin.

Aside from managing the senator's personal crises, I dealt with inquiries from colleagues who knew I had Edwards's ear and understood him better than anyone else. For example, when John Davis reported sighting Rielle on the trail, I reassured him that although she was no longer on the payroll, she and the senator were probably just friends and there was nothing to worry about.

Rielle's travel arrangements required fancy footwork, and here my experience as a campaign aide came in handy. When I knew where the senator was staying, I made reservations in my own name, faxed copies of my credit card and state identification card, and told the hotel staff that my "wife" would be checking in on my account. This ploy allowed Rielle to get into the hotel and wait for the senator, who then called and signaled her to come to his suite. Rielle would leave before the aides came to get the senator at the start of the workday.

The routine worked perfectly except for on one occasion in Florida, when the campaign bus left a swanky resort where the senator had spent the night so early that Rielle was still in the suite when he departed. She planned to go back to the room I had arranged for "Mrs. Young" but decided to get into the shower first. That's when she heard pounding on the door. She got out, wrapped herself in a towel, and looked through the peephole to see someone from the campaign. (The staffer had a key card, but fortunately Rielle had fastened the security chain on the door.) Afraid to respond, she hid in the bathroom and called the senator on the Bat-phone. When the senator heard what was going on, he called me.

Accustomed as I was to having the phone ring at all hours with emer-gency requests from John Edwards, it still rattled me when the phone rang before the alarm clock, and it took me a few seconds to wake up. The sena-tor, who was calling from the campaign bus, where he was surrounded by staff and press, spoke in an upbeat voice—as if nothing were wrong—but his breathing sounded panicked, and I could tell he was faking it.

"Our friend is having a problem," he said. "Can you give her a call right now?"

I soon understood what was wrong. Someone from the staff had gone to the room with a key card to make sure the senator had not left behind any confidential papers. This was standard operating procedure, and whoever it was had been surprised to find the door bolted from the inside. I told him I would fix it, and as he hung up I immediately heard from Rielle. There were now two security guards and three campaign aides, including my old assistant, banging on the door. Rielle was scared, but also excited and gig-gly. (I think she wanted to get caught.) She agreed to tell them she needed to get dressed and would open the door in a few minutes.

While Rielle dressed, I called the hotel, which was the Westin Diplomat Resort & Spa in Hollywood, Florida. Using my best presidential campaign aide voice, I asked for and got connected to the manager. "I had an old friend drive through the night to deliver confidential papers to the senator this morning," I explained. "I told her that she could take advantage of the room—since it was paid for—and enjoy the resort after he left. If you want to check out who I am, call the campaign. They'll confirm who I am."

Five minutes later, the manager called me back and agreed to call his security men on the radio and have them leave the hallway. But this still left the Edwards staffers who were upstairs and wanted an explanation. I called Rielle again, then had her open the door a crack and, since Mrs. Edwards had turned my former assistant against me, I told her to hand the phone to one of the other staffers. When he got on I said, "Who the hell is this?" with as much authority and impatience as I could muster.

With my opponent back on his heels, I said, "This is Andrew Young." I then said that all he needed to know was that the woman in the room was someone I had sent with confidential documents because every call I had made the previous night had gone unanswered by staff people, who were out partying. (This was an assumption that turned out to be true.) "I had to get one of my friends to do your damn job, so leave her alone."

The bluff worked and they left Rielle alone. I then instructed her to pack up and call me as she left the room. She did as I told her, and I kept her on the phone to calm her as she walked down the hallway, rode the elevator, crossed through the lobby, and went outside to a cab stand. She noticed the Edwards staffers who had come to the door of the room outside the hotel, but they saw her on the phone and didn't intercept her. She breathed a huge sigh of relief and then started laughing as the cab departed the hotel, with her aboard, safe and still secret. I called the senator and told him the crisis was over.

Senator Edwards thanked me up and down on the day I got Rielle out of the Florida hotel, but the next time I saw him, he'd developed a case of amnesia about this event. Having had my daytime driving privileges restored, I had picked him up at the airport, following our usual routine. I had continued to tease him by putting down the armrest. He looked at me and said, "Why do you keep doin' that?"

I stayed silent as he handed me the Batphone, enjoyed a sip of wine, and sighed with relief. I then casually mentioned the tight scrape we had just survived. He turned to me and with a perfectly straight face said, "I don't know what you are talking about. Rielle wasn't in Florida."

I looked at him, amazed, and said something about how he must be joking.

Of course Rielle was in Florida with him. She had been discovered by the staff, and I had come up with a brilliant scheme to explain why there was a woman in the shower of his suite. The senator looked at me blankly, repeated that "Rielle was never in Florida," and asked me how I could say such a thing.

We were hurtling down the interstate, and since I had to keep my attention on the road, I didn't stare into his eyes directly. But I could tell from his tone of voice that he truly believed what he was saying. I decided that he was either the best liar in the world or he was having some sort of psychological episode. My phone records showed more than thirty calls with him, Rielle, and the Westin on the day of this incident. Clearly, I could prove to him that something big had happened that day. But I decided to drop the subject.

The way I saw it, Rielle presented a problem with three possible outcomes. If Edwards ended the relationship, she would probably go to the press, reveal the affair, and, I assumed, supply enough solid evidence to make the story stick. Since he had presented himself to the country as the handsome and brilliant man of the people who was standing by his wife through her illness, news of an affair would end Senator Edwards's political career. If he followed the second option, he could keep seeing Rielle and, if Elizabeth found out, risk a divorce that would expose him in the same way. The difference here was that Mrs. Edwards's desire to live in the White House was as great as, if not greater than, his. She had already accepted his personal betrayals as part of the price for the real estate at 1600 Pennsylvania Avenue. The third option would be to continue to see Rielle and hope to keep Mrs. Edwards in the dark until after the election. Callous as it was, the senator chose this last option and pursued the presidency with all the energy he could muster while talking to me about how much easier life would be without Elizabeth. I thought all of this was repulsive, but since she had forced me out of her life, I felt there was nothing I could do about it.

Ironically, once the senator was relaxed about discussing Rielle with me, he frequently aired the same kinds of complaints about her that he had expressed about Mrs. Edwards in the past. He said Rielle was overly demanding and emotional, and he frequently called her "crazy." But just as he counted on his sometimes "crazy" wife for counsel and support, he depended on "crazy" Rielle's input and advice. Along with her commitment to do everything and anything he requested as part of her spiritual mission to see him become a world leader, she offered political guidance, comments on strategy, and criticisms on every aspect of his performance from wardrobe to cadence. Although it came mixed with horoscope readings and other New Age mumbo jumbo, the senator genuinely valued Rielle's input. He called her before every debate or major public appearance and generally called her afterward for a critique. I know, because I was the go-between who used three-way calling to connect them so no record of Rielle's number would appear on his phone.

Strange as it may sound for a man raised a Southern Baptist, I think the senator was open to the idea that Rielle might have a special power to see into the future—a startling number of powerful people believe in such things—and that her age and social background meant she could speak for a part of the electorate he wanted to reach. Finally, in listening to her and including her in the campaign, he rewarded her for accepting the mistress role and staying in the background. She clearly loved playing secret adviser to a future president, and he fed her feeling of importance by having me send her the daily schedule, clippings from the national press, and important memos so they could discuss them. Regardless of her flakiness, she did provide an interesting and creative perspective on his campaign.

Besides information, Rielle needed money. She had worked in the past as a spiritual adviser, but now believed her life's purpose was serving John Edwards. The senator wanted to keep her happy but had difficulty getting money to her. He once gave her his bank card, but when Mrs. Edwards saw that a large sum had been withdrawn in New York when her husband was in California, she sent out an alarm. He was able to make some kind of excuse to cover up this incident, but from that point on he asked me to handle Rielle's finances. I used my credit card to book hotel rooms and airline flights for Rielle. I even gave him cash to give her—a few hundred dollars at a time—when I took him to the airport for outbound flights. He promised I would be repaid when a wealthy benefactor was recruited to cover these costs or when Mrs. Edwards died.

"I'll take care of you, Andrew," he said. "You know I'm good for it."

Elizabeth Edwards's cancer had hung over her family and the senator's various organizations ever since it was discovered in 2004. At that time, it was described as a metastatic form of breast cancer that is almost always fatal, and the senator talked about the future in the bleakest terms. But three years after it was discovered and her treatment was begun, Mrs. Edwards seemed as robust as ever. She was so active that I sometimes forgot she had been diagnosed.

In many ways, the senator acted as if she were gone already. In March he arranged to celebrate Rielle's birthday at the Hotel Fort Des Moines while he campaigned in Iowa. When the date arrived, I got an urgent call from John Davis, who was with him. The plans had been changed, he said, and the boss was coming home. He gave me the time to pick him up at the private hangar at Raleigh-Durham International and warned me that the senator was "very upset." He didn't know what had happened, but he knew it was bad.

At the airport, Edwards skipped the usual handshakes he offered the ground crew and hustled to my Suburban. He didn't say a word until we had left the airport proper and had merged onto the interstate. "Elizabeth's cancer is back," he said, "and it's bad."

The senator looked out the window and cried as he told me that Elizabeth's cancer had spread to her bones. He told me she had heard one of her ribs break as she was moving a box "and cussing you out, Andrew, for putting it in the wrong place." Publicly, she would say the fracture happened when Senator Edwards had hugged her too hard. I wondered what she thought she gained from this version of events.

Imaging done at the hospital had turned up a fracture on one side of

Mrs. Edwards's rib cage and a mass on the other. A biopsy had shown a malignancy in one rib, and further tests indicated the cancer had spread to other areas of the body. As he talked about his wife's condition, the senator used words like "fatal" and "terminal" and seemed to be genuinely grief-stricken. But then, as we reached a point halfway to his house, the conversation turned to the campaign and he made it clear that they both wanted it to continue. Within days they agreed that this diagnosis would generate positive publicity after frustrating months when the press ignored him. They actually believed the cancer would give the senator's poll numbers a boost.

From a coldly political perspective, they were correct. If people believed the campaign was intended to serve others, the brave pursuit of a victory despite the cancer would seem heroic. Anyone else whose spouse had received a death sentence diagnosis might decide to chuck all current plans and devote the time to a sail around the world or anything else his or her heart desired. But the White House was what the Edwardses desired most, and they weren't going to give up the dream just because of a fatal illness. Instead, they planned to bring them on the campaign trail so the family could be together as much as possible. (They would be "home-schooled" along the way, with lessons taught from books and trips to museums and historic sites wherever they traveled.)

As we exited the interstate and turned west toward Chapel Hill, the senator recalled that Rielle was waiting for him in Iowa. He used my cell phone to call her and explained why he would not be there to celebrate her birthday. When he finished going through his wife's diagnosis and describing how it would be revealed to the press, he paused to let her respond. She cussed him out so loudly that I could hear almost every word. He let her complain and then kept saying he was sorry until we approached the long driveway that led to his house. The senator repeatedly tried to end the call and finally asked me to pull over since we were near his home, but Rielle wouldn't stop talking. After the senator finished placating Rielle and ended the call, we then went up the drive, and I let him out. Before he went inside, he told me to send Rielle some flowers but to leave the name John off the card.

The Edwardses told the world about the recurrence of her cancer at a packed press conference conducted in Chapel Hill at the Carolina Inn, a graceful old place made of soft red brick where they had held their wedding reception in 1977. Mrs. Edwards explained how she had broken her rib—the senator joked, "Actually, I was beating her"—and then recounted how her doctor had said there was no reason for her to give up the campaign. She also said that her treatment would consist of a less debilitating type of chemotherapy that could put the cancer into remission and be used again and again "for the rest of my life."

After watching this performance, most people believed that Elizabeth Edwards was riddled with cancer and not long for this world. (Cheri and I thought she might live weeks or a few months at best.) At headquarters, where many people owed their jobs to her, talk of her courage and strength dominated conversations, and I heard more than one person say, "We should try to win it for Elizabeth."

Outside of the campaign, the response to their decision to keep on with the quest was mostly positive. A few criticized the Edwardses for their ambition, but in the main they were honored for their courage and forthrightness. Frank Rich of *The New York Times* would even publish a column titled "Elizabeth Edwards for President." Others cheered the open way they were dealing with the illness and said they were grateful that the news reports put breast cancer awareness on the public agenda, which might motivate more women to perform self-exams and go to the doctors themselves.

On the Saturday after they announced Mrs. Edwards's cancer had returned, health care was the focus of a seven-candidate forum sponsored by the Service Employees International Union in Las Vegas. Senator Edwards mentioned his wife's illness in the course of presenting the most complete prescription for fixing the health care system anyone offered. Compared with Barack Obama, who hemmed and hawed and never offered specifics when asked to cite his priorities, Edwards made a brilliant case that included honest talk about how his plan would require raising taxes. As he made this point, he added, "I think it's really important, particularly given what's happened in the last six or seven years in this country, that the president of the United States be honest with the American people."

In fact, he was being honest about the things he considered to be the public's business, like taxes and health care, even as he maintained an elaborate fiction when it came to his personal life and the image he projected. Many politicians have taken this approach and said that the ends justified the means. In other words, the illusions they projected were merely the kind of advertising that is required in the age of mass media. Few mortals, and even fewer with the kind of narcissistic drive required to run for president, could really be as upright and decent as the public expects. Similarly, the unrealistic expectations of the press and the public discourage many qualified people from running for office.

A small but telling example of the art of political deception could be seen in the suit Senator Edwards wore for the Las Vegas union event. As he prepared to depart for the debate, he had realized that the label inside the coat read "Made in Italy," because, in fact, he loved expensive Italian suits and wore them routinely. Trouble is, a union crowd is likely to harbor a wiseacre who will ask a politician if he's wearing an American, union-stitched suit. When he thought of this possibility, the senator asked me about the label on my jacket—"Made in USA"—and had me take his to a tailor, where the tag from my coat was switched for the one in his. After the debate he said with some anger that he was disatisfied with the tailor's work. He played a video of the debate and pointed out a wrinkle where the label was installed.

If other candidates haven't switched labels in a suit, they have done comparable things to avoid embarrassment or promote themselves. Everyone who works at a high level in a campaign knows it goes on and goes along for the good of the candidate or, if you really believe in him or her, for the good of the country. On the day after the health care forum, John Edwards told the audience of *60 Minutes* that he was continuing with his run for the White House because he had "a responsibility to this country." In other words, he was so sure that America needed his leadership that he simply had to stay in the race. Mrs. Edwards agreed and explained that in the time she had lived with cancer, she had learned to accept and even live with the prospect of her death. When Katie Couric pressed her for a more complete explanation, Mrs. Edwards said:

> You know, you really have two choices here. I mean, either you push forward with the things that you were doing yesterday or you start dying. That seems to be your only two choices. If I had given up everything that my life was about—first of all, I'd let cancer win before it needed to. You know, maybe eventually it will win. But I'd let it win before I needed to.

It was a good answer, and for the next few weeks the Edwardses offered a version of it in a series of interviews and at campaign stops. The attention they received was so broad, and lasted so long, that media commentators recognized it as a national phenomenon. Howard Kurtz of *The Washington Post* noted that John Edwards couldn't get on *60 Minutes* with his proposal for health care, but the cancer story "mesmerized people who don't give a fig about politics." Polls taken after the publicity about Mrs. Edwards's cancer showed that her husband was finally gaining ground on Hillary Clinton and Barack Obama. On the road, Mrs. Edwards drew big crowds and loud cheers. In Des Moines, she went to a TV station to do a live interview via satellite with Larry King as a solo act. In that performance, she was a far cry from the nervous lady who sat next to Teresa Heinz Kerry to speak to Lesley Stahl in 2004. She was confident and relaxed, and after it was over I heard people say she should be running for the United States Senate.

Rielle watched with envy as Mrs. Edwards became a star. With her growing popularity, she was able to stand in for her husband and double the amount of ground the campaign could cover in a day. But as she expanded the reach of the organization, she also put more stress on the staff, most of whom were young and inexperienced. Although I continued to work as a fund-raiser, Mrs. Edwards had told the people in charge of the day-to-day campaign to take away all my responsibilities and to keep me away from her husband and her house.

I knew she was angry because she believed I had helped the senator communicate with Rielle. (I still didn't know the senator had told her I was carrying on an affair with Rielle and thereby endangering her husband's career.) Her fear that something was going on was well-founded, of course, because I had kept the senator's secrets in the past and I was continuing to help him stay in touch with his onetime camera girl. For months I had been in charge of the Batphone. He kept it with him on the road and then gave it to me when he returned. It then became my job to sneak it back onto the campaign plane and into the pocket of the seat in front of his before he departed again. Security at the airport made this a difficult job, and one time I actually raced off the plane and out of sight as Elizabeth was bringing him by car to the waiting aircraft.

Because she identified me with her husband's infidelity, but also knew I remained one of his trusted assistants, Mrs. Edwards obsessed over what I knew and what I may have done. She called me over and over again, demanding information I wouldn't give her. If I didn't answer, she left angry messages. At various times she accused me of lying, cheating, and even stealing from her household. In furious fights, she insisted her husband fire me, which he couldn't do because he needed me to take care of Rielle. Of course I hadn't taken anything from her family, and by pushing me out of campaign operations and putting untested people in charge, she set the stage for mistakes and mishaps.

For example, until Mrs. Edwards barred me from the campaign, I had managed many of the day-to-day expenses the senator incurred, including his haircuts, which were more of an issue than you might imagine. Naturally thick and lustrous, his hair was a fixation with him. He insisted on using just one kind of shampoo—HairTec Thick & Strong Shampoo for

Fine, Fragile Hair—which Mrs. Edwards bought by the case. His hair also had a tendency to grow in a way that made him look like Opie Taylor on the old *Andy Griffith Show*. A gifted barber could make him look mature and presidential, and when the senator found one with this skill, he was willing to pay whatever it cost to obtain his services. In 2006 his favorite was Joe Torrenueva, a Beverly Hills stylist who charged between three hundred dollars and five hundred dollars per appointment.

For years, I had used my credit cards or the Edwardses' personal credit cards to pay for the senator's personal items so that they wouldn't be charged to the campaign and then turn up in the public reports filed with the Federal Election Commission. Political opponents and news reporters scoured these documents as they were submitted each quarter, hoping to see something juicy in the spending. The senator's pricey haircuts would certainly catch the eye of any journalist interested to see if the man who was the champion of the poor was a spendthrift. I made sure that no one ever knew about them. When the new, inexperienced staff got the job of arranging for the senator's personal on-the-road needs, they pushed two bills for four-hundred-dollar haircuts through the normal campaign channels, and the payments were included in the big public quarterly report submitted to the FEC.

The revelation of the four-hundred-dollar haircuts, which was discovered by the Obama campaign, would have been bruising for any candidate under any circumstances, but it was worse for Senator Edwards because of his antipoverty focus and because of a video on YouTube that showed him having makeup applied and fussing over his hair to the tune of "I Feel Pretty" as sung by Julie Andrews. For a few weeks the "Pretty" video, which went viral at the start of spring, was one of the most viewed political items on the Internet, and it revived a mean-spirited line of attack that officials in the Bush White House had devised to use against John Edwards in the 2004 campaign.

Back then, Maureen Dowd of *The New York Times* made public the Bush team's decision to refer to Edwards as the "Breck Girl" and emasculate him by playing on his boyish good looks. Dowd has a habit of using gender issues to attack people, often suggesting something's wrong with any man showing so-called feminine traits. In this case, she gave currency to the Bush rhetoric, which just happened to be accurate.

Unstated, but always part of the context when it came to their public image, was the idea that John Edwards was actually prettier than his wife. This was an issue inside their marriage, and it contributed to her insecurity and his roving. It was also an unstated factor in the campaign and in the minds of many women voters who found him attractive and were reassured that his attachment to Mrs. Edwards remained strong as she aged more rapidly than he did and cancer stole some of her beauty. He gained political capital by loving the real Elizabeth, no matter what age and childbirth and illness did to her body. He lost a little of it when he spent too much time and money attending to his hair. And as they both knew, he risked losing all of it if his relationship with Rielle Hunter became known. Since Mrs. Edwards assumed that I was responsible for keeping Rielle around, she connected me with the threat inherent in the haircut problem. I thought she should have realized that I had always protected the senator from similar unpleasant episodes and that this one arose because she had tried too hard to marginalize me. Mrs. Edwards also didn't know that my work for the senator was going to yield a remarkable offer of aid that would prove essential to keeping alive the senator's hope of becoming president and Mrs. Edwards's dream of being First Lady.

In the midst of the negative publicity, which forced Senator Edwards to tell the press he didn't know his haircuts were so expensive and confess the issue was "really embarrassing," a letter from our friend in Upperville, Virginia, landed on my desk. Written in delicate script on pale blue stationery, it was decorated with a sketch of a graceful tree with the Blue Ridge Mountains in the background.

As she wrote, Bunny Mellon was appalled by the treatment John Edwards was receiving. "I see jealousy coming from somewhere in this news report," she said, and then she volunteered to pay whatever expenses the senator incurred that could not be covered by the campaign, including the employment of a valet. She instructed me to simply send the bills to her attorney, Alex Forger, and rest assured that they would be paid.

Bunny had written the letter as she sat in the room of her disabled daughter, Eliza, something she did many afternoons, talking to her and conducting correspondence with prominent people all over the world. I was charmed to imagine her in her beautiful house, thinking up ways to use her fortune to make life a little easier for people she admired and believed in, like Senator Edwards. I remembered the story she had told of offering her plane to help Jackie Kennedy Onassis attend Martin Luther King Jr.'s funeral and how she had accompanied her on the trip to Atlanta, carrying baskets of food. This woman had been coming to the rescue of various people for four decades. This offer to Senator Edwards was just the latest expression of quiet support for those she believed to be worthy. Little did I know how much support he would soon require or how generous a kind lady in Virginia would be.

Ten

RIELLE

Heather North, the nanny, was one of the few people who knew what I knew about the Edwardses and Rielle Hunter, and there were times when she and I compared notes. These talks were part gossip and part mutual support, which we needed, considering the stress that comes with keeping secrets. We were both struck by the midlife crisis aspect of John Edwards's affair and how he had obviously found in Rielle someone who was his wife's opposite. A New Age drifter who made her own rules, Rielle was always working the "fun-and-single-blonde" angle. She was someone who offered sex, spiritual advice, or good company as you had a few drinks. Mrs. Edwards looked like who she was—a highly educated, middle-aged mother, cancer victim, and wife of thirty years.

As different as they were in style and background, Rielle and Mrs. Edwards were both ambitious and self-confident. Both were certain that John Edwards should be president and that if he was elected, the world would be a much better place. And they both believed in the power of their own insight and intuition. Mrs. Edwards followed hers to guide the campaign. Rielle relied on hers to advise the senator personally. Finally, they were both insecure about the future and the senator's true intentions. These feelings led Mrs. Edwards to try to push me out of John Edwards's life.

They led Rielle to depend on me to connect her to him. I was squarely in the middle.

On the day the senator went home to deal with the recurrence of his wife's cancer, Rielle called me at least half a dozen times to complain about spending her birthday alone. "He loves *me*," she would say, "and it's just not right that we're not together."

In the weeks that followed, Rielle seethed over the attention Mrs. Edwards received from the media, but she also celebrated the jump in the senator's poll numbers. We spoke every day, usually more than once. With his schedule in hand, Rielle was able to meet him in various hotels when he was campaigning without his wife. However, the rules of engagement, so to speak, had changed as Mrs. Edwards had become keenly aware of Rielle Hunter. She monitored call histories on phones (at least those she could locate) and called her husband many times a day when he was away. Mrs. Edwards also forbade hotel operators from transferring calls from women to his room and regularly changed his check-in pseudonym.

More concerned than ever about being caught, the senator required Rielle to be as furtive as possible. When he was in New York, she could no longer wait in the hotel lobby and then go up to his room. Instead, she had to hang out in a bar next door and hope to either catch sight of the entourage entering or wait to receive a cell phone call. During one of these stake-outs, she looked up to see John Davis, the body man, enter and take a seat at the counter, which was between her and the door. Panicked, Rielle ran to the restroom and hid. After a long wait, the woman who had served her a drink came to ask if she was all right. Rielle told her a tale about how she was hiding from one of the customers, and the kindly waitress let her slip out a back door.

The drama excited Rielle, as did the sense of power she felt as a secret insider with a direct line to a man who could become president of the United States. She followed his every move on the twenty-four-hour news channels and the Internet and spoke to him numerous times every day on the Batphone or via a three-way call. He felt calmed by Rielle and wanted to talk to her before every debate and major event. She believed her spiritual blessings were vital to his success. When she couldn't get through to him directly, because he was at home without the special phone or Elizabeth was around, she called me incessantly.

In late April, Rielle called and left me a message while she was watching a televised debate. It was the first to include all eight Democratic Party candidates. She seemed happy with the senator's performance until the end, when he was asked to name a person he considered a moral leader. After mentioning Jesus Christ and before naming his father, he said, "My wife, who I think is the finest human being I have ever known, is a source of great conscience for me." Over the phone, Rielle groaned and said that if Elizabeth Edwards was anyone's moral leader, "we're all going to hell."

Although it's difficult to say she showed a whole lot of conscience about the way she conducted herself (I never saw her troubled by doubt after she indulged in a tirade or fired a staffer), Mrs. Edwards was quick to criticize others for what she believed were displays of moral weakness or bad behavior. This trait was on full display when she publicly scolded Ann Coulter for lying about her husband.

The Coulter conflict arose after the right-wing commentator used the word *faggot* in connection with the senator and talked about how she wished he had been assassinated. Mrs. Edwards surprised her by calling into the Chris Matthews TV show *Hardball* and getting on the air to ask her to quit the personal attacks. It was good theater, but I didn't understand why a potential First Lady would engage in debate with an insult comic like Coulter. But influencing Coulter was not the point. Mrs. Edwards called the show on an impulse. It caught the senator and the campaign staff by surprise. She wanted to defend her husband, and her ever stronger performance as a campaigner had given her the standing and the courage to act.

Unfortunately, Mrs. Edwards's courage often empowered her to express frustration and anger in clumsy ways. In the call to *Hardball*, she was more emotional than reasoned, and she came off sounding like a scold. She was similarly off pitch when she gave an interview in which she complained about the media focus on Barack Obama and Hillary Clinton and the advantage minority status gave their campaigns.

"We can't make John black, we can't make him a woman," she said. "These things get you a lot of press . . . [and] fund-raising dollars."

These comments brought criticism from those who thought she was whining and found it awfully hard to work up sympathy for a white Southern man with enormous wealth and privilege. But like the *Hardball* call, they did energize Mrs. Edwards's more fervent supporters, who saw her as the spunky wife saying what needed to be said on behalf of the best candidate. Of course, they didn't know that even as she stood up for him, John Edwards was continuing to betray her and that the threat posed by the force of nature that was Rielle Hunter had already become much worse.

By May 2007, Rielle and I were in constant communication. I had never known a woman who needed more attention, but on the day I received four calls in the space of an hour, I knew something unusual was going on. The senator was traveling with his wife (no Batphone) and about to begin taping an interview with George Stephanopoulos of ABC News. Having deflected Rielle three times, I answered the fourth call feeling irritated and almost angry.

"Somebody better be dying or pregnant," I said.

"Nobody's dying," sobbed Rielle. She then threatened to go to the press with evidence of their affair—she was Camera Girl, and she had plenty of pictures—if I didn't find a way to connect her with Senator Edwards immediately.

The senator had told John Davis to always accept my calls, no matter where he was, and he was one of the few people in the campaign who had expressed suspicions about Rielle. He tried to brush me off, but I was adamant and said, "I'm not asking you, I'm telling you."

During a break in the taping, Davis managed to pull the senator aside and get him to call me from a private spot. I shouldn't have been startled by his initial response to what was happening—he asked me to "handle it"—since I had fixed a thousand problems for him in the past. This time I said, "I can't handle this one," and he agreed to talk to her.

Whatever he said kept Rielle quiet, temporarily. Later that day, cussing and barely under control, he would tell me that Rielle had long claimed she was physically unable to get pregnant and that since she was "a crazy slut" and they had an "open" relationship, he thought there was only a "one-in-three chance" that he could be the father of her baby. He told me she should get an abortion and asked me to help persuade her to do it.

The next time I spoke with Rielle, she said that the senator had told her to get an abortion. I am pro-choice, but when she asked me what I would do, I thought about my kids and said I wouldn't go through with an abortion. She talked about how she was a forty-two-year-old woman who wanted to have a child before she got too old. She also believed that the baby she was carrying—a combination of his intellectual brilliance and her spiritual superiority—was some kind of golden child, the reincarnated spirit of a Buddhist monk who was going to help save the world. There was no way she was going to have an abortion.

Instead, pregnant Rielle would require more attention and support than ever before, and this would cost a lot of money. Even though he possessed a fortune worth tens of millions of dollars, the senator had no way to access this money without his wife finding out. This problem had become especially acute in the months since Mrs. Edwards had learned about Rielle, and was complicated by the financial stress related to their new home.

For years the Edwardses had spent freely, but as they built their mansion, they realized that more money was going out than was coming in. First they accused their closest aides—including me—of abusing the access to funds they had granted us in order to help keep their various households going. Once these spending streams were stopped, they then imposed stricter accounting for their own expenses. Unable to sneak any cash out of this system, the senator asked me to pay for Rielle's silence. He suggested I draw on the profit Cheri and I had realized in the sale of our Lake Wheeler house, which was reserved for the new place. (He promised I would be re-paid.)

I had already covered some of Rielle's expenses, and as a minor player in the macho games of scheming, high-powered men, I think a part of me would have felt proud to say I was rich enough to offer the senator this fa-vor. But even as he asked me to use money that was, by rights, Cheri's as well as mine, the senator begged me to hide everything about Rielle from her. He asked this because he understood that what he was doing was shameful, and sensed that Cheri had never trusted him as I did. Of course, I couldn't do what he asked. I had already told Cheri everything. She was well aware of Rielle, and disapproved of the way the senator was putting his wife and children at risk. And now that Rielle was pregnant, this was obviously a long-term project and we didn't have the funds to support her lifestyle.

Once I was crossed off the list of potential donors, Edwards suggested David Kirby. The senator thought that Kirby owed him support because of all the big jury awards he had won for their firm, but Kirby did not agree. I suggested an appeal to Fred Baron, but the senator said, "Fred's got a big mouth, and he's too close to the Clintons." Finally we focused on Bunny Mellon, who had made it clear she would give Edwards money for extraneous expenses with no explanation required. Edwards called her, and "the Bunny money" began to flow. To make her feel rewarded for this aid, the senator stayed in touch by calling her from the road. In June, he called her from backstage in Manchester, New Hampshire, just prior to a nationally tele-vised candidates debate. (On that same evening, I was attending a function at my kids' school—it was "Spanish Night"—and the senator called demanding I help him contact Rielle. Cell phone reception was poor at the school, so I had to leave the event to facilitate a three-way call.)

Bunny's checks, written for many hundreds of thousands of dollars, were made as payments to her decorator, Bryan Huffman, so that she wouldn't have to offer an explanation to the professionals who handled her accounts. These funds (and the money that came from Fred Baron later) were gifts, entirely proper, and not subject to campaign finance laws. She did not know that the money was being used in part for Rielle. Bunny sent the checks to Bryan hidden in boxes of chocolate and with notes discussing her contributions to "the confederacy." Bryan sent them to me with notes of his own. One said, "A little table money," because the memo line indicated it was payment for an antique table. Another said, "For the rescue of America," which was how Bunny referred to the way she used her money on behalf of Democrats in general and John Edwards in particular. After I received each check, it was deposited in joint accounts I held with Cheri, to be used to keep Rielle happy and hidden from the media, Mrs. Edwards, and anyone who might divulge her existence. This was the arrangement the senator expected me to follow, so that he would have "plausible deniability."

In accepting the checks and responsibility for Rielle, I plunged myself, Cheri, and my kids into hot water. The temperature wasn't so high that it was uncomfortable, so we stayed in the pot. And like frogs that will remain submerged in a pot on a stove while an experimenter raises the temperature ever so slowly, we would stay in this situation far too long, enduring as each new demand increased the heat by a fraction of a degree. Unlike frogs, we would get out before it was too late. But looking back, I find it hard to believe that we didn't hop away on the day Rielle arrived at our house with photographers from the *National Enquirer* hot on her trail.

For months, Rielle had complained to me about how her boyfriend, now the father of her child, neglected her. She also talked to her "close friends," who she said would never betray her because of their "spiritual connections." One of these friends was *Newsweek* writer Jonathan Darman, who spoke with her on the phone from time to time and once had lunch with her. (She talked with him about having an affair with a very powerful man but wouldn't divulge his identity.) When I talked with her, Rielle requested my help with financial and emotional concerns and every once in a while threatened to go to the press and reveal the affair. Rielle was especially outraged on July 30 when the Edwardses marked their thirtieth anniversary by renewing their wedding vows and celebrating at Wendy's.

The event got extensive coverage from the media, including pictures in *People* magazine and a bit of fawning from Diane Sawyer of ABC-TV's *Good Morning America*.

Besides my having to deal with the senator's mistress, the summer brought new personal demands as the builder began work on our new house and we moved out of the smelly purple mansion and into a big, luxurious house owned by former UNC and NBA basketball player Eric Montross. I knew him, and when he told me he had been having trouble selling the place, we made a deal for a lease. The house was in a gated development called the Governors Club. It had four bedrooms, and the screened backyard gave our dog, Meebo, a great place to hang out. The only odd thing about the house was that all the furnishings—sink, shower, countertops, cabinets, and so on—had been built for someone seven feet tall.

In this time period, I was especially busy at work, which meant Cheri couldn't rely on me as she helped the kids adjust to new schools and a new neighborhood. She was driving hours every day to take care of my mom's second husband, Warren, a wonderful man whose health was deteriorating rapidly. Warren's decline and death took a terrible toll on my mom, and as I focused on helping her, the *National Enquirer*, notorious for revealing then presidential candidate Gary Hart's affair with Donna Rice in 1987, found Rielle in South Orange, New Jersey. On September 27, 2007, they confronted her at her friend Mimi Hockman's house, where she stayed when she wasn't on the road.

How did the *Enquirer* even know to start looking for Rielle Hunter? The answer to this question may never be known, but she would be a good person to ask. With all of her threats, she certainly had in mind a call to the media. Mimi Hockman would be another person to question. Inside the campaign there were no likely suspects, but the Internet had begun to buzz with innuendo. The most prominent source for speculation was Sam Stein of the Web site HuffingtonPost.com.

On the day before the photographers confronted her in New Jersey, Stein posted a report on his attempts to find and view the webisodes produced for the Edwards campaign. Once readily available online, they had suddenly disappeared. Stein couldn't locate the producer, Rielle Hunter, and his effort to find her company led him to Mimi Hockman, who answered his e-mail request for an interview with, "Nope. Not a chance." More digging brought Stein to an article about Rielle in a New Age magazine called *Breathe,* which said she was a "formerly hard-partying girl who claims that she found enlightenment."

Stein reported all he had discovered and the fact that he was given the runaround by the Edwards staff, especially Jonathan Prince, who also had suspicions about Rielle. Prince had offered implausible explanations for the disappearance of the videos, claimed that the campaign no longer had them, and then offered to let Stein view them, but only with Edwards's representatives in the room. Prince's handling inflamed the situation, and all the bobbing, weaving, and mystery allowed Stein to write in a way that made any reader imagine hanky-panky was involved. He ended with a quote from Edwards that said, "I've come to the conclusion I just want the country to see who I really am," and a quip of his own: "I'm still waiting to see." The senator was outraged by this and said that "Clinton is behind it" and that Bill and Hillary Clinton were friends with Stein and had urged him to write the article.

Given the number of people who saw Rielle on the campaign trail, staffers who suspected something was going on, and those—including Rielle—who could confirm the affair, it was no surprise that rumors had been swirling for months. According to the whispers, clean-cut John Edwards, who made an issue of morality, was stepping out on his cancer-stricken wife. The staff of the *Enquirer* almost certainly had the story staked out, and the Stein article could well have added the piece to the puzzle that brought them to Mimi Hockman's house.

Panicked, Rielle called me several times during the day, insisting I connect her with the senator. Now that Rielle was pregnant, I never had any trouble getting through to him. John Davis took my call, asking, "Can't it wait five minutes?" I told him no, and he pulled the senator away from whatever he was doing and gave him the phone. I told him the *Enquirer* was outside Rielle's house and patched him through to her. After he soothed her, he called me back and said he was afraid that Rielle was going to crack and go outside to meet the *Enquirer* team and tell all. She obviously needed to go someplace and hide, and according to the senator, she had no trustworthy friends or family to visit. The temporary solution, he decided, would be for her to come to stay behind the gates at the Governors Club with Cheri and me.

"This is bigger than any of us," he said, evoking the many causes—peace, health care, poverty, and so on—that he represented. This struck me as disingenuous and I really wasn't listening. I was thinking about what I was going to tell Cheri. We were both mourning my stepfather, and were about to fly to Shelter Island, New York, for his funeral. This wasn't going to go over well.

When I finally agreed with his plan, the senator said, "Andrew, nobody has ever done something like this for me. You are the best friend I ever had in the world." I put down the phone and walked into the kitchen to find Cheri. Her reaction was what you might expect.

"Are you kidding me?"

"We just have to deal with this. I know it's ridiculous. But it's not going to be for very long."

Cheri had seen so much crazy stuff where the Edwardses were concerned that she wasn't exactly surprised. Instead, she was angry and disgusted. But she trusted me enough to just shake her head in a weary way and say okay.

Rielle caught a flight on American Airlines and arrived at the Raleigh airport at about nine-thirty P.M. She came out of the terminal wearing tight jeans, sunglasses, and the long pink scarf that was her signature accessory. I drove her to the house in the four-wheel-drive convertible Jeep I had bought once Mrs. Edwards barred me from driving her husband and I no longer needed the Suburban. I had the top off, and Rielle complained about the rough ride all the way down Interstate 40 and through the security gate at the Governors Club. When she got to the house, which was a pretty impressive million-dollar place, her mood changed. She followed me up to the door as I carried her bag. As she entered the foyer, which was lit by a big chandelier, she took a spin like Mary Tyler Moore's whirl in the opening of the 1970s TV show and cried, "I'm heeeeere!" As she squealed, her sunglasses flew off her head.

Cheri was as kind as she could be for a wife greeting the mistress of her husband's boss at ten-thirty P.M. She welcomed Rielle and listened as she excitedly told us how she had evaded the photographers and escaped to North Carolina. Rielle has an almost childish voice and the Valley girl habit of making statements in a tone that rises at the end of the sentence, making it sound as if she's asking a question. She laughed a lot and spoke about her day as if it had been an adventure. She seemed to like the idea that she was being pursued. She genuinely admired John Edwards and believed she could help him present himself to the world in a more effective and appealing way. But she also liked the power that came with being the woman with a secret that could bring down a presidential candidate.

The next morning, when the kids awakened to find a strange lady in the house, we explained that she worked with me and she needed our help. This explanation seemed to be enough (we had had many staffers stay with us over the years), and since Rielle barely interacted with the kids or even showed much interest in them, they didn't ask many questions. We had to leave town for my stepfather's funeral, and when we came back, the senator told me to rent a house in the Governors Club where Rielle could live by herself. This seemed the best option for keeping her quiet and safe during the pregnancy. It would also allow the senator to come visit by claiming to have an appointment with me.

With funds supplied by Bunny Mellon, who did not know the nature of the expenses she covered, I signed a yearlong $2,900-per-month lease on a house for Rielle that was less than half a mile away from mine. We went together to buy her a $28,000 BMW. (She approved the "energy" of the car based on color, styling, and extras like a sunroof and premium sound system.) And I got her a credit card under the name R. Jaya (Sanskrit for "Victory") James. This name change was her idea, and it was inspired, of course, by Jesse James. We tried to call her Jaya but often slipped and called her Rielle. For my purposes here, I'll stick with Rielle.

Rielle lived with us for about two weeks while waiting for the lease on her place to start. She had some annoying habits, like using her hands to pick at her food or refusing to let the kids watch cartoons on TV if she was interested in catching the news. The senator came to see her at least twice in this period, and I was there for one of his arrivals. He drove from his place in his Chrysler Pacifica, which I had arranged for him to buy as a symbol of his all-American family man persona. For a disguise, he wore aviator sunglasses and a ball cap pulled down low, which was pretty silly considering the EDWARDS FOR PRESIDENT bumper stickers plastered all over the rear end of the van. I met him at the security gate, and he followed me through the development to the Montross house; the garage door opened automatically, and he steered into the garage so he could access the house without being seen. Cheri and the kids and I stayed away, and later Rielle told me they had exciting, clandestine, we're-in-this-thing-together sex. Fortunately for us, they used the guest bedroom.

The senator's risk taking made Rielle feel she was his true love. She talked constantly about how Edwards was fighting against his "destiny" and that he should "let the universe take him where he is supposed to go." At the top of this agenda was honesty, she said, and for this reason she protested how he asked her to "live a lie" by hiding the relationship. Every time she heard the senator mention how much he loved his cancer-stricken wife—this line was a campaign staple offered primarily to women voters—Rielle became angry and resentful. Over and over again, she said she didn't know how much longer she could violate her superior moral code by staying silent. But then we would go shopping for a car, or the deliveryman would arrive with something she'd bought over the Internet, and her impatience would subside. It seemed like every few minutes I got an e-mail confirming a purchase Rielle had made from Pierre Deux, Restoration Hardware, or The Children's Place.

Empowered with a credit card and money that unknowingly came from Bunny, through me, Rielle furnished all four bedrooms (including one for the baby) along with the other living spaces, and bought clothes, kitchenware, draperies, and linens. I was on call whenever she needed curtains hung or furniture assembled, and we gave her a reference to use the obstetrician who delivered our babies. Cheri did Rielle's grocery shopping and other errands so she wouldn't be caught by paparazzi. We did notice that Rielle was willing to take the risk of being sighted when she zipped off in her Beemer to a boutique, but she didn't want to greet the cable repairman at her door. But since this was supposedly a short-term arrangement, we kept our mouths shut.

Other people, however, talked. Within days of Rielle's arrival in North Carolina, the *Enquirer* quoted a "friend" of the mistress who explained how the two met and that "sparks flew immediately."

The tabloid report made Mrs. Edwards furious, and as the senator told me time and again, she screamed and yelled and cried and repeatedly threatened suicide. In the coming months, she would do everything possible to monitor his movements and track his contacts. Her telephone calls and demands for attention would make him late for many campaign appearances. But through it all, he never seemed to grasp the magnitude of the trouble he faced. Instead, he would tell me that if the truth ever came out, it would be, at worst, a one-day news story because "everyone knows" that politicians screw around on their wives. What this position denied was the fact that his wife had cancer and he had sold himself to the American public as a devoted husband and family man who talked about his faith in order to appeal to Christian voters.

The senator's minimizing may have been a psychological strategy, a way for him to stay calm while heading down the path to self-destruction. I say this because if you look at what he did rather than what he told me, the fear is obvious. Why else would he work so hard to get me to serve as his protector? Almost immediately after the paper reported on Rielle, he issued a statement denying the affair and accusing the paper of fabricating the whole thing. "The story is false," he said. "It's completely untrue, ridiculous." Speaking to reporters, he added that he had been "in love with the same woman for thirty-plus years" and that she remained "loving, beautiful, sexy, and as good a person as I have ever known. So the story's just false."

The accusation and denial rippled through the mainstream media but did not build into a wave. In fact, if you got your news from the big papers or TV networks, you probably didn't know a scandal was rumored. In the blogosphere, however, people feverishly shared insights, information, and gossip in an attempt to piece together the truth. Many bloggers announced that *The New York Times* was investigating another possible affair between the senator and a woman recently graduated from Duke University. A *New York Post* item that had been published weeks earlier about a politician visiting the city to see a mistress suddenly made sense. To others, the fact that the *Enquirer* was owned in part by Clinton backer Roger Altman's investment company was proof that the charges were pure politics. When her name began to appear in many posts, Rielle gave a statement to Democratic blogger/strategist/consultant Jerome Armstrong: "When working for the Edwards camp, my conduct as well as the conduct of my entire team was completely professional. This concocted story is just dirty politics and I want no part of it."

Remarkably, the senator's denial, Rielle's statement, and our effort to keep her away from reporters and photographers dampened interest in the story advanced by the *Enquirer* and a few other outlets. From mid-October to mid-December, we heard barely a peep from the press. Political insiders, however, remained alert to the possible scandal and the senator's vulnerability. First and foremost among them was the senator himself. Every time we spoke, he reminded me that I was his main protector. He wondered aloud whether interest in the story might fade permanently (he hoped so), and he speculated whether Hillary Clinton's camp might have been behind the *Enquirer*'s interest in Rielle. After one debate, the senator told me that Mrs. Clinton spoke to him privately to say she was sorry that he was in tabloid hell and to assure him that her campaign had nothing to do with it. Coming from someone he trusted, Hillary's words would have been reassuring. But he didn't trust her, and he didn't believe her.

No ambiguity could be heard in the message Elizabeth Edwards left on my telephone in mid-October, which I saved. Apparently, someone had told her that I had been helping her sister look for a house. (Obviously my inquiries about a rental to accommodate Rielle—whom I had referred to as *my* sister—got relayed to her in a mixed-up way.) After complaining about this, Elizabeth went on to say, "Do not communicate anything about our family to people. You have no authority. I don't want you talking to anyone as if you have some position with my family. You do not. And I want you to stop. If I hear about it again, I'm going to see what kind of legal action I can take."

The threat was unmistakable, and so was the anger in her voice. Although I didn't know it at the time, the senator had persuaded her that although he had spent one night with Rielle, I had been involved with her for some time. If she believed this fiction, Mrs. Edwards also believed that I was a bigger threat to her husband's dreams—and her own—than any of his political opponents. All they had worked for, from their personal ambitions to causes such as health care reform and ending the Iraq war, was being undermined by my supposed sexual sins and betrayal. No wonder she hated me.

I wouldn't have blamed Cheri if she hated me, too. Rielle was a very demanding and self-absorbed person who focused intently on her social life and fashion and had the manners of a teenager. If we prepared a salad for dinner and set it on the counter, she'd come in and start eating it with her hands. If we ran out of bottled water, she expected Cheri to run out for more immediately. To her credit, Cheri was patient about all of this and struggled to be helpful to a woman whose values were almost an affront to her own. Cheri cared about our family and our future, and therefore she worried about the way our lives had become entwined with the life of John Edwards. These concerns motivated her to help Rielle, not any sense of obligation to her as a friend or as someone important to the future of America, which was how Rielle increasingly viewed herself.

The senator and Mrs. Edwards were just about the only sources of conflict in our marriage, but they provided enough trouble to spark frequent arguments. Although I was disillusioned, I was stubborn about my commitment to the senator and to the issues he represented. Ever since 2000, when he was hailed as the future of the Democratic Party, I had operated as if I were helping to make history. Cheri had long since stopped trying to stand against the cause and agreed to follow my lead if possible. But this didn't mean she was happy about it. In fact, eight years after I started working for a politician, she still didn't like or trust any of them. And she was furious about the time one particular politician demanded from me. But it was a good time for me. In this period I raised almost $3 million in donations and was paid a percentage of the money I made, which increased my income substantially. It was a long way from the days of the phone banks.

I would have had an easier time persuading Cheri to have a little faith in politicians if the one I worked for hadn't become so reckless and selfish. These flaws had always been part of his character, along with the small-town insecurity bred in Robbins and the immaturity that comes with being Mama's favorite boy who could never do anything wrong. But the more people told him he could and should be president and invested their time and money in making it happen, the more pronounced these flaws became. As he was welcomed into the seats of power in Washington, New York, Los Angeles, and other places, Edwards came to believe his place there was part of the natural order of things. When he told me, "This thing is bigger than any one of us," he meant that his destiny was practically born in the stars. This status could justify almost anything.

The senator wasn't the only one who got intoxicated by power. Mrs. Edwards had knowledge of her husband's affair and understood that if he won the nomination, the Democratic Party and the country could be traumatized if the truth about Rielle came out. She also had the power to demand he drop out, but she did not. Instead, she pressed on with the drive for the White House and became increasingly strident and critical. On November 9, 2007, after she and the senator had finally hired a few more professionals to help the campaign, she sent this blistering e-mail to Joe Trippi (who had helped make Howard Dean a star in 2004), Jonathan Prince, and pollster Harrison Hickman:

> The videos I saw (which Kathleen forwarded me, as if it was somehow forbidden for anyone to speak to me directly) were well-shot (with the exception of the set piece that had the dismal background, a visual completely inconsistent with the message) but that is all I can say good about them.

The complaints that followed were numerous. Mrs. Edwards charged Trippi, Prince, and Hickman with "doing a lousy job" and being so focused on undermining one another that they had not developed any coherent advertising strategy. She dubbed them a dysfunctional "white boys' club," and her litany of failures criticized the negative content of the material, and bitterly complained about what she presumed was their expenditure of "money John raised (by being away from his family) to focus group that lousy bunch of advertisements. . . . Testing lousy material to see what is the least lousy is hardly the way to run a presidential campaign." According to Mrs. Edwards, they had "the best candidate in the race with which to work," but were "producing the worst possible product." Rather than presenting John Edwards as a "contemplative" or "energetic" candidate, or a "candidate with hope," she claimed the videos made him look like "[j]ust a sanctimonious bellower." In a particularly vivid barb, she charged, "You may end up having crapped on one another, but it all sticks to John." She claimed they hadn't listened to her in the past, and doubted they would listen to her now. Finally, in closing, she issued the following imperitive: "And Jonathan, you can keep testing me but this is a test I will win. Send it now."

These last two lines in the message, copies of which went to eight additional staffers, referred to Rielle Hunter's phone number. For months, Mrs. Edwards had been demanding that Jonathan Prince hand it over, and he had dodged these requests. Eventually, he would be able to tell her that he didn't have the number, because, in fact, we changed it many times. I thought he was wise to avoid being triangulated between the senator and his wife. Joe Trippi responded this way:

> It has been an honor working for you and John. I have done the best I could under the circumstances. But I will step aside. Your email makes it clear to me that I have outlived any usefulness to the campaign. I am sorry for that.

Mrs. Edwards's outburst had revealed how her dark side was coming to the fore to obscure all of her better qualities. The better parts of John Edwards were as real as his faults, and these gifts—his intelligence, compassion, energy, and courage—had led me, over the years, to invest my future in his success. In that same time I had learned that many, if not most, powerful men operate with the same sense of entitlement shown by the senator.

By the year 2008, Internet outlets had buzzed with rumored affairs involving Barack Obama, Hillary Clinton, Bill Clinton, and both John and Cindy McCain, so I thought that all of the viable candidates for president faced potential scandal. Republican rule had been such a disaster for America that I was almost desperate to see a Democrat win, and I believed Edwards had the best shot, especially since he might win a few states in the South that I believed were beyond the reach of the others. This concern, combined with our long-standing relationship, explains why, even after I knew so much about his shortcomings, helping him remained a reflex.

I thought we would get a break from Edwards duty at Thanksgiving. Cheri and I took the kids to her parents' house in Illinois while Rielle entertained her old roommate from New Jersey, Mimi, and Mimi's two adolescent sons. Most of the communication I got from her over the holiday was innocuous. Comically, after the turkey feast she sent me a text message that said she was watching the movie *Knocked Up* and "it's great." Two days later, she wrote that her holiday was going well except for the fact that she was "not hearing from him." I was off duty until Sunday, when I would have to go home to North Carolina to get the Batphone and deposit it in the campaign jet before the senator left on a speaking tour.

Leaving Illinois ahead of my family, I flew into Raleigh and drove to the Montross house. Thinking I was late, I grabbed the phone and raced to the fixed base of operations (FBO) that served the jet Fred Baron had bought to lease to the campaign. The only help I had for this mission would come from a personal assistant (who was paid by the campaign) at the Edwards mansion who was still my friend. She called my cell phone to warn me when they left the house for the airport.

I was relaxed when I reached the FBO because I now thought I had plenty of time. I saw Fred's plane, which had the tail number N53LB, and I talked my way past the maintenance crew and out to the stairway. Once on board, I could see the plane was dirty and hadn't been stocked with food, drinks, or periodicals. Realizing something was wrong, I went back down the steps and noticed that one of the two engines had been removed for repair. This jet wasn't going anywhere.

A quick call to the personal assistant brought me the name of a different FBO where Edwards was to board a replacement jet. I talked one of the ground crew into driving me over there in a golf cart. When we reached the plane, I persuaded the pilots to let me board. Here all the skills of bluff and bluster that I had acquired as a political operator came in handy. They had never handled a presidential candidate's schedule, so I explained that they should always expect an advance man to come for a preflight cabin check. As I walked down the narrow aisle, I slipped the phone into the right seat-back pocket. After giving the pilots a thumbs-up, I emerged from the cabin doorway to see the Edwards caravan approaching. I jumped onto the tarmac, trotted to the golf cart, and left before I got caught. From a distance, I saw Elizabeth outside the plane, kissing her husband good-bye.

They caught me, Andrew! It's the *National Enquirer*. They surrounded my car taking pictures. What should I do?"

Rielle was calling from her BMW as she drove away from a supermarket near her obstetrician's office. She was giddy with excitement, but also a bit worried about what it might mean for the paper to publish photos of her, heavy with child—and possibly not so pretty—running errands just a few miles from the Edwards mansion. She asked me to connect her with the senator, and I did, immediately. When their call was finished, he rang my phone. He sounded both desperate and demanding. "This is bad, Andrew," he said. "You have to get her under control."

In a rapid-fire conversation, we reviewed what had happened and concluded that Rielle should come to my house. Before he hung up, the senator asked me if I had any idea how the *Enquirer* had found Rielle in North Carolina. "Just between us," he said, "I suspect she's talking to them. Do you think so?"

I told him, "Hell yes. All she does is talk on her damn phone about you."

He didn't want to believe it. He preferred to theorize that the paper had staked out Mimi's house and followed her by car to the Governors Club at Thanksgiving. Ultimately, it didn't matter how Rielle had been discovered. All that mattered was the picture they had captured and the fact that the Iowa caucuses were three weeks away. Edwards was neck and neck with Barack Obama for the lead in the polls. (Hillary Clinton was a distant third.) After years of work and a huge investment in cash, the hopes of the millions who saw a bright future in John Edwards might be realized if he won Iowa and received the inevitable rush of donations that could power him through the primaries. Of course now, with the *Enquirer* guys chasing Rielle as if she were Princess Diana (a thought that both scared and thrilled her), the campaign could be ruined by scandal. After all, as Rielle said, she was "tired of living a lie."

As far as I could tell, no one followed her to our place, but I had Rielle park in the garage behind the closed door just in case. She came inside grinning and shaking and talking excitedly about how the photographers had rushed up to her and barked questions while they took her picture. She was happy to think that she looked cute in her jeans, a flowing black top, Louis Vuitton handbag, and silver shoes. But she was also worried about how the senator might react.

By the end of the evening, after we fed Rielle dinner and Cheri started the roundup for bed, I drove the candidate's mistress to her house, leaving her car in the garage. It was visible because we had opened the door to walk out. As I arrived back home, I saw that a dark-colored Jeep Liberty (a boxy sport utility vehicle with four doors) had been backed into our driveway. All of its doors were open, and no one was in sight. I stopped my car in a spot where I blocked the Jeep from leaving and walked into the garage. I could hear the kids squealing inside and thought for a moment that some friends must have come to visit. When I opened the door to the house, I saw they were all running around half-naked (it was bedtime), and Brody screamed, "There are two big men looking in the kitchen window!" Cooper and Gracie ran to me and grabbed my legs.

In an instant I figured it was probably the *Enquirer* guys, which meant they weren't burglars or rapists. But I still felt we were being threatened, even violated, and I could feel anger rising through me. I called out to Cheri, telling her to take the kids upstairs and get behind a locked door. I went back out to the garage and, before reaching the driveway, grabbed a broom and hit the switch to close the big door.

It was now dark outside, which meant the prowlers would have trouble seeing me. I shouted, "Cheri, where's our gun?" as if she could hear me and we actually had a gun (we didn't), and then I pressed the broomstick against the driveway and used my foot to snap it in half. The noise was surprisingly sharp, almost like a gunshot, and in an instant two men came scurrying out of the darkness with their hands up.

One of these fellows was an older British-sounding man. The other was a young American. The Brit tried to explain that he and his colleague were from "the American Media Corporation of Los Angeles," as if they represented a prestigious company, perhaps the *Los Angeles Times*. He did not say "the *National Enquirer*."

At this point, Cheri came outside. She was shaking with both fear and anger. Above and behind her, the kids peeked out of the second-story windows, pushing apart the blinds so they could get a view of what was going on. I told her to go back inside "and call the sheriff." Cheri was pleased to turn the tables on these guys with a call to the authorities.

As she retreated, the two men, who couldn't leave because I had blocked their Jeep, tried to talk me into letting them go. They also pressed me for information about Rielle and the senator. "Why are you covering up for him?" they asked.

I wasn't bothered by their questions. In that moment, I thought they were scummy guys who had terrified my kids, and I was hoping they would be arrested. But as it turned out, they knew more about the laws on trespass than I did.

The sheriff's deputy soon explained to me that the local law would allow him to make an arrest only if our property was posted with "No Trespassing" signs (it wasn't) or if they had been peeping at naked people inside. Since the kids had their pajamas on halfway, we couldn't claim they were violated. The deputy had to let the two men go, but as he did he made sure to tell them, "If you had come to my house, I would have shot you first and asked questions later. That's what we do in Chatham County."

Once the deputy had informed us of the law and I had discovered how the skulking journalists had gotten inside the Governors Club—they had posed as golfers headed for the clubhouse—I moved my vehicle and let them depart. Inside, I apologized to Cheri for being so gruff in the middle of the confrontation. While we talked, the kids hugged us and asked about the men who had been peering in at them and about the deputy who had come to our house with the lights on his cruiser flashing. They were scared, and all we could say was that the men were not supposed to be on our property, they had made a mistake by coming to our house, and the deputy had protected us.

In the next hour, I spoke to the senator several times. He was remarkably calm and absolutely certain that he could control the *Enquirer*. Determined to stick with his denials about the affair, he decided to confront the editors and publisher with their Clinton connection and argue that going to press with baseless charges would make them look like a tool for his opponents. If this argument failed, he said, he would attack the *Enquirer* report as "tabloid trash" and offer to sign an affidavit denying that he was Rielle's lover and the father of her child.

I thought his strategy was wrong. Attacking the paper would only invite more aggressive reporting, and a false affidavit is always a bad idea. I counseled him to wait. Even if the story leaked out, it would take many days, if not weeks, for it to reach a mainstream audience. By then the caucus would be over and we could have a more coherent strategy. Nothing was settled that night, in part because the senator was too busy preparing for the final debate of the Iowa campaign, which was set for the next day in the Des Moines area.

It was almost midnight by the time things got quiet at our house. The kids were so upset that we let them all come into our big bed to sleep. This would be the first night of many that all five of us slept together, heads and feet everywhere. It would also be the first night of many that I would keep a knife at the bedside and get up frequently to check the windows and doors. Somehow, we were supposed to go back to our regular lives in the morning. Cheri and I planned to drive the kids to school and then shop for a turtle habitat and food at a big pet supply store called PetSmart. We needed turtle stuff because Cheri had found a cute orange-and-brown eastern box turtle on the dirt road leading to our building site. She had put him in the car and brought him home for the kids. They loved Mr. Turtle, but Cheri and I worried they might handle him a little too roughly, or a little too often, and thought he would be happier in his own secure home. Anyone would.

Eleven

THE COVER-UP

Although we had moved out of the purple mansion, for the sake of stability we had kept Gracie and Brody at Scroggs Elementary School in Southern Village. It was just a few blocks from the campaign office I had helped set up for John Edwards but where I was no longer welcome. On the morning after the deputy sheriff came to our house, we actually saw several of my former colleagues on the street. They turned away, either pretending they didn't see us or snubbing us intentionally. At school, Brody told his class that "the police were at our house last night."

After we made sure the two older kids were safely inside Scroggs and delivered Cooper to his three-hour preschool class, Cheri and I ran a few errands together. (We were feeling a little paranoid and didn't think we should separate.) The last stop on our schedule was the turtle supply department at PetSmart. If you have never been to one of these places, imagine a supermarket-size store filled with rawhide bones, aquariums, catnip toys, and every other item a family pet might require. As we went inside and looked for the right aisle, Cheri and I went through a little routine we have, where I predict that whatever we're shopping for is going to be exorbitantly priced—say, five hundred dollars for a clear plastic turtle house—and she says we can get everything we want for next to nothing.

When we finally found the spot in the store where they sold the terrariums, heaters, misters, food, rocks, decorations, and other turtle items, I knew that outfitting Mr. T was going to cost us far more than Cheri expected. I became more certain when the young man in charge greeted us and began his monologue about what we owed this little critter when it came to his care and feeding. I was almost relieved when my cell phone rang and I saw it was the senator. I told Cheri I was going outside to speak to him, and she nodded.

The weather was warm for a day in December, and the sun felt good on my face. I sat on the curb in front of PetSmart and listened as the senator told me he wanted to find a "way out of this thing," which meant he wanted to kill the *Enquirer* story or, barring that, prevent the rest of the media from picking it up. He talked about how he and John Kerry had lost by a few hundred thousand votes in Ohio in 2004 and he knew how to win in November but would never get the chance if we didn't act decisively now. "A black or a woman can't win the general election," he said again.

Sensing that this was going to be a hill that would require all of my focus, I got up from the curb and walked to my minivan with the cell phone still held to my ear. I got inside and noticed, in the pile of mail on the seat, that Edwards was on the cover of the *Newsweek* that had just been delivered. (The article about him, which I read later, noted his surging popularity and quoted him saying, "I'm going to speak the truth.")

The senator talked as if he had all the time in the world, even though the Des Moines debate was just two hours away. (His demeanor made me think that he possessed at least one presidential quality: the ability to stay cool in a crisis.) Gradually, he came around to the real purpose of his call. He wanted me to issue a statement taking responsibility for Rielle's baby—to insist I was the father—and then disappear with her, Cheri, and the kids for a few weeks. The senator's rich trial lawyer friend Fred Baron would let us use his private jet and pay for our expenses as we enjoyed the equivalent of a multiweek luxury vacation.

I was dumbfounded. How, I asked, was I supposed to explain to my wife that I should confess to an affair I never had, claim an unborn child that was not mine, and then bring her along with our family as we attempted to vanish into thin air? Although he couldn't begin to tell me how I might accomplish these tricks, the senator did appeal to my commitment to the cause that is "bigger than any one of us" and to our friendship. When I told him that he was asking me to ruin my career and my ability to support my family, he said that was not true. He would make sure I had a job in the future, he said. "You're family. A friend like no friend I've ever had," he added before concluding that if I helped him, I would make Mrs. Edwards's dying days a bit easier. "I know you're mad at her, Andrew, but I love her. I can't let her die knowing this." He said he thought her days were short.

Sitting there on the curb in front of PetSmart, I didn't know whether to laugh or cry. My wife and children had been so shaken by the creeps from the *National Enquirer* that they were no longer comfortable at the Governors Club. My colleagues at the office I had opened, but where I no longer had a desk, were shunning me. All of my professional contacts, made through my work for Senator Edwards, were slowly evaporating. And the much beloved and respected Elizabeth Edwards was telling mutual friends, donors, politicians, and anyone else who would listen that I was the worst kind of scoundrel. (The senator had obviously told her the lie about my being the baby's father long ago.) In short, I was fucked, and at that moment I couldn't see that I had any options but to continue playing John Edwards's game.

As I hung up the phone, Cheri came out of PetSmart hauling turtle stuff. When I didn't say anything about her purchases, she realized that the content of the phone call must have been serious. I told her that I needed a few minutes to think before I tried to tell her about it. With about a half hour left before Cooper would be ready for pickup at preschool, I steered the car toward McDonald's.

The drive-through was backed up with the cars of other parents buying Happy Meals, so we moved slowly toward the intercom station where you place your order. After I finally got to holler for Chicken McNuggets with chocolate milk and the right toy, I turned to Cheri and in the time it took us to reach window number one (where you give them the money), I said, "Edwards wants me to say I'm the father of Rielle's baby, and then Fred's gonna fly us off to someplace where we can all hide."

At this point in the "conversation," I had reached the pay window, so I pulled out my wallet and handed the young McDonald's cashier a twenty-dollar bill. She gave me the change, and as I pulled forward to collect the food, Cheri began to sputter.

"Are you out of your mind? Why would you even tell me about this? Why didn't you just say no?"

Cheri wasn't exactly yelling, but she was loud. At the delivery window, I reached out and took the McDonald's Happy Meal box from the clerk and said, "Thank you." The clerk didn't bat an eye. My guess is that she had seen plenty of women talking loudly to their husbands at the drive-through.

Once she had vented her outrage, Cheri sat quietly for a few minutes. Among the thoughts that raced through my mind in the silence was that I had gotten us stuck in a big mess involving two billionaires, a presidential candidate, a pregnant mistress, and a whole lot of money. Cheri was having the same thought, and she was recalling the run-in with the men from the *Enquirer*. That ruckus had only added to the sleep debt she had been accumulating ever since Thanksgiving, as Gracie and Cooper seemed to get one cold or ear infection after another. We were both exhausted and afraid, and once we started talking about the John Edwards/Rielle Hunter problem, we could see it only in the most threatening way. What if the press kept hounding us? Who would ever hire me after the collapse of my career and Mrs. Edwards savaging my reputation? I started to feel light-headed, and Cheri could see I was upset. We were already deep into this mess. I had signed an expensive lease for Rielle's rental house. I had bought her a car, and I had agreed to be responsible for her into the foreseeable future. These facts hung over our decisions.

The trip from McDonald's to Cooper's school was so short that we got there before we could settle anything. We stopped talking when Cooper got into the car and let him tell us about his experience in class. He chattered all the way home, where we went inside so he could eat his Happy Meal and we could get ready for Rielle to come over. She wanted to watch the Iowa debate with me, and since I couldn't go to the campaign office anymore, and Cheri was not the least bit interested in what John Edwards had to say, I had told her she could come over for it.

According to the analysis I read later, the debate was a boring one. Hillary Clinton talked about the looming Social Security and Medicare deficits. Obama pandered to the locals by saying he would cut federal payments to agribusiness and give more aid to family farms. Edwards made a faux pas in his opening statement, saying, "We should make this country better than we left it." Laughter from the audience made him correct himself. During the rest of the session, he talked about the "two Americas" and fighting corporate greed and otherwise went through the motions, as though he were distracted. Rielle and I were distracted, too, as I laid out the plan the senator had suggested.

Initially, Rielle was foursquare against it. "There's no damn way I'm doing this," she said. "I'm not going to live a lie." But as we talked, she said she could "handle" the prospect of having both a wealthy presidential candidate and a billionaire benefactor devoted to her care and support. "Not too bad, considering I was sleeping in my car a few years ago," she said. She could keep up contact with Senator Edwards and, in the meantime, live in luxury until events played out. With these thoughts in mind, her nay vote quickly turned to yea.

My wife was not so receptive. She pointed out that the senator had offered no definitive end point for the scheme, other than a vague assurance that it would be over in a few weeks and then he would take responsibility for Rielle's baby. She also didn't trust the senator's promise that if I continued to be a good team player, I would have a job for life with either him or Fred.

Cheri reminded me of promises the senator had made and broken, including his offers to give me more prominent roles in his campaigns. With her words in mind, I called Fred, who assured me that my salary—including a recent 130 percent raise—would be continued along with my health insurance until my new career was established. "You can do anything," said Fred. "We will make it happen."

Exhausted and under intense pressure to make a decision, we finally agreed that even if we followed through on the senator's plan, no one who knew us would actually believe the story he wanted everyone to tell, so we took the plunge. I would work with a lawyer named Pam Marple, who was recommended by Fred Baron, to craft a statement to release to the media. Once that was done, we would fly off in Fred's plane to a place where no one could find us.

As he listened to me accept his scheme, a prospect that anyone outside the situation would say was ridiculous, the senator breathed a huge sigh of relief. Over and over again he said that he loved me, he loved Cheri, and he was going to support us in every way he could for many years to come. When we discussed the details, he said, "It's going to be a one-day story, Andrew. No offense, but the press doesn't give a shit about you. They want me. But if we give them a story they can understand, a story about two staffers, they'll go away."

While Pam Marple and I worked on the statement that would be issued to the press, the senator and his allies failed to persuade the editors at the *Enquirer* to hold the story. No one knew what they planned to say exactly, but we assumed that as soon as a photo of Rielle with child went into circulation, Elizabeth Edwards would go on a furious emotional rampage. The senator was as concerned about this as he was about the prospect of his candidacy being destroyed. On many levels, he still loved Elizabeth and didn't want to hurt her. We all knew that in her fury Elizabeth could do a lot of damage to innocent people.

To get ahead of the situation, the senator said, he would have to tell his wife a version of the story—the version in which *I* was the baby's father. (In fact, he had done this already.) He said he expected that she would make him call to confirm the tale while she listened. With this in mind, he left a message on my cell phone. It said, among other things, "I'm gonna leave you this message just in case you get a call from me where I ask you what's going on . . . the reason we are calling is because Elizabeth is standing there . . . so, be aware of that. If I am calling saying, 'What happened? How did this happen?' or 'What's going on?' then that's because Elizabeth is standing there with me. . . . I've gotta tell her about this because it's moving."

For once, I didn't give John Edwards what he wanted. I refused to be on any call involving the two of them. In five days, he left half a dozen messages, asking me to return his call. Mrs. Edwards, who officially loathed me, even left one asking me to call back on a "hard line" instead of a cell phone, presumably for security purposes. I continued to ignore her, but I did stay true to my word, approving the following statement, drafted by Pam Marple, on December 15, 2007:

> As confirmed by Ms. Hunter, Andrew Young is the father of her unborn child. Senator Edwards knew nothing about the relationship between these former co-workers, which began when they worked together in 2006. As a private citizen who no longer works for the campaign, Mr. Young asks that the media respect his privacy while he works to make amends with his family.

This single paragraph was to be offered to the *National Enquirer* or any other media person who called the Edwards campaign about Rielle Hunter. The senator and the advisers who worked closely with him on this issue— Jonathan Prince and Mark Kornblau—expected the onslaught to begin on Wednesday, December 19, when the new edition of the *Enquirer* would be posted online. Accordingly, Cheri flew with our kids to Illinois, where they would stay for a while with her parents. She couldn't tell them exactly why we needed their help, where she was going, or when she might come back. This frightened her mom and dad, but they were supportive. I offered a similar nonexplanation to my family, telling them we were going away, that we were safe, but that I couldn't tell them anything more.

The *Enquirer* story, posted online on a Wednesday and distributed to the nation's newsstands on a Thursday, was as damaging as it could be. The front-page headline screamed JOHN EDWARDS LOVE CHILD SCANDAL! and Rielle's picture was included. The most important part of the text came in the first two paragraphs:

> Presidential candidate John Edwards is caught up in a love child scandal, a blockbuster *Enquirer* investigation has discovered.
>
> The *Enquirer* has learned exclusively that Rielle Hunter, a woman linked to Edwards in a cheating scandal earlier this year, is more than six months pregnant and she's told a close confidante that Edwards is the father of her baby!

Besides these most pertinent paragraphs, I was struck, of course, by a reference to "Andrew Young, who's been extremely close to Edwards for years." The paper added:

> And in a bizarre twist, Young—a 41-year-old married man with young children—now claims HE is the father of Rielle's baby! But others are skeptical, wondering if Young's paternity claim is a cover-up to protect Edwards.

The *Enquirer* was right: From any outsider's perspective, the explanation we had offered to the questions about Rielle was bizarre. But to our relief, no serious newspaper or TV network picked up the story because they couldn't find a source to confirm it. Our phones and those of our friends and relatives rang constantly with calls from reporters and producers, but we ignored them all. Rielle and the campaign followed the same strategy, and since they still play by the multi-source rule, the big print and broadcast news organizations were stymied.

The reaction was different in the online world, which exploded with speculation. Two prominent bloggers—Mickey Kaus and Matt Drudge—simply ignored the claim that I was the baby's father and announced that Edwards had a girlfriend who was six months pregnant. A few radio talkers, most notably Don Imus, also made snarky remarks, but since these comments were all based on unconfirmed facts, the news didn't seem to affect the candidate or the campaign. As I talked to the senator and Fred Baron, we began to think that perhaps our strategy had worked. All that remained was for us to disappear until the more persistent reporters and photographers got frustrated enough to give up the hunt.

While Cheri had been in Illinois, Mr. Turtle ended up in a lake, and Meebo went to stay with her brother along with Granny, the cat. Rielle took charge of the decisions about where we might hide out and chose the same resort—the Westin Diplomat Resort & Spa in South Florida—where she had been caught in the senator's room by the campaign staff and hotel security. The destination dictated a light wardrobe, so I packed summer-style clothes for Cheri and me. I also grabbed a small number of the Christmas presents Cheri had bought, because I couldn't be sure where we might spend the holidays, but I knew I would demand that we be together with the kids.

At four A.M., Cheri and I left the Montross house in my car and went to pick up Rielle, who traveled light—just a few clothes and a bag of makeup—and wore a black bandanna over her hair and her signature bright pink scarf around her neck. Although Cheri and I were both exhausted, Rielle was wide awake and excited. We drove around aimlessly for a bit, making sure no one was following us, and then went to the acres in the woods where our new house was going up. My friend Tim Toben met us there so I could hide the car and he could drop us at the airport. He didn't ask a single question about why we were dashing out of town or where we were going. (Later, Tim explained that he had supported Edwards's campaign because of his interest in energy policy. He wasn't much interested in the nuts and bolts of electioneering, like who was flying where and when.)

At the FBO, we drove into the hangar and parked next to the jet so no one could see Rielle get out of the car. We were met by a pilot and copilot who ushered us aboard. I noticed that the cabin had been stocked with food, coffee, and liquor. We were the first flight out when the airport opened for the day. The takeoff was smooth, and the plane climbed sharply until it reached an altitude where we could see the sun breaking over the eastern horizon. Rielle grabbed a copy of *The New York Times* and pored over it for political news. She and I talked quietly about politics while Cheri fell asleep.

A hired car and driver met us at our destination airport and took us to the hotel, where Rielle went into full diva mode. Unwilling to accept just any room, she left the luggage in the lobby while we all traipsed upstairs to inspect the accommodations. The first room had "bad energy," the second exuded the wrong "ambience," and the third simply "didn't feel right." Since, as she said, "Fred was paying and wouldn't care," she kept harassing the desk clerks until we wound up in expensive adjoining suites overlooking the ocean from the top floor. While I booted up my laptop and began nervously checking for news about us, Rielle took off her traveling clothes, put on the thick robe she found hanging in the closet, and called room service.

While Rielle kept the resort staff busy by returning half the food she ordered from the kitchen—including toast—Cheri and I found it difficult to relax at the Westin. I kept checking the Internet for news stories about me and my philandering, and although I got lots of hits on gossipy Web sites, I saw nothing in the mainstream media. My phone rang constantly with calls from reporters, whom I ignored. I also heard from Heather North, who said, "You've been nothing but good to every person you have ever encountered, especially to the Edwards family." And Tim Toben offered a joking observation about a *USA Today* article on rising fertility rates and said, "Way to be a trendsetter!" (I would later learn that Tim didn't believe I would ever betray Cheri, and he suspected the senator was the father of Rielle's child.)

Of all the people who tried to contact me during this first stage of our life on the run, the most persistent was John Edwards, who, despite being on the road as a presidential candidate, managed to leave a message every few hours:

12:51 A.M.: "Uh, Andrew, it's John. If you could call me back at 402-998-3400, room 8030.

6:47 P.M.: "Andrew, it's John. Call me back on this number. Thanks."

6:49 P.M.: "Andrew, if you get this message, too, you can call back on this number. Thanks."

7:13 P.M.: "Uh . . . Andrew, call me back as soon as you can on this phone. It's now—" (Cuts off.)

7:26 P.M.: "Andrew, I keep trying to reach you. I have called you a bunch of times. I have talked to Elizabeth and I think it's under control, so I just wanted to talk to you about it, but I have to go into an event now. I will try to call you guys later. Thanks. Bye."

9:09 P.M.: "Andrew, it's John. It's nine-ten P.M. East Coast time. I just got out of my last event. I'm on my way to the airport to get on a plane. I've got about ten or fifteen minutes if you can call me back. If not, I will talk to you from Des Moines. Thanks."

When we did actually speak, the senator talked anxiously about the scandal-related press calls coming into the campaign but also kept telling me how grateful he was for my help. He went out of his way to make me feel important, as if I were saving him and therefore the country from a catastrophe. He said he was worried about calls the campaign had had from a reporter for *The New York Times* who said he had evidence that I had undergone a vasectomy after our last child was born with heart problems. He claimed that Rielle's child couldn't be mine. This wasn't true, of course. I hadn't had a vasectomy

In this conversation, the senator told me his wife was now calling supporters and saying derogatory things about me but that he would try to get her to stop. He acted as if we were partners now more than ever, and he reinforced this connection by sharing inside information. When Benazir Bhutto was assassinated in Pakistan, he told me about how Pervez Musharraf had called him directly to consult. Strangely, he made these observations on world and national affairs with less urgency than he brought to his comments about keeping Rielle happy and quiet. He was careful, though, to avoid using her actual name. Typical was this message:

> I'm in Nashua, New Hampshire, about to get on a plane to go to Iowa . . . I'm sorry I couldn't reach you, but we're just, you know, I've got four CBS reporters on the plane with me so I'm standing out in eighteen degree temperatures to call you. And please tell her I said hello and I will call later tonight. Thanks.

Rielle required the senator's constant attention, because now that she was playing "fugitive on an expense account," she was even more demanding and, at times, less careful. Although her picture was displayed on the front page of the *National Enquirer*, which was on the rack in the lobby newsstand, she traipsed around the resort as if she owned the place. With

Rielle indulging in this risky behavior, and Cheri and me anxious to re-
unite with our kids for the holiday, Fred Baron arranged for us to get out of
Florida on Christmas Eve aboard another private jet. At checkout, I noticed that we had racked up a bill totaling more than eight thousand dollars
in seven nights. The clerk also gave me a FedEx envelope from Fred. It
held one thousand dollars' cash and a note that said, "Old Chinese proverb:
Use cash, not credit cards."

The plan called for us to travel to southern Illinois to pick up the kids
and then to Aspen, Colorado, where we would stay in Fred Baron's vacation home. Aspen was going to be our temporary haven until we found a
place where we could live together in seclusion until Rielle gave birth. The
only hitch in the plan, other than the fact that we were giving up our normal lives, involved a friend—a trial lawyer from Georgia—whom Fred
had invited to use the house from December 27 to January 2. During this
time, we would have to hide ourselves at a hotel in San Diego which Rielle
chose. Complicated as these arrangements may sound, I was used to juggling campaign travel for the senator, who might take half a dozen flights
in a single day, so this itinerary seemed easy to me.

As we left Florida, we phoned Cheri's dad to ask him to bring the kids
to the MidAmerica Airport, a little-used facility outside St. Louis where
we would be unlikely to attract any attention. We asked him to come
alone, because her mom wasn't too crazy about me. (She had good reason
to feel this way.) To his credit, he didn't say anything even after he saw
Rielle and her swollen belly and realized she was with us. Like everyone
in my family, Cheri's folks were aware of what was on the front page of
the *Enquirer* and must have guessed what was going on, but her dad said
nothing as he said good-bye to his grandchildren and they climbed aboard
a private jet for some mysterious adventure.

Because we knew the kids would miss their regular Christmas celebration, Cheri and I had bought a tiny artificial tree with lights and installed it
inside the plane, so as they climbed aboard it looked as if they were getting
a ride on Santa's private jet. We had never been separated from all three of

them for so long, and they hugged us as though we had been lost in the jungle for a year. Rielle, whom they called "Jaya," did her best to smile and be friendly during the flight, although she must have felt like an outsider at a family picnic. The kids ate candy, visited the pilots in the cockpit (where they helped "fly" the jet), and screamed with roller-coaster delight when we landed and the plane wobbled from side to side as the crew applied the brakes to bring us to a halt on the icy runway.

At the FBO, which is a stone-and-timber building that looks like a ski chalet, the crew shut down the engines, opened the door, and lowered the steps. The kids ran outside and immediately grabbed some of the fresh snow to throw at one another. Two SUVs waited for us, and the driver of the one that carried our family narrated the journey through a development started by the singer John Denver: "That hundred-and-fifty-million-dollar house belongs to Prince Bandar bin Sultan, the former Saudi ambassador to the United States; this one belongs to Robert Wagner, the actor. . . ." When we drove up Fred Baron's driveway, we discovered a stone-and-wood mansion secluded by evergreens and staffed by a house manager, a chef, and a masseuse, who were all on call.

Fred's sprawling house was lavishly furnished. Pictures of his frequent guests Bill and Hillary Clinton were placed in conspicuous places, and the coffeepot in the kitchen was, we were told, the property of Lance Armstrong, who had lived in the place during training. I was impressed by the home gym, which was filled with equipment. The kids loved the racquetball court, which they called "the ballroom," and the indoor pool/Jacuzzi/sauna complex, which was enclosed by a ceiling painted to look like the night sky, with twinkling lights to represent the stars.

Within an hour of our arrival, the kids were splashing and floating in the pool as Cheri, Rielle, and I watched them. For a moment, we forgot the craziness that had brought us to the place and allowed ourselves to enjoy it. Rielle got so relaxed that she again started talking about her sexual escapades with the senator, including specifics about where, when, and how they performed certain acts. We interrupted her with cries of, "Whoa!

TMI!"—too much information—and she retreated from this subject. But the details about their affair would come up again and again in our time on the road.

After Cheri and I put the kids to bed and the quiet overcame us, we remembered that it was Christmas Eve and we were far from friends and family and unable to give our kids the holiday they usually enjoyed. On Christmas Day, we managed a small celebration with a tree Fred had arranged and the few presents we had brought from home. Cheri and I called our families and had some awkward conversations, and we had fun playing in the snow with the kids. Rielle was unhappy to be out of contact with the senator over the holiday and impatient to move on to California, where she hoped that Fred Baron would set us up in a house in either San Diego or Santa Barbara. The latter was her first choice because it was the home of her spiritual adviser—a guy called Bob—who was her most important source of "spiritual" support.

Anyone who spent any time around Rielle knew that Bob McGovern was the source of wisdom who guided many of her decisions. She called him "an intuitive," which in her world meant that he possessed a sort of sixth sense that he could use to acquire special insight into any situation and to predict the future by reading the stars. Although I had never met him, I heard Rielle consult him on the phone many dozens of times. Often she would just leave a message describing her problem and requesting he intervene. A little while later, she would say she could "feel" the changes Bob was "creating" in the spirit realm. Because we paid her bills, I learned that Bob charged for his cell phone consultations—two hundred dollars was typical—and that Rielle relied on him for help with everything from the profound to the ridiculous.

The ridiculous was on display in Aspen on the one occasion when we all went out to eat together. With the kids in mind, we picked a burger-and-shakes place called Boogie's Diner. With 1950s-style music and decorations, the place is as casual as you can get and still have sit-down service, so most people order something greasy and chomp away. Rielle left Bob two voice mails about her Reuben sandwich. To be precise, the issue was the Russian dressing, which she found lacking, and she wondered whether she should send her meal back to the kitchen. She did. Twice.

The impatient and self-indulgent attitude that led Rielle to make a double fuss over a Reuben sandwich would get worse as her due date grew closer. But as much as she appalled us, we also tried to empathize with her because she was alone, without emotional support from her baby's father, and scared of everything, including giving birth. She also knew that a major effort was being made to control her and that my loyalties were with Cheri, the kids, and John Edwards, in that order.

After just four days in Aspen, we all packed our stuff and got back on the private jet to spend a week in San Diego. We landed there on December 27, crammed ourselves and our luggage into a rental car that was way too small, and drove to the Loews Coronado Bay hotel. After check-in, when another envelope full of cash was handed to me, we all got back in the car so we could hit an ice-cream shop for the kids and a drugstore so I could pick up a few necessities like toothbrushes and shaving supplies. While I was in the store and everyone waited outside, I spotted a new edition of the *Enquirer* on the news rack and was relieved to see we weren't on the cover. I thumbed through a copy while at the register and still didn't see anything about Rielle or the senator. When I brought the paper to the car, I said, "Hey, good news. We're not in the *National Enquirer*." Then I glanced down at the paper as it fell open to page six, where I saw a nice picture of Cheri next to a larger and very unflattering photo of Rielle with her mouth hanging open and her left hand extended, clawlike, making her look like a *Tyrannosaurus rex* in a maternity smock.

"Oh shit," I said without thinking.

"What?" said Rielle and Cheri in unison.

Cheri took the paper out of my hand and got into the backseat of the car to look at it. As I drove, I could see she was studying it carefully. The article didn't offer anything new about Edwards, Rielle, or the Young family but was instead a breathless report titled "Edwards Love-Child Bombshell

Causes Nationwide Frenzy." (The last two words, "Nationwide Frenzy," were printed in red ink.) Since no new facts were offered, the only real new tidbit was the picture of Cheri, which she didn't like but I thought was fine. Rielle, as you might expect, was unhappy with her photo.

During our week at Coronado Bay, we ran up a $10,000 tab as Rielle used every service the hotel had to offer while Cheri and I took the kids to Legoland, SeaWorld, and the San Diego Zoo. I authorized our biggest single room service purchase on December 29 when I realized as we were leaving the hotel for the zoo that it was Cheri's birthday. (I got a little help when Cheri said, "You don't even know what day it is today, do you?")

After apologizing, and apologizing, I spent the time at the zoo walking a step and a half behind Cheri and performing child care like the world's best dad. When I was able to get a private moment, I used my cell phone to call Rielle and ask her to help me out. She called the concierge, who went to the hotel gift shop and bought a bunch of odd presents. The concierge also got Cheri balloons, flowers, and a birthday cake, and the kitchen sent a small banquet to our room. It was a celebration, but nothing like the all-stops-out birthdays I had arranged for Cheri in the past. The proof was in the pictures, which show my wife and supposed mistress seated together at a well-appointed table, forcing smiles.

Cheri's birthday was just one moment in what was becoming an unnervingly surreal misadventure. Unable to tell anyone where we were, and barred from speaking honestly with colleagues and friends, I began to feel as if I were watching the world turning from a spot on the moon. The Internet became even more important to me, and I followed news sites closely for some hint that the bargain I had struck with John Edwards was going to help him win Iowa and grab the momentum to propel him to the nomination. Everywhere I looked, I saw that he was gaining on the front-runner, Obama. This success came from a new campaign strategy that stressed taking a tough approach to the election battle with Republicans. Edwards told his audiences, "You try and nice them to death, they'll trample you."

This message worked with activist Democrats who had seen too many of their guys take the "high road" to defeat.

As Senator Edwards barnstormed across the state, the press took note of the fact that he was significantly tardy—an hour late wasn't unusual—for every event. But no one knew that the delays were caused, in part, by the time he used on the phone listening to his angry wife, comforting his lonely mistress, and maintaining his relationship with me. In the ten years I had known him, John Edwards had never tried harder to strengthen our bond, by sharing information and expressing concern and gratitude. In one call, he said to me, laughing, "[Former president] Clinton's been calling around trying to hire you. . . . He said he would still be president if he had you to cover for him." On another call, he left a message noting he had just finished an interview on CNN with Larry King but wanted to make sure "you're safe and in a place where you are good."

By "place," the senator meant state of mind, and I didn't expect to be in a good place until we got our normal lives back. If he got the nomination and Mrs. Edwards survived, we would be hard-pressed to find a way out of our arrangement with Rielle before November. If he didn't win the nomination but wanted to pursue either the vice presidential slot or a place in some future Democratic administration, we'd be in the same predicament. Barring a sudden surge of honesty, the only way we were going to get out of our commitment would be if Mrs. Edwards died. And we still loved her too much to hope for this terrible outcome.

The three of us watched the reports on the Iowa caucus results in Fred's house in Aspen. (We had returned there once his friend from Georgia had vacated the place.) Barack Obama won handily, becoming the genuine front-runner for the nomination. John Edwards offered a raspy thank-you to the voters who had given him second place. Unfortunately for him, Edwards had gone "all in" in Iowa, and he finished with just 1 percent more of the vote than Hillary Clinton. And while Obama and Clinton had big organizations in the next battleground state, New Hampshire, Edwards had no real organization there, and was quickly running out of money.

"It's not about me," said Edwards in New Hampshire. "It's about the families who deserve a real chance in this country."

With Obama trumpeting "change" and Hillary turning on the emotion (her eyes welled with tears when a voter asked about the rigors of the campaign), Edwards continued with the basic themes he had used in Iowa, stressing that he would fight for the average American. But as he faced opponents with far more resources and depth of support, he was eventually reduced, in his last days of campaigning, to pleading that a vote cast for him would not be wasted.

On New Hampshire primary day, the senator actually took time to call me in Aspen. I was out playing in the snow with the kids, so he left a message. It said, in part, "Just wanted *all* [his emphasis] of you, including her, to know that I am thinking about you. I will be in South Carolina tomorrow, flying in there in the morning, and should be by myself tomorrow night, so I will talk to you then."

Rielle, whose belly was approaching basketball size, was now living for the moments when she could talk to the senator at length. Uncomfortable and lonely, she consulted Bob on a regular basis, watched the TV news channels, and when there was no election news, searched for reruns of *Law & Order*. This show and her pink cell phone, which now displayed a photo of her lounging with the senator whenever it was on, were comfort objects for her. She used them to pass the long hours in the house because she was unable to go out because of the paparazzi. Aspen was crawling with them.

Rielle knew long before the polls closed that the results of the New Hampshire primary were going to be worse for Edwards than the Iowa caucuses. We watched the results in the library, which overlooked snow-covered mountains. He got clobbered, finishing a distant third behind the winner, Hillary Clinton, and the runner-up, Obama. Mrs. Clinton claimed the title of "Comeback Kid," and Obama finished just three points behind her. This success, in a largely rural and almost entirely white state, would help propel his fund-raising toward a record-setting total. It also suggested that Democrats were ready for either a black candidate or a woman. Edwards gamely declared, "Two states down, forty-eight to go. I'm in this race to the convention, and I intend to be the nominee of my party."

Realistically, the Democrats in New Hampshire had just made the contest for the presidential nomination a two-person affair, and if Edwards was running for anything, it was to be as candidate for vice president or for a spot in some future Democratic administration. After New Hampshire, even Fred Baron's enthusiasm began to wane, but he remained interested because his friend might win the veep slot or be named attorney general. In either of these spots, Edwards could help protect the nation's trial lawyers from Republican efforts to cut their business by imposing tort reform.

While some Democrats began calling for the senator to drop out, we turned our attention to finding a more permanent hideout where we could give our kids some semblance of a normal life. School was starting, and Cheri and I wanted to go home. But now Fred and the senator were insisting we stay away and keep Rielle under control until his part in the election was over or Mrs. Edwards died. Santa Barbara was now the only place Rielle was even willing to consider for her hideout. This decision had been made during a blowup that began with a suggestion from Fred Baron. He told us of a place in the Southwest "where they take care of situations like this" in utter privacy for wealthy clients. Rielle took this to mean that Fred wanted to send her to a clinic for late-term abortions. In fact, Fred was recommending a secluded retreat, with staff, where celebrities and other pregnant guests get the utmost privacy. But nothing anyone said could reassure Rielle, and the argument made her even more eager to live near Bob McGovern. On January 10, we took another private jet flight, this time from Aspen to Santa Barbara. While we were in the air, Fred left me a voice mail that confirmed how things might be changing now that the dream shared by John and Elizabeth Edwards (and the shared ambition that held them together) was breaking apart:

> Andrew, it's Fred. I just want to give you a heads-up on something. I'm gonna be meeting with the principal tomorrow, but they want you to know that he is not taking your calls or her calls right now because of his circumstance, uh, with EE [Elizabeth Edwards] and not to take it personally, but it will get better soon. But right now he is in a bad place . . . When you get settled out there, give me a buzz.

By calling the senator "the principal" and referring to Rielle as "her," Fred Baron displayed a little of the lawyer's impulse to assure himself plausible deniability. He may have spoken this way out of habit or because he worried about future legal problems. To me it just sounded strange, as if Fred were backing away emotionally. This turned out to be true. As Fred later told me, in the weeks after the New Hampshire primary the Clintons put extra pressure on him to abandon Senator Edwards and get him and the nation's trial lawyers behind Hillary's campaign.

Fred's account squared with comments I heard from the senator, who was worried about losing his support. He had talked to me about how Fred's cash would be only "our short-term solution." Edwards believed this because he thought Fred would soon shift his interest to another candidate. He also knew that Fred had been diagnosed with cancer and, like Mrs. Edwards, might not be around for very long. With this in mind, he said that Bunny Mellon was more likely to provide "the long-term solution" to his need to fund both Rielle's lifestyle and an organization to keep the Edwards name in front of the public after the election. (Bunny's support would also keep me employed.) He was confident about Bunny's loyalty because he had been building a relationship with her. She was so fond of him that she had given him one of her gold necklaces to carry as a good-luck charm.

Despite the concerns the senator expressed, in the winter of 2007–2008, Fred Baron's short-term support was unwavering. He spent time on the phone with Rielle when she needed comforting and enlisted his wife, Lisa

Blue, to do the same. Fred also said that money was "no object" and told me to spend whatever it took to placate Rielle and Cheri, and he would pay the bills. But because Mrs. Edwards's condition was not as dire as the senator had told us, this was beginning to look like a long-term project. Believing Fred would eventually stop writing checks, we set aside the money Bunny had sent for future use. As the senator kept saying, "Fred's the short-term solution and Bunny is the long-term solution."

On January 10, we boarded Fred's jet to leave Aspen for good and landed in Santa Barbara to start house hunting. Encouraged by Fred to "make everyone comfortable," I checked everyone into the Biltmore Four Seasons at Butterfly Beach. Although Rielle was disappointed that we couldn't get suites at the exclusive Bacara Resort & Spa, the Biltmore was a luxurious five-star place. Built in Spanish colonial style with red tile roofs and bubbling fountains, the hotel offered attentive service from the moment you arrived and were greeted by bellmen wearing argyle sweaters. Rielle had to inspect three different rooms and request upgrades, but to her credit, we wound up with blissfully quiet accommodations overlooking the croquet green. When the kids ran to look at the ocean, they saw a pod of dolphins jumping in the water about a quarter mile from the beach.

The main task I had to accomplish in Santa Barbara was finding a home where Rielle could wait out the end of her pregnancy and raise her baby through the first few months of life. Cheri flew home for a couple of days to clean Eric Montross's house (and take down the Christmas tree there) so he could put it back on the market. When she got there, she discovered reporters had left about a dozen notes and business cards slipped under the front door.

In Santa Barbara, Rielle and I met real-estate agents, who were told that she was my "stepsister," and we scoured rental listings on the Internet. I found several nice houses in the $5,000 to $10,000 (per month) range and was sure I had discovered the perfect spot when I stumbled upon a mountaintop home owned by Herb Peterson, who had invented the Egg McMuffin for McDonald's. Mr. Peterson, who was going into a nursing home, offered me a

Heineken, and we shared his last beer in that house while Rielle looked around and decided it did not have the right karma.

The winner in what became a dream house contest was a huge, single-level home in the gated Montecito neighborhood of Ennisbrook. Adjacent to Oprah Winfrey's estate (where Barack Obama had recently held a fundraiser) and hidden behind its own secondary gate, the hacienda-style home had nine-foot-high steel-and-glass entry doors, a great room with a grand piano and a view of the ocean and mountains, and a library with a fifteen-foot ceiling. The layout of the place, which offered separate wings for our family and Rielle, provided a measure of privacy for all of us. The final stamp of approval came from Bob McGovern, whom I met for the first time when he arrived in his BMW 740i to perform a blessing, which Rielle said would "clear the energy" of the place.

Roughly six feet two and well over two hundred pounds, Bob was not at all what I expected. A few years past sixty, he had bushy hair that was silvery gray and a big belly that made him look like Captain Kangaroo. His voice was extremely measured and soothing, and his smile seemed genuine. I didn't go inside to watch him do his thing, but whatever it was, it made Rielle happy and calm, and I appreciated his effect on her.

When Cheri got back, we all moved in. We had gone to great lengths to hide from the press and the public, so we couldn't risk enrolling the kids in school. Instead, we found a teacher who would come to homeschool the kids and establish a routine for them. Ennisbrook isn't exactly teeming with kids, so I regularly took them to the park and the local YMCA, where they met lots of playmates, and I let them run on the beach as much as possible.

Because Rielle was late in her pregnancy and her picture was in the *Enquirer* and all over the Internet, she stayed home most of the time. She spoke often with Senator Edwards and told us that it didn't matter that he was losing his bid for the nomination. "The universe" had other things in store for him, she said, including a life with her and a new baby.

When I spoke with him, the senator grumbled about John Kerry—
"that asshole"—endorsing Barack Obama and speculated about how he
could parlay his own endorsement into a position for himself. Cheri and I
fell into a routine of taking care of Rielle's basic needs almost as if she were
our child. When we cooked meals she was included, and when we went to
the store we bought her supplies along with ours. As an expression of rebellion, I ran these errands while listening to Hank Williams cranked up loud
on the stereo in my redneck Jeep, which I had had shipped out from North
Carolina. I waved to our neighbors, who drove Bentleys and Aston Mar-
tins, and I didn't care that they never waved back. Once, as I pulled up to
the front gate of the development, the guard looked at my four days'
growth of beard and my Jeep, and when I said, "Andrew Young, Ennisbrook," he said, "Is he expecting you?" He didn't believe me at first when I
said, "*I'm* Andrew Young," but a call to the manager, who confirmed the
identity of the redneck in the Jeep, convinced him.

When the sun was shining and the breeze carried the scent of the ever-
blooming flowers through the air, Santa Barbara was so beautiful that I almost forgot we were on the run with John Edwards's pregnant mistress.
But then I would get back to the house and discover that Rielle was ranting
about some bit of praise John Edwards had offered to his wife during a TV
interview or that my wife had received a hostile message on her cell phone
from Elizabeth. In one, which we saved, she said, "We thought you should
know that this is not Andrew's first woman," and then she cackled into the
phone.

Listening to this stuff, I became convinced that her husband's infidelity,
the inevitable end of the campaign, and her ongoing battle with cancer had
become too much for Mrs. Edwards to bear with any grace. She didn't want
to recognize the doubts sown in the minds of voters by the *Enquirer* or the
possibility that Obama—with the help of several Edwards castoffs, including David Axelrod and Julianna Smoot—was simply a better candidate.
She preferred to believe that I was responsible for John Edwards losing his

advantage and the caucuses in Iowa and getting clobbered in New Hampshire.

The last straw for the campaign came on January 26, when the senator finished third in the primary in South Carolina, where he was born. After this defeat, he quit the race. However, anticipating a convention split between Obama and Clinton, where his handful of delegates could determine the winner, he didn't officially end his campaign but merely "suspended" it. "It's time for me to step aside," he said, "so that history can—so that history can blaze its path." Ironically enough, Rudy Giuliani, whose sign had annoyed Elizabeth Edwards every time she left her house, dropped out of the Republican race on the same day her husband ended his run for the Democratic nomination.

When I spoke to him next, Senator Edwards sounded defeated, but he was already scheming about how to turn his endorsement, and his hold on a few delegates, into a top position in the next administration. It was impossible to get him to focus on resolving Rielle's status and mine. Fred Baron was similarly evasive when I pressed him.

But at night, when the house turned quiet, Cheri and I questioned every decision we had made in the previous year. As the days passed and the birth of Rielle's baby drew closer, we became less confident about the promises the senator and Fred Baron had made to help us get back to our old life. When the kids asked for the umpteenth time, "When are we going back home?" and we said, "Soon," we felt hollow. My decision to cover for John Edwards, a choice made out of loyalty, friendship, and hope for my own future as well as the country's, was turning out to be a foolish mistake I was powerless to correct. As far as the world was concerned, I was now the guy who had confessed to an affair and taken responsibility. If I recanted, I would then be the guy who foolishly took the blame for the sin of a man who didn't deserve to be protected.

Twelve

"MY LIFE IS HELL"

John and Elizabeth Edwards held their "farewell and thank-you" party for the people who had worked for, volunteered for, and funded the 2008 campaign in the barn-style gym at their estate, where a stage and sound system had been included in the design for just such an occasion. The crowd numbered about five hundred and included friends, family, donors, staff, and a smattering of celebrities, including basketball coach Dean Smith and actor Danny Glover.

This kind of get-together is a lot like an old-fashioned Irish wake, where people have an opportunity to both celebrate and begin mourning. The comparison seems even more appropriate if you consider that those who idolize and devote themselves to a candidate come to feel that the campaign is like a big family. In this family, John and Elizabeth played the role of mom and dad, and at their party they were so obviously angry with each other that they made all the children nervous.

I'm confident writing about an event I didn't attend because I received dozens of texts and phone calls from people who did—many came *during* the party—and they all reported the same thing: The senator mingled easily, thanked people profusely, and gave a brief talk that my friend Tim Toben reported was heartfelt and kind. Toben had once been captivated by John Edwards, but unlike others, he had developed powerful doubts. He said that at the party Elizabeth told several people what a truly bad person I was.

Other friends who attended the farewell told me that the senator and his wife were noticeably cold to each other. They spent most of the night in different corners of the room and rarely came together. When it was time for them to speak, they stood at opposite ends of the stage. The way they related to each other made the members of the "family" feel as if the parents were fighting. If you recall from your own family what that's like, then you know that the folks the Edwardses were supposed to be thanking felt awkward and uncomfortable. During the campaign, this kind of thing happened far too often, as the candidate and his wife argued while staffers waited and wondered what to do.

Hearing about how Mrs. Edwards had behaved made it easier for me to accept that I didn't attend the party. I resented being shunned, especially when I thought about all I had done to help the Edwardses build their public lives and the very house where the party was held. And certainly the sacrifices that Cheri, the kids, and I continued to make as political fugitives made me feel angry. But giving up the stress of being around the Edwardses when they were fighting was no sacrifice at all.

As the weeks passed at our Santa Barbara hideaway, Cheri worked especially hard to make our existence normal. With their homeschool teacher coming every day, the kids made spectacular academic progress. We returned to the nightly routine of home-cooked dinners and enrolled the kids in various lessons and activities. Gracie went to a theater program, and Brody played every organized sport available. And at night when we said our prayers, we included blessings for "Fred, and Jaya and her baby" as well as Pepper (the cat) and Mr. Turtle.

In her part of the house, Rielle set up a nursery, lit candles to promote spiritual harmony, and talked on the phone with friends and her adviser Bob. We tried to give her privacy because it's hard enough by itself to carry around a full-term, about-to-be-born child. She didn't need us staring at her all the time. The one thing we all did together, without fail, was gather around a TV set to watch the *American Idol* talent contest every week.

By the middle of February, almost everyone at the house had selected a favorite idol contestant. Rielle and Cooper liked David Archuleta. Cheri and Gracie favored David Cook, and Brody was fond of a pretty young woman named Brooke White. I had trouble settling on just one, so I changed my vote from week to week, which made the debates we had about the talents of the various singers that much more fun.

The *Idol* show moved from the audition phase to the true competition in mid-February, just as the due date for Rielle's baby came and went. Feeling ever more uncomfortable, Rielle didn't move much off the sofa, where she waited for the senator's calls and scanned the TV news channels for stories about him. On February 17, I got a voice mail from Rielle saying she'd just seen a picture of the Edwardses meeting with Barack Obama, who had gone to Chapel Hill seeking an endorsement. "Johnny and Elizabeth could not be farther apart from each other," she said, laughing. "I mean, like, they're on separate sides of the driveway."

Although she took pleasure in seeing the Edwardses look alienated from each other, Rielle was always pained by the sight of Elizabeth Edwards and frustrated over being unable to contact the senator whenever she wanted to talk. On the night after she saw the "Obama visits Edwards" TV report, Rielle found Cheri's phone and used it to try to call him at his home. It was eleven P.M. there, and when Mrs. Edwards answered, Rielle hung up without saying a word. The senator's wife promptly called back and left a message that began in a pleasant tone as she said, "Cheri, I don't know whether it was you or Andrew who called us. You are welcome to call us anytime you want." But then, as she got wound up, she became contradictory and scolding. "You have a pretty screwed-up life right now, I understand, with . . . uh, another child . . . [pause] and I am willing to talk to you, Cheri, but I don't want Andrew to call us, and you all can't be a part of our lives. We are trying to wash our hands of this filth."

After we heard this message, I called the Batphone, which the senator now kept hidden somewhere in the barn/gymnasium, where he spent most of his days and nights in a form of marital exile. The phone wasn't set up to receive messages, but every once in a while he would tell Elizabeth he was going to exercise or shoot baskets so that he could check the call history. When I talked to him this time, he told me I needed to control Rielle more closely and to just ignore his wife. We talked politics for a while, and I encouraged him to find something to do that would connect him to his main issue of fighting for the poor and middle class.

"Imagine if instead of Hillary and Barack seeing you at your house, they met you at a Habitat for Humanity work site in New Orleans or even in Greensboro, a few miles away," I said. "That would have been a better picture."

He brushed off the suggestion by saying something about how he was going through a difficult time and needed to be home. He then went on to gush about his encounter with Obama. He said he was leaning toward endorsing him, but Elizabeth had been appalled by Obama's lack of detailed ideas about health care reform. However, the senator was most excited by how his onetime adversary was impressed by the basketball court at the mansion, which is a replica of the floor at UNC, where they traded shots in a game of H-O-R-S-E. (Edwards crowed about how he had won.) Hillary Clinton had already made a similar pilgrimage to Chapel Hill (no H-O-R-S-E), and although Mrs. Edwards wanted her to get the endorsement, he wanted only to endorse the eventual winner. He believed his endorsement was influential enough to determine the winner. He told me he offered it to both Clinton and Obama—first come, first served—in exchange for their commitment to his being named vice president.

Three months would pass before the senator announced his preference for Obama. As he used that time to angle for either the vice presidency or a spot in the cabinet of a future administration, the one Chapel Hill friend who still spoke to me, Tim Toben, became ever more agitated about the man's audacity.

A decade of being "the good soldier" had reinforced my tendency to be loyal to the extreme. And besides being loyal to the senator, I had been boxed in by Elizabeth Edwards, who had called every person who might have helped me start over in a new job to say that I was a liar, a cheat, and a thief. She spread the rumor that Rielle was just "one of Andrew's women" and I had delivered her to the senator as if I were a pimp. Under the cloud she had created, beginning when the campaign was still in full swing, only John Edwards was in a position to clear my name and help me start over. The only hope I had was that once his new child arrived, he would be moved to do the right thing.

On February 26, when she was roughly a week overdue, Rielle was scheduled to have her delivery induced. When she was ready to go to the hospital, she came to our side of the house and said, "Let's take a picture." She also said, "Will you call him for me, Andrew?"

Our kids knew what was going on and started to run around and shout, "The baby's coming!" After we shushed them, Cheri went to call Bob McGovern to come with his car, and then she helped Rielle get ready. I tried the senator's Batphone. When Rielle returned and I told her that he hadn't answered, she barked, "Call Fred!" but then caught herself and said, "Sorry, Andrew. I'm a little emotional right now." Fred did answer and spoke to Rielle, wishing her good luck.

When Bob arrived we took a few pictures and gave her a hug, and Rielle left for the hospital with him. About twenty minutes later, Edwards called me. I had trouble hearing because of the kids. He was abrupt and sounded irritated.

"Hey, what's up?" he said.

I was in a good mood and said, joking, "The eagle is about to land."

"What?"

"Just kidding. She is on the way to the hospital and wanted to talk to you. Hold on, I will patch you through."

As I removed the phone from my ear to hit the buttons, I heard him raise his voice: "Andrew . . . Andrew, don't patch me through!"

I put the phone back to my ear and said, "What?"

"I don't want you to patch me through. Just tell her I couldn't talk because of Elizabeth and I will call you later. Tell her I am thinking of her."

"Senator, you have to talk to her. She will freak out if you don't." Pause. "Boss, you have to. Just for a minute." He insisted it was a bad time and he would call back later. I didn't hear from him all night.

While I talked to the senator, Bob McGovern delivered Rielle to Cottage Hospital in downtown Santa Barbara. In a photo taken before they went inside, Bob has his arm around Rielle. She's wearing a white turtleneck that doesn't quite cover her enormous belly and has her signature pink scarf looped around her neck. Over their heads, a sign announces, EMERGENCY TRAUMA CENTER.

At the admissions desk, Rielle signed in under the name Jaya James and let them run one of our credit cards to pay the bill. (Yes, the mother of John Edwards's baby did not have health insurance.) The initial authorization was for five thousand dollars. When they went to the obstetrics ward, Bob blessed the room ("cleared the energy," in Rielle's words).

Rielle labored all night, but her cervix never dilated. Cheri was there at a little before nine A.M. on Wednesday, February 27, when Rielle agreed to a cesarean section, and a baby girl came into the world. She was twenty-one and a half inches long, weighed eight pounds one ounce, and had blue eyes and a full head of brown hair like her father. Although the baby scored high on the scale they use to assess neonatal health, she had had her umbilical cord wrapped around her neck during the labor and her heart rate was a little fast, which caused some concern among the professionals in the delivery room. After letting Rielle visit with her briefly, they transferred the baby to an intensive care unit for observation. Cheri and Bob followed the baby to the ICU, where the nurses, assuming Bob was the father, made sure he got to hold her first.

Fortunately, the baby's heartbeat normalized quickly, and she was soon reunited with her mom. In a photo taken during this reunion, Rielle looks peaceful and relaxed as the baby rests on her chest. The picture also shows that Rielle is wearing the long heavy gold chain that Bunny Mellon gave Senator Edwards as a good-luck charm.

When I got the news about the baby, I called and texted the senator again. I then called Fred. About an hour later, Edwards called me and I was short with him. "You need to call her. Let me give you Cheri's cell. Be sweet—Rielle is very scared right now." He gave me a vague assurance that he would call her, and I asked him if he wanted me to send her flowers from him.

"Yeah, that's a good idea." He paused. "But don't sign it from me. Someone might see it."

In this moment, I felt as though a switch had turned in my heart. After watching and hearing John Edwards practice a thousand little deceptions and tell a thousand different lies, ostensibly in the service of some greater good, I finally recognized that he didn't care about anyone other than himself. A precious living, breathing human being—his daughter—had come into the world, and he wasn't inclined to even call the woman who had given birth to her. Instead, I had to prompt him to do the right thing, to do the most basic, human thing. My faith in him died almost instantly, and I felt both ashamed of my naïveté and very afraid for the future of my family.

The senator eventually did call Rielle at the hospital, and Cheri told me that she seemed happy about what he had told her. I knew that he had merely played the role of the concerned father, transforming himself for the few minutes that he had to spend on the phone with Rielle and then dropping the pose as soon as he hung up. I knew he had this chameleon ability, and I no longer considered it a talent or a tool. I saw it as a symptom of something deeply flawed in the man, and it disturbed me to think about how he had used this ability to fool me and others so many times. It had taken me almost ten years to figure out the truth about the senator. Rielle had known him for only two years, and when they spoke she was drugged with painkillers and flooded with the feel-good endorphins that come with labor. She believed him.

Because she'd had a cesarean, Rielle stayed in the hospital for five days.

During this time, Cheri offered her expertise as a nurse to help her adjust to breast-feeding and learn all the other duties that come with a newborn. (Despite her years of experience with new moms, Cheri was a little taken aback when Rielle asked when she could resume having sex.) When Rielle and the baby were ready to be discharged, Cheri and Bob were there to help her. Cheri brought along a baby's shirt that Rielle had asked our kids to decorate with the logo "I Am the Granddaughter of a Millworker." Rielle wrapped the shirt around her baby, whom she had named Frances Quinn, for the journey home. (She chose Quinn, a derivation of the Latin word for "five," because she was Edwards's fifth child.)

The hospital's final bill was paid with our credit card, and Rielle signed out under the name Rielle Jaya James Druck. The space for "father" on the child's birth certificate was left blank. Bob drove mother and child to Montecito and through the gate at Ennisbrook and then to the house.

Within an hour of Rielle's arrival at the house, I could see that she was not going to have an ordinary relationship with her child. I had witnessed the bond Cheri made with each of our children and watched other new moms with their infants, so I knew the attachment could be fierce. But Rielle believed, as she said, that the baby had been "sent to save the world." Accordingly, she just couldn't let anyone else hold her. In fact, in her first few days at the house with the baby, Rielle almost never put her down. With the slightest cry or snuffle, she would pick up the baby, coo something like "You are just soooo beautiful!" and try to nurse her.

In more relaxed moments, Rielle would do a funny imitation of Barack Obama's famous campaign line "Fired up, ready to go." Before it became annoying, it was actually heartwarming to see a mother with her baby, chanting, "Fired up! Ready to go! Fired up! Ready to go!" as the baby's eyes widened and focused on her face. Unfortunately, Rielle's positive spirit was reserved entirely for Frances Quinn. With us, she was irritated and impatient. She couldn't bear the slightest noise from our kids and would try to get them to be quiet even when they were playing outside.

When Bob visited we had a few private minutes with him, and he tried to explain Rielle's demanding and needy nature. He said that Rielle had suffered terribly as a child. With Frances Quinn, he said, "she's trying to fill the void inside her." Knowing that her father had been involved in an insurance fraud scheme and actually killed his own daughter's beloved prizewinning horse, we found it easy to believe she carried deep psychological wounds. But although this information helped us have compassion for Rielle, it didn't make living with her any easier. After a couple of days, we decided to go to North Carolina and check on our house, which was now months into construction. Rielle invited an old friend named Wendy to come up from Los Angeles and keep her company while we took a risk and flew back to Raleigh-Durham. (We left the kids with Cheri's parents as we traveled.) I hadn't been home since December.

At the construction site, we were able to see what the builder had done. Because we were forced to make decisions by phone, guided by our architect, the house had gotten much bigger and more expensive than we had planned. During the visit we offered whatever suggestions we could for bringing the project under control, but we could hardly blame the builder, because we had told him to do what he thought was best. "Best" in any contractor's mind is going to be big and expensive, and in the world we now inhabited, which included private jets, Aspen vacation homes, and Santa Barbara rentals that cost twenty thousand dollars per month, a thousand dollars this way or that way didn't seem to matter.

When we weren't at the building site we were at the Montross house, which hadn't yet sold. We went through piles of mail and a stack of notes left by reporters and photographers. We didn't respond to any of them but brought the notes with us as we traveled back to California. We didn't know when we would ever get to North Carolina again.

In Santa Barbara, we discovered that Rielle had just about driven her friend Wendy crazy with demands and criticisms. (Wendy actually broke down crying as she talked to us about the experience.) Rielle also had been calling Senator Edwards's phone several times a day and was threatening both him and Fred Baron with going public about the affair and the baby. I wouldn't have thought it was possible for anything to make Rielle more difficult to deal with, but motherhood had in fact given her an even greater sense of her own power and a willingness to use it.

One seemingly small incident from this period illustrates the point perfectly. After calling Cheri for a cup of coffee, Rielle let it sit for a moment and then summoned her back because she needed more sugar put in it. Cheri got her what she requested and left, only to receive another phone call from Rielle. The coffee now needed more milk. Cheri added milk, but now it was too cold. "Put it in the microwave," said Rielle. A mother, nurse, and wife who was accustomed to caretaking, Cheri actually did this chore, but she was obviously unhappy and said something sarcastic about how Rielle must have been especially tired.

Soon Cheri and I were both fit to be tied as life with Rielle became more difficult and weeks passed without any sign of the senator telling the truth or any suggestion of a long-term resolution of this crazy mission. Communication with him was becoming more difficult. Where he once called several times a day, he now never dialed my number. When I got through to him, he kept the calls brief and guarded what he said. In the middle of March, I was shocked to hear that he had booked himself onto *The Tonight Show* with Jay Leno and that after the taping he was going to visit Rielle and the baby at a hotel in Beverly Hills.

Rielle told us of this plan with both excitement and anxiety in her voice. The meeting was set for March 19, which was about ten days away, and she was self-conscious about her physical condition. She instantly began fasting and exercising madly. (I'll never forget how she chanted along with special recordings of Buddhist monks that she listened to as she worked out on the treadmill. The sound of the chants, with Rielle joining in, echoed through the house.) Rielle was also worried about how to relate to John Edwards now that she was the mother of his child and their relationship was more complicated. Cheri, who was overloaded with the stress of Rielle's demands, responded to this concern with one of her rare (considering the circumstances) displays of hostility.

"Well, of course you are worried," she said. "Your whole relationship has been about nothing other than hanging out in hotel rooms, drinking, and having sex." This time Rielle would get the hotel room, Cheri allowed, but since she was nursing, alcohol was out, and it was a little too soon for her to engage in much sexual activity.

As snarky attacks go, Cheri's little commentary was fairly mild, and Rielle didn't react. On March 18, Bob came to pick her up for the drive to Los Angeles, where they would stay in two of the more expensive suites available at the famous Beverly Hilton Hotel. I received text messages from Rielle that referred to the senator and his new daughter. The most telling one arrived at 1:39 A.M.: "Yeah he is burping Quinn going to sleep when he is done. Soooo tired."

The next night, I watched on television as the senator walked onto the Leno set, shook hands with the genial host, and answered questions. Like everyone, Leno was most interested in whether he had made an endorsement decision. The senator said Hillary Clinton was the choice he'd make with his head, but Barack Obama might be the candidate chosen by his heart. When asked if he might try one more time for the White House, he said, "I'm not thinking about running again. But never say never."

It was mind-boggling to me that the senator was able to take the stage in such a relaxed manner and discuss national political affairs with such a sense of his own power, knowing that he could be brought down in an instant by a mistress lounging in a hotel across town with his newborn baby. Worse still, he was sitting on the same sofa he had shared with Elizabeth just months earlier, when they spoke lovingly of their thirtieth anniversary.

Cheri had had enough of Rielle, John Edwards, Elizabeth Edwards, and the freakish existence we had accepted and now seemed to be trapped in-

side. She wanted our life back, and so did I. But I had signed for the
$20,000-per-month lease on the Santa Barbara house, and my income was
tied to John Edwards. Every time I talked to Fred Baron about ending the
charade and helping us get back to a normal life, he said, "Don't worry
about it, we're going to take care of you. We need to focus on getting him
the vice presidency." When I tried to call and text the senator myself, he
refused to answer the phone or respond to my messages. He had no problem responding to Rielle, however, and called her half a dozen times a day.
Once when I answered her phone when he called, he responded with cold
indifference to my pleas for him to come clean and changed the subject by
accusing my wife of talking to bloggers who were speculating on the Internet about Edwards's connection to Rielle.

I could barely contain my anger. "Rielle tells everyone she knows about
you. We haven't even told our families. What the . . . ?" I shouted at him. I
let him know that she had told her friends Mimi and Wendy everything
about him, and when she talked to her friend Pigeon O'Brien in St. Louis,
they laughingly referred to him as "Love Lips." Our families still weren't
sure why we had disappeared, and our kids were beginning to forget their
lives back in North Carolina. Senator Edwards didn't seem to care about
our distress, but he did ask if I could get a diaper to send for a DNA test. He
still didn't believe he was the baby's father.

When the call was over, it was clear to me that I would have to take
some action to solve our problems. I still heard from a few people who were
connected with the campaigns and refused to judge me harshly. One of
these friends actually gave my name to a prominent attorney in Tampa who
had started a national nonprofit organization to help disabled people. Blinded
in an accident when he was a teenager, Richard Salem called this group
Enable America. Its goal was to help people with various disabilities gain
access to employment. The project had stalled for lack of donations, and
my track record as a fund-raiser got his attention. After he reviewed my
history and we spoke several times on the phone, he flew Cheri and me to
Tampa for an interview.

My first contacts with Richard Salem had restored my sense of confidence and given me some hope for the future. After a night in a hotel, where we talked about living in Tampa and decided it would be okay, Cheri and I went to meet him. We had breakfast at a restaurant that was high up in one of the city's tallest buildings, and I thought an offer was pending. Toward the end of the breakfast Salem motioned to his assistant, who began riffling through her briefcase. While the assistant continued her search, Salem said, "Andrew, I want to tell you about a case in which I represented a Mob boss." He proceeded to explain how he was up front with the jury about his client's crime connections because "you should never ignore the elephant in the room." His aide then handed over copies of *National Enquirer* articles about me, Rielle, and the senator. This was my elephant, said Richard Salem, and he couldn't ignore it.

Unable to defend myself without the risk of blowing the entire cover-up, I thought the fact that I was sitting there with my wife showed the story was false. I said, "I would hope people would see what's been printed and look at us together and know what is true."

Although he obviously couldn't "see" us, I know that Richard Salem could hear the strength of Cheri's support for me when we had talked about the job and moving our family to Florida. Nevertheless, after recruiting me quite aggressively, he told me I could not have the job. We went home feeling ashamed and angry. When we got back to Santa Barbara, nothing had changed with Rielle. She was still extremely needy and so focused on her baby that she hardly ever left her alone to sleep. I never actually held Frances Quinn, and Rielle let Cheri, who had years of neonatal intensive care experience, handle her only a few times. She was happy to let us do chores for her, however, and would call us on the telephone when we were just two or three rooms away to help her with a task.

When we resisted her, Rielle became petulant but also tried to handle a few things on her own. On one morning she actually put coffee in the coffeemaker, filled it with water, and switched it on to brew. When she returned, she found that she had missed something in the setup and both coffee and grounds had flowed out of the machine, over the counter, and onto the floor. She saw the mess, made a fresh pot of coffee so she would have something to drink, but decided against cleaning up. A little later in the morning, Cheri wandered into the kitchen, where the countertop and floor (both made of limestone, which was easily stained) were still wet with Rielle's mess. She came back to our side of the house, where I was on the treadmill.

"I've had it," she said, flushing with anger. "I've really had it."

After Cheri told me what happened, I went with her to Rielle's side of the house. We found her in her bedroom, where several candles were lit and she was chanting some incantations to the baby. Cheri said, "Are you going to clean up the mess in the kitchen?"

No answer from Rielle.

"Do you expect me to clean it up?"

No answer from Rielle.

I thought Cheri was going to explode as she told Rielle that she was a capable adult and responsible for cleaning up her own messes. Rielle then held up her hand, like a cop stopping traffic, and said, "I'm not talking to you." Then she added, "You know, Cheri, you're not very smart, but you are perceptive."

I got Cheri out of there before things deteriorated even further, but there was nothing I could do to change her mind about what was going to happen next. She said that either Fred Baron was going to move Rielle out of the house "or I'll move her out." That day, Fred invited us to visit him in Dallas to talk things over.

Leaving Rielle alone in the great big house in Montecito, we took the kids to Illinois to be with Cheri's parents. After telling them only that we were trying to get our lives back to normal and needed their help with the kids, we flew to see Fred in Dallas. We landed at Love Field and got to his house in a town car he had sent to deliver us.

Fred lived in a compound carved out of about a dozen acres, including an artificial lake, within minutes of the airport. The house he built just for his domestic staff would have been one of the most impressive mansions in Chapel Hill. His own home resembled a grand château in France. (It was where he hosted his famous Christmas parties, where as many as one thousand guests would take in entertainment from the likes of the Doobie Brothers and Three Dog Night.) Determined to give us a tour, he showed us the enormous reception area by the front door, big first-floor rooms for public events, and a private library where he kept a valuable oil portrait of George Washington.

Someone else would have shown us around the house with the sense that he was flexing his muscles a bit, impressing us with his wealth and power. Fred just seemed thrilled by life, amazed that he was as rich as he was, and excited to show us how he lived (you couldn't help but like Fred). When we finally sat down to talk, we were joined by his wife, Lisa Blue, who was a lawyer and held a doctorate in psychology. Cheri kicked off her shoes and put her feet on the coffee table to show that she was not at all intimidated. Together, we then made three demands:

1. We wanted to know why John Edwards hadn't yet told the truth.
2. We wanted to separate from Rielle and her child.
3. We wanted a long-term plan for our future and a commitment to see it through. Specifically, we wanted to know if Edwards was going to establish the antipoverty foundation that was supposed to supply me with a long-term job and health insurance.

Fred said he understood our worries but that we should have confidence in him and the senator. Although I had tried to tell him the truth, he still believed I was the father of Rielle's baby, and he expected that Edwards would be a big player in the next administration. "Hold on until August," he said, referring to the Democratic National Convention. Lisa and Fred both said they felt (and Lisa is a trained psychologist) that Elizabeth was a threat to us, our kids, and herself. Repeating an argument he had begun to make with me several weeks before, Fred also said we had no special ties to

Chapel Hill and could settle anywhere in the country. He said we should finish the house, sell it, and start a new life far from the prying eyes of the press. Fred soon wired several hundred thousand dollars to our builder to help with all our expenses. He offered this as a gift.

Talk as they might, Lisa and Fred couldn't persuade us that we should stick it out with Rielle in Santa Barbara until August, when somehow everything would be resolved. We knew John and Elizabeth Edwards better than they did. We also knew the truth. Empowered by what we knew, I insisted that John Edwards call me and that we meet, face-to-face, as soon as possible.

> Uh, hey, stranger! It's John. I hope you are doing well . . . Just calling 'cause I miss you. I haven't talked to you in a while. I wanted to see how you are doing. Umm, you can call me back on this phone . . . Anyway, hope you are doing well. I miss talking to you, Andrew. We'll see you, pal.

The message was recorded on my cell phone account on May 21, 2008. The tone was contrite, and it came as a signal that Edwards was ready at last to deal with me. For months the senator had neglected not just me, but others, and he'd used as an excuse the claim that he was carefully deliberating over whom to endorse for the party's nomination. It was a ridiculous claim, but still he used it to manipulate people who had been very good to him, including Bunny Mellon, who had sent word that she wanted to visit with him. Bunny needed his support, because her bedridden daughter, Eliza, was deteriorating rapidly. When she died in mid-May, the senator skipped the funeral, saying he was still considering his endorsement. As far as I knew, the only thing Bunny had ever asked of him—in return for more than $6 million—was that he sit on one side of her at that funeral while Caroline Kennedy sat on the other. Caroline fulfilled her wish. John Edwards did not.

Truer to his promises and responsibilities, Fred Baron located a house for Rielle and arranged to have her moved into it in early June. Cheri went out to run errands on the day she left. The kids and I actually helped her pack and took pictures with her as she said good-bye. Although no one said it, I knew that I would never see Rielle again or speak to her on the phone. She did not say thank you.

Fred also kept hounding the senator until he at last agreed to meet me face-to-face, so that I could tell him how I felt and press him to make things right. I was furious about how my family and I were being treated. Cheri and I sensed that the senator was telling Mrs. Edwards tales about me and that she was getting more upset. On Father's Day, June 15, Cheri got an e-mail that appeared to come from Heather North, the nanny at the Edwards house. It read:

> Has Rielle had Andrew's baby yet? She is such a scum. I can't believe she slept with Andrew the first night she met him. Has she really been around since August 2006? You must be sick of her. I am so sorry. She flirted with Jed that first night too, even when I was right there. :(. . . I am so sorry about the rumors that Andrew has had lots of affairs like this one . . . What a bad time this must be for you.

Although it arrived with Heather's return address, nothing in this e-mail sounded like her, and Cheri called her as soon as it arrived. Heather answered, sounding very happy that we had called, and explained that she was out on a boat.

"Then you didn't send me an e-mail?" asked Cheri.

"No, why do you ask?"

It took less than thirty seconds for the two women to agree that Elizabeth Edwards was the only person who could have had access to Heather's e-mail account and the interest in sending the e-mail in question. The tone of the message and a word like "scum" were so out of character for Heather—but consistent with the attitudes of Mrs. Edwards—and only reinforced the suspicion that she was the source. The incident bothered Heather, because of the invasion of her account, but made us feel sorry for Elizabeth Edwards. She had cancer. She and her husband had just finished a grueling and failed campaign for president. And I believe that deep in her heart, she knew her husband was the father of Rielle Hunter's baby and that her campaign against me was unfair and dishonest.

When Edwards finally set a date to meet me for a discussion that I intended to use to force an end to his deception, he insisted I come alone and asked that we meet in a restaurant. I agreed to leave Cheri home but demanded we get together in private. There was no way we could settle this in a public place. He agreed, and we settled on a date, Wednesday, June 18, and a place: the River Inn in the Georgetown district of Washington, D.C. I bought a plane ticket and was ready to depart on June 17 when Edwards sent word that he needed to delay our meeting for a day in order to attend the funeral of *Meet the Press* host Tim Russert, who had died unexpectedly. Despite the cost and inconvenience, I rescheduled my flight and arrived in D.C. on Thursday morning. (Only later would I learn that Edwards never went to the funeral.) Pam Marple, the attorney who wrote the statement declaring that I was Rielle Hunter's lover, picked me up at the airport and drove me to the hotel, where I sat in the lobby.

The plan called for the senator to ring my cell phone and tell me the room number where I was to find him. Ninety minutes after the appointed time, I started leaving messages on Fred's phone. When he called me back, he said, "He is about to call you. Calm down. Let's get this taken care of."

I called Cheri and told her it was finally about to happen. While I was talking to her, I saw one of the senator's latest body men, Matthew Nelson, walk out of the elevator. "Hey, Cheri, I gotta go," I said, and got up to speak to him. He was shocked to see me but tried to act nonchalant.

"What are you doing here?"

I told him I was visiting some friends and then asked him why he was in town. Matthew said he was there with the senator, who had just filled in for Obama at an event and gotten a five-minute standing ovation for his speech. He said Edwards believed he was going to get "V.P." (This was not idle speculation. Tim Toben had relayed to me Edwards's inside knowledge of polls that showed he would help Obama capture more votes in key states like Ohio and Pennsylvania than any other running mate.)

Just then my cell phone rang. I answered to hear Edwards's familiar voice asking me to come upstairs. I said okay and then dialed Cheri for encouragement. She said, "Try to stay calm. And whatever you do, don't hit him!"

On the elevator ride up I seethed and I thought about how only a consummate actor, or a psychologically disturbed human being, could have greeted me so cheerfully knowing what was about to happen. On the fifth floor I got out of the elevator and turned right to find the suite where he was waiting. I knocked and he answered with a Cheshire-cat grin and said how glad he was to see me. I responded that I wished I could say the same.

He led me into the suite and sat down with his legs folded up on the chair in a very casual way and acted like he was shocked to see me upset. He tried to talk about how he had just given an incredible speech and was certain to be picked to run as vice president. I cut him off, saying I had run into Matthew downstairs. For a moment he seemed troubled by this but then said he didn't care because Matthew was loyal to him, not Elizabeth.

He said he didn't know why I had come to see him and suggested I start the conversation. I began by asking why the "fuck" he hadn't called me in three months. I criticized him for missing Eliza's funeral and failing to call people whom he had promised to contact on my behalf.

After trying to minimize my complaints, he then tried to soothe my feelings. He asked why I was upset and told me he loved me. He insisted that our relationship was unchanged and that he hadn't been in touch with anyone because he was depressed about the election.

I exploded. I asked how many people did the shit for him that my family had done. I told him he owed us a call. And that it was inexcusable that he had skipped Eliza's funeral. Bunny truly loved him, had given him millions of dollars and never asked anything else from him in return.

Backpedaling, he said that Bunny had assured him that she was not up-set about the funeral. I corrected him, saying that Bunny was too dignified to complain, or say how much he had hurt her.

I hit a nerve. He put up his hands and talked about how we had been friends for years, had been through so much together, and that nothing had changed between us for him. He then used one of his old tricks, blaming someone else for his problems and trying to bond with me over marital problems. He said he knew Cheri was upset with me and that he under-stood what it felt like because Elizabeth was being hard on him.

Exasperated, I looked at him with fury in my eyes and said, "Jesus Christ."

He told me that Elizabeth screamed all the time about me to him, and that he actually defended me. Edwards said that his wife believed that I had ruined the presidential campaign and their reputation. I told him of course she thinks that—he told her all that. He insisted, "I am going through hell."

He was veering way off the main topic I wanted to discuss and I tried to bring him back in line by recalling that he had abandoned me, and my fam-ily. He denied this and said he wasn't the kind of person to abandon some-one he cared deeply about.

"Not that kind of person? Not that kind of person?" I then started to name people he had betrayed or abandoned without cause, including Elizabeth, Julianna Smoot, Josh Stein, David Axelrod, Bunny Mellon, John Kerry, Josh Brumberger, and others. Before I could finish, he lost his cool. He jumped up and slammed his fist down on the table. "No one fuck-ing talks to me like that. No one." When he ripped into Cheri, accusing her of talking to the press and others about Rielle and the baby, I shouted, "Bullshit!" right in his face.

He asked what the "fuck" I wanted.

I said, "Nothing," and stood up. Our faces were about a foot apart over the coffee table and I was ready to fight him right there. He told me to get the "fuck" out. I told him he could read about it in the newspapers.

I flung open the door and it hit the wall with a loud bang. I walked down to the elevator trying to make a dramatic exit. I could feel him nervously looking at me as I pushed the call button. As I waited for the elevator, some of the drama drained out of the moment. Finally he walked down the hall and asked me to come back.

Afraid to leave things as they were, I went back to the room. In the tense first moments, he told me not to threaten him again. I told him not to "fucking" talk to me like that again.

We then had a much calmer discussion. He promised to stay in contact with me and not delay returning my calls. He also renewed his promise to help me in the long term by establishing the antipoverty organization with funds from Bunny Mellon where I would have a good job with health insurance and he could have a solid political platform.

Within twenty-four hours of our confrontation at the hotel in George-town, he went to see Bunny. During this visit he decided that he was set-ting his sights too low. Instead of $3 to $5 million, he now hoped to get as much as $50 million and her jet so he could circle the globe combating pov-erty. As a few more weeks passed, he had me contact her accountant, Ken-neth Starr (not the same fellow who was involved in the Monica Lewinsky case), to see if the foundation was feasible. The senator and I discussed strat-egy in five different phone conversations. Following his plan, I created a nonprofit corporation for this project, which we called the New Heritage Education Foundation. I broached the topic with Starr, who thought a world-wide antipoverty effort headed by Bunny's friend John Edwards would be an ideal way to honor her life.

Once he realized that this foundation could become a reality and pro-vide him with a permanent role on the world stage, the senator pursued it with enthusiasm. After one meeting with Bunny, the senator told Bunny's friend Bryan Huffman he could be on the board of the foundation and "do great things." He then called me and left a voice mail saying, "Bunny loves me." Another message he left me said:

> Andrew, hey, it's John. I had a wonderful conversation with . . . long and wonderful conversation with Bunny . . .

she will be there no matter what. She's offered me to come up there and stay if I need to, and I may end up doing that some. Anyway, she's a terrific person. . . . and I think we can completely count on her, and I just wanted you to hear that and to once again tell you I love you . . . I really love you, Andrew.

This call, and another voice mail in which he told me he was going to see Bunny to finalize arrangements for the foundation, gave me hope that the senator was finding a way to fulfill his promise that I would be employed into the future. I was also happy to be talking about something other than a secret girlfriend and his unacknowledged child. I shouldn't have been so happy. Without someone to monitor them and clean up after them, Rielle and the senator wouldn't be able to stay out of trouble for more than a few weeks.

Thirteen

TRUE LIES

With Rielle Hunter gone and John Edwards focused on the upcoming Democratic National Convention, Cheri and I thought we could take a few days to start putting our lives back in order. The Santa Barbara lease was ending in early August. In anticipation, we flew east and dropped the kids in Illinois to stay with family, then traveled on to Raleigh. We spent a couple of days moving our things into storage and cleaning up. On top of all the other frustrations we felt, we were dealing with a house that my boss told me I could never move in to.

As we moved through the rental house and sorted things into boxes and rubbish that could be discarded, I came upon a box of trash that Rielle had left behind after she stayed with us for a few weeks at the very start of her life on the run. A few things lying on top of the cardboard and papers caught my eye. One was a sheaf of pages ripped out of a notebook with "The Slut Club" written on the top line and a list of thirty-four men's names below.

I also noticed a number of videotapes, including one marked "Special," which had the tape pulled out and seemed intentionally broken. Cheri said, "Must be the missing webisodes Elizabeth was looking for."

I couldn't resist. With scissors, a pen, and some Scotch tape, I fixed the cassette and put a TV on top of some boxes to watch the video. As soon as I pressed play, we saw an image of a man—John Edwards—and a naked pregnant woman, photographed from the navel down, engaged in a sexual encounter. The images were recorded with the somewhat steady assurance of a professional, and the senator's performance was ironically narcissistic. The video was without sound, and the angle was such that the woman's face was obscured. (She obviously held the camera.) But given where we found the tape and the fact that the woman on the tape wore a distinctive bracelet I had seen on Rielle many times, it was safe to assume it was Rielle, and that it was filmed just before the election began.

As compromising images of a former presidential candidate and current contender for vice president flashed on the screen, Cheri and I dropped to the floor and watched, speechless. When we were able to talk, we debated turning it off, but neither of us could actually press the button. It was like watching a traffic pileup occur in slow motion—it was repelling but also transfixing. We also knew immediately that we now possessed something powerful. We weren't going to use it in any nefarious way, but I planned to deposit a copy in a safe-deposit box and place at least one other with an attorney with instructions to make it public, if necessary, should anything suspicious befall us.

My fear may have been fueled by paranoia. However, it was justified. I had been uprooted and then isolated from friends, and I had read enough John Grisham novels to believe that superlawyers empowered with endless amounts of money could do terrible things. We were dealing with lots of rich and powerful people. The tape, I thought, might protect us.

We returned to California via Illinois, arriving on July 21. After seven months of being trapped with Rielle, we felt like celebrating. We used a credit left over from a hotel to stay overnight at Venice Beach, where the kids got to see Rollerbladers, fortune-tellers, and a few "You're going to hell" evangelists on the boardwalk. In the morning, we drove back to Santa Barbara so we could close up that house. I turned off my cell phone and rolled down the windows to enjoy our last drive up the coast. When I switched the phone on again at the house, it rang almost immediately.

Pam Marple, the attorney who had drafted the statement declaring I was the father of Rielle's baby, was calling from her office in Washington. She said someone from the *National Enquirer* had just called her asking for a comment on pictures they had showing John Edwards visiting Rielle Hunter—less than twelve hours ago—at the Beverly Hilton. A story on Edwards going to the hotel and speculating about the nature of the visit was already posted on the *Enquirer* Web site. Pam was upset and hoped I could tell her something about what was really going on. In fact, I didn't know that Edwards had been in Beverly Hills while we were a few miles away at Venice Beach. I couldn't advise her, nor could I inform her.

At first I thought they had pictures from the senator's first visit with Rielle and the baby. She had taken photos of him with Quinn, and I thought that she may have given them to the *Enquirer*. Knowing that the senator could be in deep trouble, I wanted to help him, even after all that had happened. I tried to call Rielle but got no answer. As I hung up, the phone rang in my hand. It was the senator. I answered to hear him fighting tears and struggling to talk.

"Andrew, they caught me. It's all over."

The emotion in his voice and traffic in the background made it hard for me to hear him. I let him cry and blubber for a minute, and as he did I thought I heard a man who was finally facing the truth. I felt I needed to help him pull himself together. I started by going to my computer and logging on to the *Enquirer* Web site while I asked him what had happened.

According to the tale he told me, the senator had come to Los Angeles to see supporters and had arranged to see Rielle and Frances Quinn afterward. Bob picked him up in his BMW and drove him to the Beverly Hilton, where Rielle and Bob were staying.

"Did you see any cameras?" I asked him.

"No, definitely not. I mean, I guess there could have been one—I remember a room service cart—I guess a camera could have been there. Hell, they can hide a camera anywhere these days."

"Well, they say in the article that y'all went out walking holding hands."

"No, that's BS. We didn't leave the room."

My guess was that Rielle had tortured the hotel staff in order to get an upgrade and was not in the room where the *Enquirer* guys had set up their stakeout. A glance at the *Enquirer* Web site turned up no actual photos of Edwards with Rielle or the baby. They only had pictures of him in public areas of the hotel. "I don't think they've got what they say they have," I told him. Then I asked, "What are you going to tell Elizabeth?"

"I already talked to her. I had to."

Now a bit calmer, Edwards explained that he had been so alarmed by the encounter with the *Enquirer* guys that he felt he had to call his wife. But as usual, he didn't tell her the truth. He told her that Bob and Rielle were blackmailing him. He went to the hotel because they were going to tell the world an enormous lie—John Edwards is the father of this baby—and he had to give them money or else. He also told Elizabeth that I wasn't paying child support.

The story might have been logical if he had told Mrs. Edwards that I was part of the blackmailing scheme, but he had not. "It doesn't make sense for you to be alone in a hotel room with my girlfriend for three hours, until two A.M.," I said. "It's stupid."

A call waiting signal interrupted our conversation, and Edwards told me he had to go to Los Angeles International Airport to catch a flight home. He sounded a little like a man headed to the gallows or a little boy going to see his mother after he broke a window playing ball. He said he would call me from the airport. When I hung up and checked the message on my phone, I discovered it was Fred Baron. He sounded full of life as he almost shouted, "Hey, I'm out of the hospital and feeling great. I'm gonna beat this thing!"

Fred, whose cancer was progressing, told me he had recently spent several days at the Mayo Clinic undergoing treatment. He sounded so cheerful, I thought that he must not know what was happening with John Edwards. When I called back and informed him, he finally believed my insistent claim, which I had expressed to him for months, that I was not the father of Rielle's baby. He accepted that I had never had an affair with her and that I had been protecting his friend the senator all along.

Fred was very upset. I could hear him telling Lisa Blue the news and saying, "Goddamn Edwards. What the hell was he thinking?"

Fred and I spoke nine times in the next few hours. He was devastated to learn the truth about a man he had trusted with his time, emotion, and fortune. Like someone who has been through a terrible trauma, Fred wanted to pore over the details. At one point we discussed the fact that Edwards had asked us both to see if we could get a fabricated DNA test showing he was not the baby's father. Fred laughed and said, "That's criminal. That's ridiculous. And it's not going to happen." When we talked about how the *Enquirer* staff could have known that Edwards was going to be at the hotel, we had to conclude that they had been tipped off by Rielle, Bob McGovern, or someone either of them had told. In the end it didn't matter, but it was natural to speculate. (The details in the *Enquirer* were mostly accurate, including some facts I wouldn't confirm until much later.)

The senator called me from the airport and continued the conversation we had started earlier. We talked a total of seven different times during the day.

When Cheri and I talked about what was going on, she instantly thought of Mrs. Edwards and how she might react. According to her husband and Fred Baron, she had threatened to hurt herself many times before. Genuinely concerned for her and her children, we decided it would be best to contact their old family friend David Kirby and suggest someone check on her condition. Kirby agreed and made sure someone did. The next day, I got the following voice mail from Elizabeth Edwards, who was speaking about Rielle:

> If you want to be helpful to me you can not call a bunch of people, you can call the mother of your child and pay what you owe . . . This is a completely crazy, desperate, pathetic woman with no skills and no possibility of employment. You are going to have to take care of your baby. If you do that, she won't behave in this erratic way [long pause]. And then you and your concubine and your entire family can stay out of our lives.

Cheri had predicted that one person was absolutely certain to believe the cockamamie story Edwards had devised about the blackmail scheme: his wife. She was right, and the message proved it. Considering what Elizabeth Edwards believed was true, the anger that she directed at me was understandable, but I couldn't excuse her decision to direct some of her fury at Cheri. On the same day she used voice mail to lecture me, she called Cheri's number and said in a fake, syrupy drawl: "Andrew needs to pay for that baby!"

In the days that followed the Beverly Hilton fiasco, the senator schemed to avoid future problems and actually suggested we move to Bunny Mellon's estate. That way we would never run into Elizabeth at school events. For her part, Elizabeth would continue the effort to make Cheri feel the kind of pain that comes with intimate betrayal. One of her messages recommended that Cheri call one of John Edwards's campaign supporters who lived near Figure Eight Island to hear about how I had used their home there as a love nest: "You need to call Russell at the beach and find out why we had the locks changed on the house . . . so that Andrew would not use it with his girlfriends. We were told about it by people at the beach. Ask Russell."

When I learned what was happening at the Edwards estate during the time Elizabeth was troubling herself with calls to us, I was amazed to hear she had the time or energy to even think about us. According to Senator Edwards, she was consulting with advisers and even brought a bunch of them, including Jennifer Palmieri and Harrison Hickman, to the mansion for a big pow-wow about how to handle the *Enquirer*'s false story. In a whispered phone conversation, Edwards told me that while helicopters carrying photographers circled overhead, they'd decided, with Mrs. Edwards's leadership, that honesty would be the best policy. The senator was going to go on television with a respected and fair-minded journalist—Bob Woodruff of ABC News—and tell the story. He would do it on August 8, as the opening ceremonies for the Olympic Games in China were being broadcast, in hopes that most of the world would ignore him in favor of the spectacle at Beijing National Stadium.

This plan seemed idiotic to me. First of all, the story the senator was planning to tell, of a brief affair and blackmail, was still an incomprehensible lie. Second, the supposed "spy photos" the *National Enquirer* published on August 6 were, as far as I could tell, fakes. Edwards had gone to the Beverly Hilton wearing a blue button-down shirt. The pictures showed him holding a baby and wearing a sweat-stained T-shirt. It was the wrong shirt, and anyone who knew the guy understood that he would never walk through a hotel lobby looking like such a mess.

The senator and I discussed his decision by phone after my family and I had departed for Santa Barbara for good. With the press descending on our house, we had gone to Los Angeles to hide at Disneyland before our flight home. The motel we booked near Disneyland was a Fairfield Inn, where we had a room on an upper floor. With five of us sharing a room, the only privacy I could find for the call with him was next to an ice machine. I leaned against the wall, looked out over the busy street, and begged Edwards to delay his decision. As a candidate, he had sold himself to the public as an especially moral, Christian family man. His wife had cancer. It would be far wiser, I said, to wait to see what the press really had and tell the whole truth—the real truth—only when he couldn't avoid it.

I was not alone in my assessment of the situation. Bunny Mellon, whose love for John Edwards was sincere, believed that he should simply stay silent and ride out the storm. Bunny had lived through JFK's infidelity and knew of the affairs carried on by her men in her life. In her view, powerful men should be expected to behave this way—indeed, they might even have a right to break the rules—and only unsophisticated dolts expected anything else. Her advice? Tell the whole truth or nothing at all. (Bunny also offered to send another check and to let us stay at her home in Antigua to regroup.)

In the end, neither Bunny nor I could get him out of the trap he had created for himself. Using his considerable powers of persuasion, the senator had lied to Elizabeth repeatedly and was now boxed in by his story and her need to take action.

At two o'clock on August 5, I was standing in line for the Buzz Lightyear ride when Fred called to tell me that Edwards had definitely decided to do the interview. Since the press would jump on the story, he wanted to get Rielle and the baby out of the country. Then he asked if I could get Rielle's passport, which was stored somewhere in Chapel Hill, delivered to him.

"When?" I asked.

"Well, that's the problem. She is flying out tomorrow morning."

When she heard what Fred had asked, Cheri couldn't believe they would request more favors. But I saw the drama coming to an end, and I was eager to see it all resolved even though there wasn't much time to get the passport to FedEx. While she and the kids went off to have more fun, I went to a restaurant overlooking Tom Sawyer Island. Steamboat whistles and fake cannonfire sounded in the background as I made seventeen calls. During these calls, I made notes on a cardboard lunch box (Alvin and the Chipmunks) and the price tag from a Beanie Baby toy. Eventually, I was able to arrange to get the passport delivered to a company called Mobile Air in Mobile, Alabama, care of pilot Ronald Gehlken. (Gehlken would fly Rielle to a Caribbean island for a brief stay.)

After Rielle's escape was arranged, the senator called three times. In one call, he thanked me. But in the others, he railed about reports popping up on the Internet. Radar.com had said that Cheri had told the whole story of Rielle and the senator to her hairstylist in Chapel Hill. Another blog said our landlords had been the source of the money used to fund Rielle's life in hiding. Edwards yelled at me, saying that all along he had thought we had been "the leak." Fred agreed with him. They were convinced and angry with us. I told them they were being ridiculous. "Think about it. Cheri hasn't had her hair cut in Chapel Hill since we went on the run. She couldn't have told anyone there anything."

On Friday, August 8, prime-time viewers across the country saw Edwards, in shirtsleeves, sit with the ABC correspondent and answer every question with contrite and seemingly sincere statements that were absolutely false. Here are some key passages:

JOHN EDWARDS: In 2006, two years ago, I made a very serious mistake. A mistake that I am responsible for and no one else. In 2006, I told Elizabeth about the mistake, asked her for her forgiveness, asked God for His forgiveness. And we have kept this within our family since that time. All of my family knows about this, and just to be absolutely clear, none of them are responsible for it. I am responsible for it. I alone am responsible for it. And it led to this most recent incident at the Beverly Hilton. I was at the Beverly Hilton. I was there for a very simple reason, because I was trying to keep this mistake that I had made from becoming public.

BOB WOODRUFF: I know this is a very difficult question, but were you in love with [Rielle Hunter]?

JOHN EDWARDS: I'm in love with one woman. I've been in love with one woman for thirty-one years. She is the finest human being I have ever known. And the fact that she is with me after this having happened is a testament to the kind of woman and the kind of human being she is. There is a deep and abiding love that exists between Elizabeth and myself. It's always been there, it in my judgment has never gone away.

Here's what, can I explain to you what happened? First of all, it happened during a period after she was in remission from cancer; that's no excuse in any possible way for what happened. This is what happened. It's what happened with me and I think happens unfortunately more often sometimes with other people. . . . Ego. Self-focus, self-importance. Now, I was slapped down to the ground when my son Wade died in 1996, in April of 1996. But then after that I ran for the Senate and I got elected to the Senate, and here we go again, it's the same old thing again. Adulation, respect, admiration.

Then I went from being a senator, a young senator, to being considered for vice president, running for president, being a vice presidential candidate, and becoming a national public figure. All of which fed a self-focus, an egotism, a narcissism, that leads you to believe that you can do whatever you want. You're invincible. And there will be no consequences. And nothing, nothing could be further from the truth.

The reaction to the interview was swift and mostly harsh, and the Olympics did not keep the media from covering the story. News outlets around the world published excerpts. Editorial writers, columnists, and bloggers flayed the senator in their commentaries, and political types announced the death of his relevance in national affairs. It was very strange to see reporters offering detailed accounts of a story we had lived with for so long.

Later I heard of additional developments that never reached the public. For example, Edwards told me that both Barack Obama and Hillary Clinton phoned his wife to say they were sorry about what was happening and to tell her she was in their prayers. Bill Clinton, a veteran of his own sexual disgrace and attempted cover-up, called the senator and said, in effect, "How'd you get caught?"

On the night of the Bob Woodruff interview, my phone rang constantly. Reporters from around the world were calling. I didn't speak to one of them. My main concern was to protect Cheri and the kids from the cameras, and I was glad we were leaving for North Carolina in the morning. Then, at 10:33 P.M., Fred sent a text saying that he couldn't send his plane because it was "in Guatemala with Lisa until Sunday—sorry—DO NOT talk to press!!!!!!!"

I logged on to the Web site FlightAware.com and checked to see where the plane was. The site, which tracks the whereabouts of every aircraft with a tail number, showed it was parked at Dallas Love Field. It was clear—Fred and John Edwards weren't looking out for us anymore. I told Fred I knew where the plane was. He didn't react to the fact that I had caught him in a lie but agreed we needed to travel covertly and offered to have a driver meet us near the Southwest Airlines arrival area when we landed in Raleigh-Durham. Fortunately, no one was looking for us at the airport when we arrived late Saturday. If they had been, it would have been a cinch to find us. All they'd have had to do was stand near the limo driver holding a big sign that read, "Andrew Young."

On the Sunday morning after the interview, Elizabeth Edwards again lashed out at Cheri with two messages left on her phone. The first said:

> Andrew told Rielle that he was the person responsible for the PlayStation 3 fiasco. Rielle told on her boyfriend and told John that Andrew is the one who did it. Shouldn't confide things to your boyfriend . . . or your girlfriend.

The second Sunday message said:

> Hey, Cheri, um, yeah, uh, when you move from North Carolina, Andrew and Rielle both asked if they could please be really close together. Uh, hope you like that!

The flailing nature of these remarks—recalling the years-old Play-Station issue, for example—reflected the paranoia that seemed to be falling over the Edwardses.

An army of media people had descended on Chapel Hill, and there were TV satellite trucks and photographers everywhere. My phone rang constantly with requests from Larry King, CBS News, *Good Morning America,* and every major newspaper and magazine in the country. On August 12, Fred Baron told me he believed that all the cell phones used by people close to the Edwardses were being "hit by the other side," so he told me to use only landlines to call him.

Many months later, I can recall these anxious references and tell myself that Fred and the others were just upset and scaring themselves. At the time he spoke to me, Cheri and the kids and I were living four miles from the Edwardses' mansion. We were in our yet-to-be-finished house, where the floors and plumbing were not quite completed, and we were sleeping on mattresses thrown on the floor. Unsure about the future of my job, where we might live, and where the kids would start school, we felt besieged and insecure. Very few of our old friends and colleagues would talk to us. Our friend Michael Cucchiara told us that Elizabeth was writing a book that would be extremely harsh on me. Regarded as pariahs for our role in the destruction of John Edwards, we felt self-conscious everywhere we went. However, we did try to keep a sense of humor.

When Cheri went to a grocery store, she grabbed the *National Enquirer* at the checkout and flipped it over so no one could see it. The man standing behind her said, "Hey, are you embarrassed that you are buying that magazine?" She turned and saw he had an armful of similar magazines. After a flash of fear, she realized that the man didn't know she was one of the players in the scandal and she had to fight to keep from laughing out loud.

Laughs were a rare commodity for us in August 2008. Cheri didn't have any friends, other than me, who knew what she was going through and could talk to her with real understanding and laugh at the ridiculous elements of the scandal. I was lucky to have Tim Toben. "I've never known anyone who could do this," he would say. "John Edwards can convince and compel in such a genuine and honest-seeming way but is really not authentic. He lies, but it's like he believes it all and so do we." His point made me think of the movie *True Lies*. That's what John Edwards was all about—constructing lies that seemed like truth and had the power of truth, until he was found out.

My last encounter with Edwards came on August 18, when I got an urgent call from Fred Baron. He said that Mrs. Edwards had left the house and the senator would have access to David Kirby's car for just a short time. He begged me to agree to see him. I was furious with Edwards and all the people around him, but I needed to meet with him to hear what he had worked out with Bunny on the matter of the big poverty foundation. When I agreed, Fred told me to drive to an intersection on a deserted two-lane road near the Edwards estate. It was just before one o'clock in the afternoon. I got in our minivan, drove to the spot, and parked.

At 1:15 P.M., Fred sent me a text to tell me, "He is in a black suv." Just then, Edwards pulled up in a black Chevy Tahoe and waved at me through the open window. I rolled down the window on the minivan, not knowing what to expect.

"Follow me," he called out. Then he drove off.

I followed as he drove down the country roads, making one awkward turn after another. (He was talking on a cell phone and anxiously checking the rearview mirror as he drove the borrowed car.) Finally, he stopped and signaled for me to get in his car.

When I opened the door of the Tahoe, I saw that Edwards looked fit and tanned as usual, but when I got in I noticed he was fidgety, and as he drove off, he seemed to have a little trouble controlling the car and maintaining his train of thought.

Two months had passed since I'd last seen John Edwards, and in that time I had come to understand that I had never really known him at all. I began to worry just a bit about my own safety. In the movies, this would be the scene where the rich guy would deliver the man who knows too much to an assassin in the woods. I knew this was probably a paranoid thought, but it remained in the back of my mind as he actually tried a little small talk.

"How are you doing?" he said. "How are the kids?"

"We're doing pretty shitty," I answered. "Where's your car?"

"Elizabeth's taken all my keys."

"Elizabeth's taken your keys?" I wanted to embarrass him by making him explain.

"Yeah, and she's got me sleeping in the barn. She yells at me all night, and when I sleep she gets in my face and screams."

As this line of conversation died, Edwards grew nostalgic. He said he missed hanging out with me. "I don't have anyone to talk to anymore."

I wasn't interested in his loneliness. I asked him what he was going to do about me now that my reputation was trashed and I had no chance of finding a job. What about the foundation he was supposed to start with a big donation from Bunny Mellon? The last I heard, he was increasing his request to $50 million.

He said that when he saw Bunny, her lawyer and accountant had attended the meeting and told him she wasn't in a position to give him what he wanted. The senator then started talking about the checks Bunny had written to cover Rielle's expenses and the cost of our great escape.

"I didn't know anything about this," he said. "Did you?"

I didn't know what was going on. I wondered if he was secretly recording our conversation. Panicked, I told him I didn't know what he was talking about.

"What about your promise to take care of things?" I asked him. "What about you coming clean?"

"If you apply for a job, I'll give you a good reference. Just let me know who to call."

After a decade of devoted service, untold sacrifice on the part of my wife and children, and an act of extreme loyalty that left my reputation ruined, John Edwards proposed to compensate me with a good reference. I could no longer contain myself. I looked at him and in dead seriousness said, "You know, I'm not sure we can really control what happens next." I then explained that I had the sex video, a small library of pertinent text messages, voice-mail recordings by the score, and contemporary notes I had made almost every day since I began working for him. If he wasn't willing to clear my name by telling the truth, then I would do it.

"Andrew, I've told Elizabeth everything," he said. "You can't hurt me."

With this statement, Edwards communicated two important things. First, in the strange universe he occupied, he and his wife were the only two beings who mattered. Second, he was a remorseless and predatory creature, unaffected by the suffering of others, even suffering he had caused with his reckless behavior. I told him to take me back to my car. When we got there I got out, closed the door of the Tahoe, and stepped aside. As he drove away, I stole one last glance through the window of the driver's door. I saw a man I couldn't recognize at all.

Almost a year would pass before I would be near John Edwards again, on a ball field where our two boys played for different teams, and he would look past me. I heard nothing from him directly in those ten months, but his wife would continue to bad-mouth me and Cheri to folks in Chapel Hill and around the country. The worst of what she did was accuse me of trying to bilk a helpless old woman—Bunny Mellon—out of funds for a fake foundation her husband knew nothing about. She said this much and more in a voice-mail message recorded and played for me by Tim Toben:

> . . . I thought that perhaps you should know that John visited Bunny Mellon, Andrew Mellon's widow, with whom Andrew had met in the course of fund-raising. And Andrew apparently tried to . . . told her that Andrew was starting a foundation, that she needed to give several million dollars in cash to the foundation.
>
> She said she didn't have that cash, and he suggested that she should mortgage her property. She is ninety-eight years old . . . she should mortgage her property for John's foundation. The only problem is John didn't have a foundation, did not ask Andrew to do anything. This was a totally bogus scam of a ninety-eight-year-old woman.

The senator later told Tim that I had been setting up a fake foundation without his knowledge. Tim reminded him that they had actually discussed the foundation long ago over dinner, when Edwards was under consideration as the Democratic candidate for vice president. Tim recalled this because he had been impressed when Edwards explained that Bunny had said she was going to help him "be to poverty what Al Gore is to climate change."

Despite the fact that Tim had revealed Edwards to be lying about me, the senator and his wife would continue to spread such stories about me for many months. They even accused me of stealing a baseball card collection that had belonged to their son. On the day Cheri and I celebrated our ninth wedding anniversary, Mrs. Edwards left a message on my phone that said, among other things:

> Andrew, it's Elizabeth, mother of Wade, who wants Wade's cards back. I know that you took them . . . they gave lie detector tests to everybody else . . . it leaves you . . . Are you that low that you would steal from a dead boy?

(For the record, Elizabeth knew the police had arrested someone who tried to pawn the cards. When she couldn't identify the cards in detail, he had to be released.)

Five days after Elizabeth Edwards left her final message, Fred Baron died. In 2009, Elizabeth published a book that she called a reflection on "facing life's adversities." In it I was no longer the young man she asked to be "family." I was some sort of deranged groupie or "obsessed fan." When I read this I was hurt, but I didn't have time to dwell on it. The FBI and federal prosecutors had been to my home to talk about an investigation of the Edwards campaign. With the help of David Geneson, a brilliant and compassionate lawyer, I began putting together all the records they requested for a grand jury that had been convened.

Edwards started telling people he wanted to "get this baby mess" behind him so he could return to national politics. He and his wife continued to tell people that I was responsible for all their problems, from the failure of his campaign to the discord in their marriage. As my grand jury testimony approached, few of our old friends even spoke to us. Among the notable exceptions were Glenn Sturm, a former big Edwards supporter, and my brother-in-law, Joe Von Kallist. These two stood up for us when no one else would and immediately offered to represent me pro bono. Glenn spoke to me several times a day and would even fly us to his ranch in Wyoming for a break.

When I eventually testified before the grand jury, the U.S. attorneys questioned me for seven or eight hours. The members of the jury then got the chance to ask their own questions. They only asked one. A man in the back row raised his hand and said, "Is the government providing you and your family protection?" I didn't answer but the prosecutor did, saying that the authorities would provide it if necessary. When I left the room, I bumped into Bryan Huffman, who was nervous about taking his turn in the witness chair. I told him the lawyers were actually "very nice." Bryan called me when he was finished testifying. He told me that the prosecutors had asked him how Bunny Mellon would feel if she learned that the funds she sent for poor people in Greene County and the College for Everyone Program were used instead to support the senator's girlfriend.

Even though I was relieved when I finished testifying, my advisers reminded me that I might be required in the future to appear as a witness at a trial if John Edwards was indicted. This concern was added to all the other worries I carried as I tried to recover from my decade-long involvement with him.

I had no job prospects, and the house we had built in the woods was as yet unfinished and threatening to bankrupt me. But I had time to reflect on my experience with a most charismatic and deceptive politician and the factors that made me vulnerable to his spell. Most important, I had Cheri, and Brody, and Gracie, and Cooper. I realized that their love, and the love of the few people who never deserted us through the scandal, were the most valuable possessions I could claim.

EPILOGUE

In late summer 2009, my father, who had declined gradually over many years, suddenly became terribly sick and was hospitalized. Tests revealed that his degenerative heart disease had progressed to the point where his once-mighty heart was reduced to five percent of its normal function. The doctors, who didn't know how he was still alive, sent him to hospice, where they thought he would die in a few days. I went with him and stayed as his body fought death for nearly two weeks.

My dad's dying came as I was about to finish writing this book, and the break that it forced me to take allowed me to reflect on my own choices in life, on the nature of such basic human values as love, loyalty, commitment, and justice. During long days and even longer nights of waiting and listening to the sound of my father breathing, I dwelled on my relationship with him, my attachment to John Edwards and his cause, and my own motivations, values, and actions.

With the exception of an admittedly long period—a decade—when I strayed, I have tried to live by the values given to me primarily by my father. He was my unquestioned hero and my role model until his fall from grace when I was a senior in high school. In his sermons and his daily life, he stood for the rights of every person to be treated fairly and to have an equal chance at success and happiness. He did this with a faith-powered commitment that endured despite attacks that included a cross burning on our lawn. Listening to him as a child, I came to believe that once you adopt a cause, you stick with it, come what may.

But as an impressionable child, I couldn't grasp the more subtle messages my father also tried to deliver. In between his calls to the best in us, he alluded to the darker side of human nature, to excessive ambition, selfishness, greed, and deceit, and he asked the people in his congregation to face these universal qualities in themselves.

When I learned of my father's darker nature, of how he had betrayed my mother, I rejected all of him and was unable to allow the good to exist with the bad. Not surprisingly, as I committed my own errors, I could not accept them in myself. Instead, I felt ashamed and began to live in fear that every mistake I had ever made would be used against me. I couldn't see that this was the fate I had imposed on my father in the years I had rejected him for his mistakes.

Armchair psychologists will say that when John Edwards came along, I adopted him as a substitute for my father. He became my hero, and my commitment to him was like a son's commitment to his father. Inside the campaigns, I found a cultlike atmosphere that eroded my ability to resist his requests for ever more extreme behavior. This analysis is correct, as far as it goes. But if you want to understand how I could have aided and abetted the worst in John Edwards, it helps to know that I was also trying to grasp, as an adult, what it means to take the good with the bad. I had confronted my father, watched him seek redemption, and made peace with him. But I hadn't developed a mature understanding of what I should do beyond accepting another person's flaws and moving on.

Late one night as my father lay dying, I sat alone with him and turned for comfort to some audio recordings of his old sermons. The first one I heard included the following passage, preached in his deep and familiar voice:

Love yourself. Know yourself. Accept yourself. Remember Jesus' words when he said, "You shall love your neighbor—how? As you love yourself."

Most of us, me included, never learn that to "love yourself," you must first see and understand your own failings, accept them without shame, and learn to consider them as you move through life. If I had truly loved myself, I wouldn't have been ashamed of my own mistakes and lived in fear of being found out. If I had loved myself, I wouldn't have felt the need to devote myself to a hero and his cause. If I had loved myself, I would have understood how much Cheri and the kids valued the time I spent with them and I would have said no to John and Elizabeth Edwards.

In my father's sermon, he also said that too many of us get caught up in trying to be "little Jesuses." By this he meant we try to be perfect, the way we imagine Christ was, and judge ourselves without mercy when we fail. Better, he said, to try to be a "big you" rather than a little Jesus. In fact, he thought that was all God ever expected of any human being.

With my dad's help, I know now the difference between understanding human nature—the combination of good and evil—and being able to love yourself and others through it all. I am genuinely sorry for all that I have done wrong and for all the hurt I have caused others. I don't want to be a little Jesus, and I don't expect it of anyone else. With any luck, this is the lesson we learn from personal failure. If you face who you are, what you have done, and what you have lost, you can recover from almost anything. My dad did this. After his terrible failure he retreated, came to terms with his own sins, and began again as a preacher at a church in South Carolina. He healed his relationships, and at the time of his death, he was surrounded by family who loved him. His funeral, in a church packed by hundreds of people, was a celebration of all that he was. They knew about his shortcomings, accepted them as real, but loved him anyway and allowed him to give what he had that was good.

After my father's death, as I returned to the work of writing, the press began to report on the grand jury investigation of John Edwards, and this brought renewed interest in the scandal. The media revealed that I was going to "tell all" in a book, speculation swirled around the secrets I would spill, and commentators theorized about my motives. Some said I was greedy and bent on revenge. Others said I should go away and leave the sordid truth untold. I held my tongue, until now.

I have written this book to end years of gossip and lies about me, John Edwards, and a host of people who deserve better than to be remembered only as sinners or fools. I have written it to make money to support my family at a time when no other job was available to me. And I have written this book as an exercise in my own understanding, so that I could learn something from the trauma suffered by so many who believed in what they thought John Edwards represented and were willing to sacrifice for the greater good.

Gifted, charismatic, and mesmerizing, John Edwards knew what was right but was so blind to his own flaws—narcissism, greed, power lust—and so determined to hide his shame even from himself that he couldn't correct them. Mrs. Edwards pursued noble ideals but never saw how she was changed by the privilege that comes with wealth, power, and fame. She got a vision of her husband in the White House and herself at his side, and she pursued it with an ambition that became blind and destructive. Her cancer diagnosis may have clouded her judgment for a time, but it does not excuse her from her duty to seek the truth, nor does it allow her to attempt to destroy others. (Nor do I believe she would expect her illness to exempt her from any of the realities of life, including what I have to say.) I do understand, however, that she resented me more because her husband had spoon-fed her evil half-truths about me.

Sadly, John and Elizabeth Edwards could have put themselves in a position to continue their good works, if they had told the truth when they had the chance. This is what Bill Clinton eventually did, and it has allowed him to return to a productive public life as a sinner who is also good. Instead, the Edwardses held to a lie they knew was a lie and refused to do the right thing. Faced with this reality, I had no choice but to write this book in order to move forward in some way. I hope our wounds will begin to heal as the truth comes to light.

If I achieve what I hope to achieve with this book, I will begin to build a new, positive future. I will create a record that will make some sense out of my life's choices and a terrible political scandal, for my wife, family, friends, and you, the reader. Finally, I hope to give myself permission to be imperfect but nonetheless unbowed. Like my father, I want to begin again.